Project-Based Second and Foreign Language Education

Past, Present, and Future

A volume in
Research in Second Language Learning
JoAnn Hammadou Sullivan, *Series Editor*

Project-Based Second and Foreign Language Education

Past, Present, and Future

Edited by

Gulbahar H. Beckett

and

Paul Chamness Miller

INFORMATION AGE
PUBLISHING

Greenwich, Connecticut • www.infoagepub.com

Library of Congress Cataloging-in-Publication Data

Project-based second and foreign language education : past, present, and future / edited by Gulbahar H. Beckett and Paul Chamness Miller.
    p. cm. – (Research in second language learning)
  Includes bibliographical references.
  ISBN-13: 978-1-59311-506-7
  ISBN-13: 978-1-59311-505-0 (pbk.)
  1. Language and languages–Study and teaching. 2. Project method in teaching. I. Beckett, Gulbahar H., 1959- II. Miller, Paul Chamness. III. Series.
  P53.P67P76 2006
  418.0071–dc22

2006014589

Printed in the United States of America

To my mentor, Bernard A. Mohan, for encouraging me to aim high.
—Gulbahar H. Beckett

To Alan Garfinkel for his constant support and encouragement.
—Paul Chamness Miller

CONTENTS

PART II

Application: Frameworks and Models

PART III
Future Directions

FOREWORD

Leo van Lier
Monterey Institute of International Studies

This timely volume brings together a number of innovative studies about Project-Based Learning (PBL). As such it presents consistent arguments to establish a rationale for this approach to second and foreign language learning. The empirical and conceptual studies in this collection make a strong case for a project-based approach to language learning and teaching.

None of the researchers in this volume claim that PBL is new. Indeed, its antecedents are frequently invoked, and perhaps the most frequently named influence is John Dewey, dating back to the early decades of the 20th century. Dewey's advocacy of experiential and action-based learning is well known and acknowledged all over the world. However, what is perhaps less commonly appreciated is that Dewey's experiential, democratic and social-behaviorist ideals for education were themselves part of a wider stream of educational thinking that went far beyond the spatial confines of the United States and the temporal limits of the first half of the 20th century.

The reform movement that started with Dewey, Kilpatrick and others in the United States was in many ways similar to earlier educational reforms proposed in Europe, in particular the action-based, experience-based and perception-based recommendations made by numerous educational thinkers, from Jan Comenius in 17th century Prague, to Johann Pestalozzi in 19th century Switzerland, the Italian educator Maria Montessori in the early 20th century, and the giant of modern educational theory, Jean Piaget. To this list must certainly be added the special case of L. S. Vygotsky, whose influence was huge in the early years of the Soviet revolution, then went underground (but not forgotten) under Leninist and Stalinist repression, and surged to world-wide prominence in the last third of the 20th

Project-Based Second and Foreign Language Education, pages xi–xvi
Copyright © 2006 by Information Age Publishing
All rights of reproduction in any form reserved.

century. In view of these varied but pedagogically convergent antecedents, we cannot afford to look at PBL as just another fashion, bandwagon or fad that will soon fade as so many other methodologies or reforms have done in the past. Instead, we need to study and appreciate the deeper foundations of educational thought (whether it be enlightenment, democracy, or fulfillment) that underlie this approach to education. Furthermore, and perhaps even more importantly, we must study the reasons why this educational philosophy has never managed to succeed as a mainstream pedagogical approach to educating school children, language learners, or in fact any learners of anything.

In this foreword I primarily want to address two crucial aspects of PBL: first, the well-established fact that it is a sensible and sophisticated way to approach the teaching-learning dialogue; second, the clearly observable fact that PBL mostly tends to happen in elite, low-stakes courses, where performance does not make or break a student's future academic or professional success. Whenever high-stakes (standardized) tests rule the roost, project-based learning and similar initiatives tend to be pushed into the periphery of the educational landscape.

In some ways, PBL has always been part of learners' learning experiences at various times along their educational trajectory. For the most part, these experiences appear to cluster around the earlier elementary years, with perhaps some additional project work at the secondary level (e.g., the common "science project" or "senior project" in American high schools, and possibly some project work at the tertiary level as well; culminating, of course, for those who stick with it to the bitter end, with the mother of all educational projects, the Ph.D. dissertation).

Most learners and teachers are therefore familiar with project work, although generally as an addition to (or insertion into) a regular content or language driven curriculum. As the main organizing principle of a language curriculum, PBL remains relatively rare. What is proposed in the studies in this volume is a much wider role for PBL, one that incorporates curriculum design, critical pedagogy, language socialization, content learning, and much more. It also addresses the crucial question of empirical (both quantitative and qualitative) research into the effects and conditions of PBL, something that will require much additional attention and effort in the future.

I mentioned earlier that PBL is usually traced back to the Reform Movement spearheaded in the United States by Dewey and Kilpatrick in the early decades of the 20th century. Key European influences at that time included Johann Pestalozzi, Maria Montessori, and Jean Piaget. Somewhat later, the Dutch existentialist psychologist F.J.J. Buytendijk proposed a whole-body, humanistic approach to learning, and in Germany the concept of *Handlungsorientierter Unterricht* (Action-Based Teaching and Learning) began to take shape (Finkbeiner, 2000). In the Soviet Union, educators influenced by the work (still barely coming out of banishment) of Vygotsky were developing various models of educational activity theory (see Bakhurst, 1991; Wertsch, 1981). All these and many other holistic educational approaches form the foundation for what many language educators now practice under a variety of names, including PBL, action-based learning, experiential learning, exploratory teaching, holistic teaching, humanistic methods, and so on. I suggest that all of these flow from the same ideological and pedagogical well.

There is more yet. I mentioned that the second point of my look at PBL relates to the borders, limits, sanctions, proscriptions and restrictions (the issues that Bernstein calls *classification*, 2000) that are placed on the implementation of PBL and related approaches in the real, everyday world of institutional education. For example, if you draw a line that progresses over time from kindergarten to the last year of high school ("K–12" in the United States), you will probably find that PBL flourishes close to the "K" end of the line, that it still may find a reasonably or moderately comfortable home in the elementary years, but that it then starts to dwindle rapidly as we move into the secondary and college preparatory years. Once the student approaches the graduate pinnacle of the educational ascent, projects once again become prominent, but by that time the student can't remember how it felt to work like that when she was in Kindergarten all those years ago, and painful adjustments likely need to be made.

Following on from the above, I mentioned earlier that PBL tends to take place on the fringes of the educational landscape. I must now qualify this remark somewhat, since many of the studies included here in fact take place in school contexts in the United States, China, Israel, Japan and elsewhere. As such, these studies exemplify that PBL is possible and can be successful in a wide variety of school contexts. Even so, some of the most well known projects take place outside formal schooling contexts, such as Shirley Brice Heath's work with learning in informal youth centers run by at-risk youths and drop-outs (Heath & Smyth, 1999). We must also bear in mind that in an educational climate ruled by the triad of *standards—accountability—tests*, there is ever-increasing pressure to strip away everything from the curriculum that does not directly feed into test scores in reading and math. There are reports about this in the general and professional press (such as *Education Week*) on a regular basis. To give an example, in a recent opinion piece the psychologist Robert Sternberg (2006) argues that the current accountability movement in the United States fosters conformity and stifles creativity. As he puts it, "The increasingly massive and far-reaching use of conventional standardized tests is one of the most effective, if unintentional, vehicles this country has created for suppressing creativity" (p. 64). In this educational climate it is even more urgent to shine a light on approaches such as PBL that go against the increasing forces of commodification and homogenization. It is urgent to follow the advice of several of the contributors here to conduct research that carefully triangulates data and research methods, both quantitative and qualitative, since that is one of the few ways to catch the attention of policy makers.

As Finkbeiner (2000) points out, action-based learning "includes learners' hearts, bodies and senses" (p. 255). This is not mere subjective talk; it addresses hard and well-documented facts about human functioning in context (Damasio, 1994). It brings to mind the classic anthropological study of the Balinese cockfight by Clifford Geertz (2005, originally published in 1972) in which he discusses the notion of "kinesthetic perception":

> The use of the, to Europeans, "natural" visual idiom for perception—"see," "watches," and so forth—is more than usually misleading here, for the fact that ... Balinese follow the progress of the fight as much ... with their bodies as with their eyes, moving their limbs, heads, and trunks in gestural mimicry of the cocks' maneuvers means that much of the individual's experience of the fight is kinesthetic rather than visual. (pp. 84–85)

PBL is important not just as a different and more efficient way to afford language learning opportunities, but in a wider sense as a semiotic-ecological endeavor that focuses on the making and using of signs that are multisensory and multimodal (van Lier, 1994). As several researchers have pointed out, perceptual skills cannot simply be taken for granted, but must be fostered, guided, and practiced over time to facilitate effective functioning in relevant contexts (Bronfenbrenner & Ceci, 1994; Gibson & Pick, 2000; Heath, 2000; Kress, 2001). Eyes and ears are not just conduits that automatically funnel suitably pedagogized discourse to expectant information processors in the brain, rather, the human organism is an actively perceiving agent who perceives, understands, acts on and acts in relevant environments with increasing effectiveness. That is why it might be useful to see PBL as one type of instantiation of a more general action-based pedagogy that has human agency at its center (Swain, 2005). In this way the pedagogy under discussion links directly and overtly to the ideals that form its foundation, and that express the core ideas of virtually all major educational thinkers from Comenius to the present day.

I congratulate Gulbahar Beckett and her team for a groundbreaking collection of papers and research studies that makes an important contribution to the practices and ideals of curricula that treat learners as agents (and inquirers); the main principles and characteristics of the work in this volume are well summarized in Mohan and Lee's final chapter in the collection, where they draw on Charles Taylor, Halliday's functional linguistics, Allen Tough, Ruqaiya Hasan and other important present-day educational thinkers on these issues. Many of the papers in the volume broaden the research base in PBL through various kinds of—mainly interpretive—research. There is no doubt that this publication will provide a much-needed further impetus to extend the theoretical, practical and research base of PBL and other action-based learning.

I will close with a final look at the political and institutional context within which PBL must find its place. There are two themes, or tendencies, that shape the educational policies of most, if not all governments. One is to create a work force that is flexible, creative, adaptable to market changes and capable of lifelong learning. The other is to control, prescribe and predict what goes in and comes out of educational establishments. The irony is that one theme is completely incompatible with the other. Governments are pushing the door open with one hand while at the same time pulling it shut with the other. This effort exhausts their energy, even though the door stays exactly the way it was. This contradiction has been brilliantly laid bare by Bernstein (2000), and was noted earlier by Stenhouse, when he wrote that "education as induction into knowledge is successful to the extent that it makes the behavioral outcomes of the students unpredictable" (1975, pp. 82–83).

The paradox noted here should be quite visible to anyone with an ounce of common sense, yet it appears that governments and their policy-making institutions, left to their own devices, are quite incapable of seeing it. Perhaps business leaders and future employers, who are supposed to be smart, and whose own livelihood after all depends on workers who are flexible and creative, can be led to see this perplexing anomaly in official educational policy. If so, they should have enough clout (i.e., money) to change the situation. Or else teachers, parents and students will just have to take matters into their own hands and produce change from the grassroots up. Whatever the political trajectory to come, PBL and more generally action-based teaching will have a vital role to play.

REFERENCES

Bakhurst, D. (1991). *Consciousness and revolution in Soviet philosophy: From the Bolsheviks to Evald Ilyenkou.* Cambridge: Cambridge University Press.

Bernstein, B. (2000). *Pedagogy, symbolic control and identity: Theory, research, critique.* Oxford: Rowman & Littlefield Publishers.

Damasio, A. (1994). *Descartes' error: Emotion, reason, and the human brain.* New York: Putnam's Sons.

Finkbeiner, C. (2000). Handlungsorientierter Unterricht (Holistic and action-oriented learning and teaching). In M. Byram (Ed.). *Routledge encyclopedia of language teaching and learning* (pp. 255–258). London: Routledge.

Geertz, C. T. (2005, Fall). Deep play: Notes on the Balinese cockfight (1972). *Daedalus*, 2005, 56–86.

Gibson, E. J. & Pick, A. D. (2000). *An ecological approach to perceptual learning and development.* Oxford: Oxford University Press.

Heath, S. B. (2000). Seeing our way into learning. *Cambridge Journal of Education*, 30, 121–132.

Heath, S. B. and Smyth, L. (1999). *ArtShow: Youth and community development.* Washington, DC: Partners for Livable Communities.

Kress, G. (2001). "You've just got to learn how to see": Curriculum subjects, young people and schooled engagement with the world. *Linguistics and Education*, *11*(4), 401–415.

Stenhouse, L. (1975). *An introduction to curriculum research and development.* London: Heinemann.

Sternberg, R.J. (2006). Creativity is a habit. *Education Week*, 25, 24, p. 64 (back page) and p. 47.

Swain, M. (2005). Languaging, agency and collaboration in advanced second language proficiency. Paper presented at the Georgetown University Round Table on Languages and Linguistics, 2005.

Wertsch, J. V. (1985). *Vygotsky and the social formation of mind.* Cambridge, MA: Cambridge University Press.

INTRODUCTION

CHAPTER 1

PROJECT-BASED SECOND AND FOREIGN LANGUAGE EDUCATION

Theory, Research, and Practice

Gulbahar H. Beckett
University of Cincinnati

As I pointed out in Beckett (1999), project-based instruction or project-based learning was first conceived of by the efficiency expert David Snedden to teach science in American vocational agriculture classes. It was later developed and popularized for educators by John Dewey's student (and later colleague) William Heard Kilpatrick, mainly through his 1918 pamphlet *The Project Method* (Alberty, 1927; Holt, 1994). The project method, the essence of which is wholehearted purposeful activity on the part of the learner, was Kilpatrick's construction of Dewey's problem method of teaching (Brubacher, 1947). Project-based leaning (PBL) was introduced into the field of second language education about two decades ago as a way to reflect the principles of student-centered teaching (Hedge, 1993).

Project-Based Second and Foreign Language Education, pages 3–16
Copyright © 2006 by Information Age Publishing

A review of early second language acquisition (SLA) literature shows the major goal reported for project-based instruction is to provide opportunities for language learners to receive comprehensible input and produce comprehensible output (Eyring, 1989). According to Haines (1989), its goal is to provide students opportunities to "recycle known language and skills" in natural contexts (p. 1). Anecdotal reports show educators achieving these and other goals such as developing analytical skills (Gardner, 1995), time management skills (Coleman, 1992), and responsibility (Fried-Booth, 1986; Hilton-Jones, 1988) through short projects such as getting-to-know-each-other multicultural parties and learning-about-other-cultures and video-making projects (see Chapter 4).

More recently, PBL has been heralded as an appropriate approach to content-based second language education (Stoller, 1997), English for specific purposes (Fried-Booth, 2002), project-based computer-assisted English as a foreign language (EFL) education (Fang & Warschauer, 2004), community-based language socialization (Eyring, 2001), and teaching the critical and higher order thinking and problem-solving skills (Beckett, 2005, see also Chapter 4) recommended by the National Research Council (1999). There has also been growing global interest in project-based foreign language education (see Fang & Warschauer, 2004). Various project-based language learning centers have been established (see Beckett, 2005), and specialized annual conferences such as Content, Tasks, and Projects in Language Classrooms organized by the Monterey Institute of International Studies have started appearing. More empirical studies have been conducted (e.g., Beckett, 2005; Beckett & Slater, 2005; Fang & Warschauer, 2004; Kobayashi, 2003, 2004; Mohan & Beckett, 2003; see also Chapter 6). An encouraging number of research-based instructional and assessment models have also begun to appear (e.g., Beckett & Slater, 2005; Coleman, 1992; see also Chapter 15).

What the field needs now is systematic discussion of PBL work in second and foreign language education by bringing together representative work, identifying obvious gaps, and guiding the field toward future directions. This book does just this through the original work of international scholars from Canada, Israel, Japan, Singapore, and the United States. It includes chapters on various theories that have informed PBL in second language education, empirical research about ESL teacher and student perspectives and issues, various instructional and assessment frameworks and models, and a discussion of future directions for project-based second and foreign language education and research.

THEORY

As suggested by Stoller in Chapter 2 of this volume, work on project-based second and foreign language education is all over the theoretical map.

Many materials' writers, teachers, and researchers who write about PBL, however, trace its roots to Dewey in one way or another. At a general level, it has been referred to as a language education approach that reflects student-centered learning (e.g., Fried-Booth, 2002; Hedge, 1993) within the framework of experiential learning (Eyring, 2001; Kohonen, 2001; Legutke & Thomas, 1991). It has also been discussed within the theoretical framework of learner autonomy (Fried-Booth, 2002; van Lier, 2005), cooperative learning, and critical thinking (see Chapter 2). At a more specific level, it has been described as an approach that promotes comprehensible input and output (see Eyring, 1989) with emphasis on practicing listening and speaking skills and as a content-based approach (Stoller, 1997) with emphasis on teaching language and content (Stoller, 2004; see also Chapter 2). These theories and their application to project-based second foreign language education are discussed in Chapter 2, Establishing a Theoretical Foundation for Project-Based Learning in Second and Foreign Language Contexts, and in other chapters in Part I.

Specifically, Chapter 2 is a comprehensive review of the literature that includes anecdotal reports and empirical research. In this chapter, Stoller states that as much of the work on PBL in second and foreign language education is anecdotal, we cannot turn to it in order to establish a theoretical foundation for PBL. She argues, however, that it should be possible to "build a defensible theoretical framework for project work" based on many claims made by proponents of project work. She presents her arguments with an overview of varied configurations of project-based learning and a summary of the positive outcomes reported by practitioners. She then explores research findings focusing on second language (L2) and foreign language (FL) teaching and learning. The chapter concludes with implications for research and pedagogy that promotes language and content learning. Highlights of this chapter include Stoller's discussion of the breadth of theories that have influenced PBL and the complexity of theorizing it in second and foreign language education.

Chapter 3, Providing a Liberatory Theoretical Framework to Project-Based Learning in Second Language Education, extends the theoretical discussion. In this chapter, Brydon-Miller proposes the application of liberatory theory to inform project-based second language education research and pedagogy. She begins her argument citing Paulo Freire's work that demands educators understand the politicized nature of our role as educators in various educational contexts. She alerts us to the fact that second language education contexts can be marginalizing for many second language learners, many of whom are already marginalized due to inequitable economic and social forces. Application of liberatory theory to PBL, she argues, has the potential to embody the kind of politically engaged, transformative approach to education envisioned by Freire and other critical

educators. Brydon-Miller examines the basic notions that underlie Freirean critical pedagogy and discusses the intersections between this perspective and project-based learning. She then suggests specific classroom
practices that educators can use to incorporate Freirean approaches in
project-based learning through the use of photovoice and other educational action research methods. She illustrates how the proposed theory
was applied by some second language educators, paying particular attention to the challenges faced by these educators.

While Stoller gives an overview of the literature on project-based second
and foreign language education and builds "a defensible theoretical framework," Brydon-Miller adds to this discussion by proposing a liberatory theory
for project-based second language education. Missing from this discussion
are linguistic and sociocultural theories that have informed project-based
second language learning (e.g., Beckett, 2005; Beckett & Slater, 2005; Kobayashi, 2004; Mohan & Beckett, 2003; see also Chapters 4, 5, and 15). This
work on project-based second language learning takes a functional perspective that views language as a resource within a particular sociocultural context (Halliday, 1994; Mohan, 1986, 1989). This view of language is related to
the *language socialization* (Schieffelin & Ochs, 1986) that informs language
learning. In contrast to the formal linguistics' view of language learning as a
matter of learning a set of rules (e.g., the goal of project-based instruction is
to provide students with comprehensible input and output), the language
socialization view holds that language learning is the acquisition of linguistic
as well as sociocultural knowledge. From this perspective, language is a
medium of "socialization through the use of language and socialization to
use language" (Schieffelin, 1990, p. 14). The authors of these studies believe
this to be a useful theoretical framework for their studies because, as pointed
out by Schieffelin and Ochs (1986), it treats language as a focus of study as
well as a medium of studying. Beckett (see Chapter 4), for example, states
that the language socialization theory allowed her to see project-based
instruction as an activity or a sociocultural context that provides opportunities for ESL teachers to teach the English language, school and social cultures, curriculum content, and various skills. It is also an activity or context in
which ESL teachers teach the English language functionally by requiring students to listen, speak, read, and write in English to learn content material
(Dewey, 1926; Dewey & Dewey, 1915; Mohan, 1986) and to learn how to
learn in Canadian schools and how to survive in Canadian society. This is an
alternative view, a view that sees the goals of project-based instruction to be
creating contexts for learning through language. It reflects concerns for language learning as well as connects language and subject area content in
some form of language and content integration as pointed out by Dewey
(1926). For further discussion of this, see Lemke (1990), Parker (1992),
O'Toole (1996), and Rowell (1997).

RESEARCH

Empirical research on project-based second and foreign language education has been scarce (Beckett, 2005). A literature review for my dissertation revealed that Eyring (1989) was the only dissertation-level empirical study conducted in North America prior to mine, Beckett (1999). Since the completion of my study, an encouraging number of studies on various aspects of project-based second and foreign language learning have been published (e.g., Beckett, 2005; Beckett & Slater, 2005; Fang & Warschauer, 2004; Kobayashi, 2003, 2004; Mohan & Beckett, 2003; see also Chapters 4, 5, 6, and 7). Eyring's (1989) study was conducted to explore how a college ESL teacher implemented project-based instruction in the United States. One of her major findings that inspired my study (Beckett, 1999) is that a considerable number of student participants did not endorse project-based English as a second language (ESL) learning, leaving their teacher frustrated and doubtful. Eyring attributed her findings to different teacher and student expectations. I conducted my study in a secondary school in Canada examining teacher goals for and teacher and student evaluations of project-based instruction. My data analyses reached similar conclusions to Eyring's. That is, though the teacher participants in the study endorsed project-based instruction wholeheartedly, a considerable number of student participants did not. I attributed my findings to different philosophical, cultural, and linguistic mental models that teachers and students may have held in guiding and understanding their teaching and learning.

The Eyring (1989) and Beckett (1999) work led to further studies, such as Beckett and Slater (2005) and Mohan and Beckett (2003). It has also been encouraging to see the other studies mentioned previously (e.g., Fang & Warschauer, 2004; Kobayashi, 2003, 2004; Moulton & Holmes, 2000; see also Chapters 5, 6, and 7). These studies have enriched our understanding of why and how project-based instruction or project-based learning is implemented in various contexts and showed us what other potential it may have. For example, in Chapter 4, Beyond Second Language Acquisition: Secondary School ESL Teacher Goals and Actions for Project-Based Instruction, I discuss a study that focused on exploring ESL teachers' goals for project-based instruction and their actions in achieving their goals. The study takes a functional perspective that views language as a resource within a particular socio-cultural context (Halliday, 1994; Mohan, 1986, 1989), a view that is consistent with language socialization theory (Ochs, 1988). The findings of the study show that the teachers had many more goals than those stressed for project-based instruction in the early SLA literature goals that are mentioned in recent SLA literature for project-based instruction implemented in postsecondary contexts. They also had a goal that is not included even in the recent general education literature, namely, language socialization of ESL students into school and social cultures as well as teaching language in context, which was one of the early goals for project-based instruction (Dewey, 1926; Dewey & Dewey, 1915). Teachers achieved their goals through purposefully designed and carefully and systematically implemented projects. This suggests that, like their general education and postsecondary counterparts, secondary school ESL teachers perceive project-based instruction to be an activity conducive to achieving many goals with their ESL students. Readers should find the discussion of general education literature on project-based instruction and the application of the functional linguistics perspective (Halliday, 1994; Mohan, 1986, 1989) to research on project-based second language learning in Chapter 4 particularly informative.

A study conducted from the same theoretical framework is discussed in Chapter 5, Second Language Socialization Through an Oral Project Presentation: Japanese University Students' Experience. In this chapter, Kobayashi discusses a study that explored the second language socialization of Japanese university students through group project work during their year-long academic studies at a Canadian university. Systemic functional linguistics (e.g., Eggins & Slade, 1997; Halliday, 1994) and Mohan's (in press) social practice perspective revealed that the participants used different sets of linguistic resources to realize their meanings. Kobayashi concludes the chapter with a discussion of several implications for L2 pedagogy.

Chapter 6, Instructor Experiences With Project Work in the Adult ESL Classroom: A Case Study, by Doherty and Eyring, and Chapter 7, Project Work as a Conduit for Change in the Newcomers Classroom, by Case, add to the increasing number of empirical studies. The Doherty and Eyring study was conducted to explore how a theorist/researcher, a graduate student, and a teacher collaboratively implemented a learner-centered approach known as project work during a 5-week segment of an adult ESL continuing education class. The researchers found that implementing project work in an urban, multilevel, multicultural adult ESL setting can generate challenges as well as provide sociocultural and pedagogical insights for instructors. They also found that the participants adjusted or abandoned lesson plans with varying levels of comfort and to a greater degree than would be normal in a more traditional classroom. Based on learner input and feedback, they made greater efforts to introduce relevant resources, scaffold information, and adjust to learner preferences while facilitating group work.

The Case study addresses the question of how teachers face students from diverse racial, linguistic, and religious backgrounds and adapt and change their beliefs and practices about science instruction and project work. It focuses on examining the unique circumstances surrounding ESL teacher change. Data are drawn from a larger 2-year study on the practices of middle school teachers of newcomers conducted between 1999 and 2001 and a second set of follow-up interviews conducted in the fall of 2004. The author concludes that (1) issues concerning race, social class, literacy, and religion facing teachers of newcomers force teachers into a state of imbalance or questioning about how to enact constructivist-based instruction and project work; and (2) project work, because of its focus on developing curriculum based on student interest, provides a unique conduit for that change. This study adds to the literature on teachers' beliefs by documenting the experience of how one teacher of newcomers, Ms. Smith, moved from a teacher-centered model of science instruction to a constructivist framework.

In Chapter 8, Project-Based English as a Foreign Language Education in China: Perspectives and Issues, Guo reports on the findings of an informal study conducted during a research visit to China. The purpose of the study was to explore some Chinese professors' perspectives on project-based EFL instruction. According to the author, after learning about project-based instruction, most of the professors participating in the study thought that it could be a useful approach that may address some weaknesses in EFL instruction in China. However, they also raised some concerns about the applicability of this approach in China. For example, some of the professors were unsure about the impact of limited resources on project-based EFL instruction, and others were concerned about the consequences of introducing project-based EFL, as its principles may challenge traditional Chinese educational beliefs and practices. These and other discussions in the chapter contribute to our knowledge of current thoughts, beliefs, practices, and perspectives related to EFL education in China.

PRACTICE

Many resources and frameworks concerning project-based second and foreign language learning exist (e.g., Alan & Stoller, 2005; Beckett & Slater, 2005; Fried-Booth, 2002; Hilton-Jones, 1988; Stoller, 1997), but not all of them are research based and theoretically well informed. The chapters presented in this section of the volume add to research-based and theoretically informed instructional and assessment models and frameworks. These chapters begin with project-based community and professional development in the United States, continue with various EFL projects, and conclude with a chapter on assessment of project-based language and content learning. In Chapter 9, "Learners' Lives as Curriculum": An Integrative Project-Based Model for Language Learning, Weinstein explores a model for integrative project-based language learning. This chapter builds on the premise that teachers must listen for learner stories to discover the most pressing issues that will bring language learning to life. In the first part of the chapter, Weinstein contrasts "mastery" versus "constructivist" orientations to curriculum and argues for a model of learner-centered teaching that integrates these two orientations. She then discusses some possible challenges in implementing the proposed model as both English language learners and teachers as they struggle to shift from pure mastery-only orientations to a constructivist approach in which mastery of certain skills, structures, and competencies are still integral to the process, but are part of a larger meaning-making endeavor. The chapter concludes with an argument that teachers are also learners who benefit from communities of peers who engage in project-based learning for their own professional development.

In Chapter 10, Global Issue Projects in the English Language Class-room, Cates and Jacobs discuss how global education links with trends in second language instruction and, in particular, with the use of projects in second language instruction. They provide specific examples of global edu-cation projects carried out by Japanese and Singaporean EFL students as part of their second language development and highlight key elements of these projects and pedagogical issues arising from the projects. Then they articulate how they implemented content-based classroom ESL/EFL projects built around "global issue" topics linked to themes such as peace, human rights and the environment. Particularly noteworthy is their expla-nation of how second language project work designed from a global educa-tion perspective aims both at the development of language skills and at the promotion of global awareness, international understanding, and social responsibility. The chapter concludes with an outline of the features of a global education approach to foreign language teaching, discusses key fac-tors to consider in designing ESL/EFL project work around world prob-lems and social issues, and describes international examples of global issues project work by second and foreign language students.

In Chapter 11, Knowing the Other Through Multicultural Projects in School EFL Programs, Jakar, introduces various multicultural projects such as *UNICEF, Lullabies, Peacefolks,* and *Bread* carried out by teachers and stu-dents in EFL classes in the Jerusalem area. She discusses how these projects reflect the Israeli Ministry of Education English curriculum standards implemented in 2001 by creating opportunities to learn not only the English language but also critical thinking as well as cooperative and cre-ative work skills. The *Peacefolks* project described in this chapter is particu-larly relevant in the current cultural/historical period. For this project, students investigated a multicultural neighborhood inhabited by Muslim and Christian Arabs, Palestinians and Israelis, European and Middle East-ern Jews, Europeans, native English speakers, French speakers, North

Americans and more, and wrote about an imagined neighborhood where people of all races and cultures could live together peacefully and happily.

The next two chapters discuss two foreign language and content learning projects. In Chapter 12, *L'Immeuble: French Language and Culture Teaching and Learning Through Projects in a Global Simulation,* Dupuy discusses global simulation (GS) projects. She begins with an examination of the theoretical basis for GS and how it can accommodate the shifts that have recently occurred in foreign language teaching and learning. Then she describes the process of her implementation of Debyser's (1996) creative GS workbook *L'Immeuble.* Finally, students report reactions to *L'Immeuble.* According to Dupuy, most students enjoyed the collaborative work during their GS projects and the opportunity to engage in creative writing, and they appreciated having a say in the direction and shape of the project, which made it more meaningful and engaging. Students also realized how they could tap into the knowledge they had acquired in previous and current classes and experiences. Dupuy concludes that, though this chapter is about an implementation model for *L'Immeuble,* a GS project designed for a French setting, Paris, the premise is easily transferable to other cities in the French-speaking world and elsewhere. According to the author, the phases of the project can be readily transferred to other L2 contexts as well.

In Chapter 13, French Gastronomy Through Project Work in College Classes, Brown presents a curriculum model for teaching/learning French language and culture through a study of French gastronomy. According to Brown, this curriculum model established a goal of deep cultural experience of French gastronomy, a culturally prominent theme for France. By carrying out projects like this, learners can study regional cuisine, cultural festivals, problems in the food industry, authentic menus, culinary vocabulary, and even literary texts. Skills can be exercised using theme-appropriate films and music, in-class food tastings and critiques (or *dégustations*), and interactive Web exercises. Brown argues that such project-based French as a foreign language learning not only embodies the principles of student-centered learning but also ensures a highly meaningful contextualization and significance with rich L2 input.

Chapters 14 and 15 expand the scope of the work on project-based second and foreign language education to much-needed work on standards and assessment. In Chapter 14, Integrating Second Language Standards Into Project-Based Instruction, Miller, acknowledging other possibilities, argues for integration of standards into project-based instruction (PBI) as he believes that PBI lends itself to meeting many of the standards set forth by ACTFL and TESOL. Miller supports his argument through a discussion of various theories that inform language pedagogy and their relevance to TESOL and ACTFL standards and illustrates how these theories may be reflected and goals may be achieved through project-based instruction. He

shows how learners can achieve goals such as using English to communicate in social settings, to achieve academically in all content areas, and to
interact with others in socially and culturally appropriate ways. He ends the
chapter with cautionary notes about the challenges that individuals may
face as they integrate and implement various standards into project-based
instruction.

Chapter 15, Assessing Projects as Second Language and Content Learning, by Slater, Beckett, and Aufderhaar, discusses assessment issues related
to project-based instruction. The authors note the difficulties of assessing
language learning through this approach and the resulting temptation by
teachers to stick with the "easy" way of assessing. In this chapter, the
authors provide a framework for examining and implementing assessment
in project-based instruction from a systemic functional linguistics (SFL)
perspective. They offer readers a background in SFL theory as it pertains to
the topic. They then present examples from science projects that illustrate
how classroom-based tasks can be carried out to assess the development of
language as well as skills and content understanding through an assort-
ment of rubrics. The major contribution of this chapter to the literature is
the introduction of a new way of thinking about the assessment of project-
based instruction. The authors conclude the chapter with an invitation for
theorists to extend their ideas regarding the potential of SFL for constructing assessment models appropriate for the simultaneous learning of language, content, and skills through project-based learning. They encourage
test makers and curriculum designers as well as teachers to incorporate
these ideas in their work. They urge researchers and teachers to field-test
the assessment model they have proposed in various contexts and make
suggestions for improvement.

The final chapter, Linking Interpretive Research and Functional Linguistics: From Learning Projects to Teaching Projects, by Mohan and Lee,
continues the momentum of this book, which I identified in Chapter 1.
The authors do this wonderfully by linking Hallidayan SFL theory and
practice to John Dewey, Charles Taylor, Mohan as well as Beckett and
Slater's work, illustrating their points through a case study of a graduate
student who is a teacher/researcher examining issues in her own learning
and teaching that bear on PBL. They guide the second and foreign language education field towards new directions by pointing out the limited
goals early SLA literature showed for project-based instruction, i.e., the
individual language learner receiving comprehensible input and producing comprehensible output. They point out that typical research methodologies and assumptions associated with early SLA were aimed at
quantifying causal relations and framed human action within a causal-tech-
nical order rather than setting it within the moral orders that inform social
life. According to the authors, because of these assumptions, it was difficult

if not impossible for PBL to follow Dewey's well known emphasis on learner inquiry related to action and integrated into students' lives and his less well-known emphasis on a functional approach to language. As such, Mohan and Lee confirm the general direction of the present volume, which encourages greater recognition of learners as inquirers and much broader, holistic, and interpretive or qualitative approaches to research that view language and discourse, in relation to their content and cultural contexts. They take this line of discussion further by showing how these trends can mutually reinforce each other and support the learner as inquirer and language user, reflectively interpreting their world and acting on it. They argue that, with a view to systematic discussion of PBL work, there can be a close relation between certain ways of doing interpretive qualitative research and a holistic functional view of language, and that this close relation has the potential to foster inquiry and reflection that are agentive and situated. They also argue that the roles of researcher, teacher, and learner need to be brought much closer together than they were in earlier research in the field. They show how this may be achieved through the case study mentioned earlier. A central contribution this chapter makes to the field is a model which makes a link between interpretive research and functional linguistics that brings a number of the themes of this book into closer association. In this final chapter, Mohan and Lee clearly explain an emerging Social Practice theory in second language research and practice. They also provide a great example of raising students' and teachers' awareness of language and content learning through project work.

This, the first volume of its kind, brings together original work on theoretical, research, and practical aspects of project-based learning and instruction in L2 and FL by some major international experts on this topic. Many more studies should be conducted and many more instructional and assessment models should be designed from various theoretical perspectives. The chapters in this volume should inspire other theorists, researchers, and practitioners in second and foreign language education to continue the discussion and research on and teaching through project-based learning and instruction.

ACKNOWLEDGMENTS

Paul and I are indebted to the contributors to this volume. Without their insightful work and cooperation, this book would not have been possible. We are grateful to our colleagues who acted as external reviewers for the chapters. They are Becky Brown, Mary Brydon-Miller, Beatrice Dupuy, Masaki Kobayashi, Shao-Ting Hung, Bernard Mohan, Tammy Slater, Fredricka Stoller, and

Gail Weinstein. Their input and feedback greatly strengthened the book. Special thanks to Leo van Lier, who agreed to write the Foreword, and Bernard Mohan, who agreed to write the "afterword" for the book. Their insight on the topic contributes greatly to the second and foreign language education literature. We would also like to express our thanks to Frances Andersen, our copy editor, whose diligent work made this project so much more successful. Finally, thanks are also due to the series editor, JoAnn Hammadou Sullivan, and to the editorial committee of the *Research in Second Language Learning* series for recognizing the value of this work.

REFERENCES

Alan, B., & Stoller, F. L. (2005). Maximizing the benefits of project work in foreign language classrooms. *English Teaching Forum, 43*(4), 10–21.

Alberty, H. B. (1927). A study of the project method in education. Columbus: Ohio State University Press.

Allen, L. Q. (2004). Implementing a culture portfolio project within a constructivist paradigm. *Foreign Language Annals, 37*, 232–239.

Beckett, G. H. (1999). *Project-based instruction in a Canadian secondary school's ESL classes: Goals and evaluations.* Unpublished doctoral dissertation, University of British Columbia, Vancouver.

Beckett, G. H. (2002). Teacher and student evaluations of project-based instruction. *TESL Canada Journal, 19*(2), 52–66.

Beckett, G. H. (2005). Academic language and literacy socialization through project based instruction: ESL student perspectives and issues. *Journal of Asian Pacific Communication, 15*, 191–206.

Beckett, G. H., & Slater, T. (2005). The project framework: A tool for language and content integration. *English Language Teaching Journal, 59*, 108–116.

Brubacher, J. S. (1947). *The history of the problems of education.* New York: McGraw-Hill.

Coleman, J. A. (1992). Project-based learning, transferable skills, information technology and video. *Language Learning Journal, 5*, 35–37.

Debyser, F. (1996). *L'Immeuble* [The apartment building]. Paris: Hachette.

Dewey, J. (1926). *Democracy and education: An introduction to the philosophy of education.* New York: Macmillan.

Dewey, J., & Dewey, E. (1915). *Schools of to-morrow.* London: J. M. Dent & Sons.

Eggins, S., & Slade, D. (1997). *Analysing casual conversation.* London: Cassell.

Eyring, J. L. (1989). *Teacher experience and student responses in ESL project work instruction: A case study.* Unpublished doctoral dissertation, University of California, Los Angeles.

Eyring, J. (2001). Experiential and negotiated language learning. In M. Celce-Murcia (Ed.), *Teaching English as a second or foreign language* (3rd ed., pp. 333–344). Boston: Heinle & Heinle.

Fang, X., & Warschauer, M. (2004). Technology and curriculum reform in China: A case study. *TESOL Quarterly, 38*, 301–323.

Fried-Booth, D. L. (1986). *Project work*. New York: Oxford University Press.

Fried-Booth. D. L. (2002). *Project work* (2nd ed.). New York: Oxford University Press.

Gardner, D. (1995). Student produced video documentary provides a real reason for using the target language. *Language Learning Journal, 12,* 54–56.

Haines, S. (1989). *Projects for the EFL classroom: Resource material for teachers.* Walton-on-Thames, UK: Nelson.

Halliday, M. A. K. (1994). *An introduction to functional grammar* (2nd ed.). London: Edward Arnold.

Hedge, T. (1993). Project work. *English Language Teaching Journal, 47*(3), 276–277.

Hilton-Jones, U. (1988). *Project-based learning for foreign students in an English-speaking environment.* (ERIC Document Reproduction Service No. ED 301 054)

Holt, M. (1994). Dewey and the "cult of efficiency": Competing ideologies in collaborative pedagogies of the 1920s. *Journal of Advanced Composition, 14*(1), 73–92.

Kilpatrick, W. H. (1918). The project method. *Teachers College Record, 19*(4), 319–335.

Kobayashi, M. (2003). The role of peer support in ESL students' accomplishment of oral academic tasks. *Canadian Modern Language Review, 59,* 337–368.

Kobayashi, M. (2004). *A sociocultural study of second language tasks: Activity, agency, and language socialization.* Unpublished doctoral dissertation, University of British Columbia, Vancouver.

Kohonen, V. (2001). Towards experiential foreign language education. In V. Kohonen, R. Jaatinen, P. Kaikkonen, & J. Lehtovaara (Eds.), *Experiential learning in foreign language education* (pp. 8–60). Harlow, UK: Pearson Education.

Legutke, M., & Thomas, H. (1991). *Process and experience in the language classroom.* Harlow, UK: Longman.

Lemke, J. (1990). *Talking science: Language learning and values.* Norwood, NJ: Ablex Press.

Levine, G. S. (2004). Global simulation: A student-centered, task-based format for intermediate foreign language courses. *Foreign Language Annals, 37,* 26–36.

Levis, J. M., & Levis, G. M. (2003). A project-based approach to teaching research writing to nonnative writers. *IEEE Transactions on Professional Communication, 46,* 210–221.

Mohan, B. (1986). *Language and content.* Reading, MA: Addison-Wesley.

Mohan, B. (1989). Knowledge structures and academic discourse. *Word 40*(1–2), 99–114.

Mohan, B. A. (2001). The second language as a medium of learning. In B. Mohan, C. Leung, & C. Davison (Eds.), *English as a second language in the mainstream* (pp. 107–126). London: Pearson Education.

Mohan, B. A. (in press). Knowledge structures in social practice. In J. Cummins & C. Davison (Eds.), *International handbook of English language teaching.* Dordrecht: Kluwer.

Mohan, B., & Beckett, G. H. (2003). Functional approach to content-based language learning: Recasts in causal explanations. *Modern Language Journal, 87,* 421–432.

Moulton, M. R., & Holmes, V. L. (2000). An ESL capstone course: Integrating research tools, techniques, and technology. *TESOL Journal, 9*(2), 23–29.

National Research Council. (1999). Improving student learning. Washington, DC: National Academy Press.

Ochs, E. (1988). *Culture and language development: Language acquisition and language socialization in a Samoan village.* Cambridge, UK: Cambridge University Press.

O'Toole, M. (1996). Science, schools, children and books: Exploring the classroom interface between science and language. *Studies in Science Education, 28,* 113–143.

Parker, L. (1992). Language in science education: Implications for teachers. *Australian Science Teachers' Journal, 38*(2), 26–32.

Rowell, P. M. (1997). Learning in school science: The promises and practices of writing. *Studies in Science Education, 30,* 19–56.

Schieffelin, B. B. (1990). *The give and take of everyday life: Language socialization of Kaluli children.* New York: Cambridge University Press.

Schieffelin, B., & Ochs, E. (1986). *Language socialization across cultures.* Cambridge, UK: Cambridge University Press.

Stoller, F. L. (1997). Project work: A means to promote language and content. *English Teaching Forum, 35*(4), 2–9, 37.

Stoller, F. L. (2004). Content-based instruction: Perspectives on curriculum planning. In M. McGroarty (Ed.), *Annual Review of Applied Linguistics* (pp. 261–283). New York: Cambridge University Press.

van Lier, L. (2005). The bellman's map: Avoiding the "perfect and absolute blank" in language learning. In R. Jourdenais & S. Springer (Eds.), *Content, tasks, and projects in the language classroom: 2004 conference proceedings* (pp. 13–21). Monterey, CA: Monterey Institute of International Studies.

Weinstein, G. (2004). Moving toward learner-centered teaching with accountability. *CATESOL Journal, 16*(1), 97–110.

PART I

OVERVIEW, THEORY, AND RESEARCH

CHAPTER 2

ESTABLISHING A THEORETICAL FOUNDATION FOR PROJECT-BASED LEARNING IN SECOND AND FOREIGN LANGUAGE CONTEXTS

Fredricka Stoller
Northern Arizona University

Project-based learning has been advocated as an effective means for promoting purposeful language learning for more than 20 years (e.g., Fried-Booth, 1982, 1986, 2002; Haines, 1989; Ho, 2003; M. M. T. Lee, Li, & Lee, 1999; Legutke & Thomas, 1991; Papandreou, 1994; Stoller, 1997). During these two decades, most support for project-based learning has stemmed from teachers' anecdotal reports of the successful incorporation of project work into language classrooms with young, adolescent, and adult learners, as well as classrooms with general, vocational, academic, and specific language aims (e.g., Allen, 2004; Carter & Thomas, 1986; Coleman, 1992; Fer-

Project-Based Second and Foreign Language Education, pages 19–40
Copyright © 2006 by Information Age Publishing

ragatti & Carminati, 1984; Gardner, 1995; Glick, Holst, & Tomei, 1998; Gu, 2002, 2004; Hilton-Jones, 1988; Kogan, 2003; I. Lee, 2002; Legutke, 1984, 1985; Legutke & Thiel, 1983; Levine, 2004; Moulton & Holmes, 2000; Sheppard & Stoller, 1995; Tomei, Glick, & Holst, 1999; Ward, 1988; Wicks, 2000). Despite evidence of some student dissatisfaction with project work and limited numbers of controlled studies to determine the merits of project-based learning (see Beckett, 1999, 2002, 2005; Beckett & Slater, 2005; Eyring, 1989, 1997; Gu, 2002), the reports of second language (L2) and foreign language (FL) students who have completed projects with improved language skills, content learning, real-life skills, sustained motivation, and positive self-concepts attest, at one level, to the perceived successes attributed to project-based learning.

While anecdotal reports provide interesting insights into project work, we cannot, in good conscience, turn to them for a theoretical foundation that supports project-based learning. What we can do to build a defensible theoretical framework for project work, however, is consult research in the broader fields of L2 and FL teaching/learning that is inextricably linked to the many positive claims made by project work proponents. For example, many practitioners report that students have increased motivation and enhanced self-esteem as a result of project-based activities; by exploring research on motivation and self-esteem, we might gain an understanding into why project-based learning, or select aspects of project-based learning, lead to these positive outcomes. By means of such an approach, we can possibly ascertain the roots of the benefits often associated with project work and then use that information to build a strong case for project-based learning as well as inform our instructional practices in principled ways.

The goal of this chapter is to establish a theoretical foundation for project-based learning in L2 and FL contexts. To accomplish this goal, I begin with an overview of varied configurations of project-based learning and a summary of the positive outcomes reported by practitioners. These sections are followed by an exploration of research findings—from areas within the fields of L2 and FL teaching and a few areas outside these fields—that can help us build a theoretical foundation that supports project-based learning. The chapter concludes with implications from this research that extend common definitions of project work in language-learning settings and a call for further research that could inform the practices of teachers, curriculum and course designers, materials developers, and those involved with assessment in instructional settings that make use of projects to promote language and content learning.

PROJECT-BASED LEARNING AND ITS MANY CONFIGURATIONS

Project-based learning is a more complex instructional concept than the term suggests. As any experienced practitioner knows, there is much more to project-based learning than the simple incorporation of projects into the curriculum. The scope of project-based learning is captured, in some ways, by the many labels given to classroom approaches that incorporate projects:

- Experiential and negotiated language learning (e.g., Eyring, 2001; Legutke & Thomas, 1991; Padgett, 1994)
- Investigative research (e.g., Kenny, 1993)
- Problem-based learning (e.g., Savoie & Hughes, 1994; Wood & Head, 2004)
- Project approach or project-based approach (e.g., Ho, 2003; Levis & Levis, 2003; Papandreou, 1994)
- Project work (e.g., Fried-Booth, 1986, 2002; Haines, 1989; Henry, 1994; M. M. T. Lee et al., 1999; Phillips, Burwood, & Dunford, 1999)

Though not necessarily synonymous with project-based learning, these labels reveal many of the features commonly attributed to it: experiential learning, negotiated meaning and experience, research and inquiry, problem solving, and, of course, projects.

Project-based learning conjures up other images as well. It has been equated, by some, with in-class group work, out-of-class activities, cooperative learning, task-based instruction, a vehicle for fully integrated language and content learning, and a mechanism for cross-curricular work. For some, project work involves fairly nonelaborated tasks; for others, project work entails elaborate sets of sequenced tasks during which students are actively engaged in information gathering, processing, and reporting, with the ultimate goal of increased content knowledge and language mastery. Some so-called projects are confined to a single lesson, yet most projects extend into weeks, an entire semester, or even a full school year. Most projects are content driven, though they vary in terms of their content emphases (cf. Skehan, 1995; Willis, 1996, for discussions of task-based instruction that might be project oriented but not strongly content driven). Some projects focus on real-world issues (e.g., elections, the environment, public transportation), while others are linked to themes in mainstream curricula (e.g., anthropology, biotechnology, catering and hotel restaurant management, social studies). Some projects emphasize an understanding of the target language culture (e.g., Allen, 2004) or issues related to cultural adjustment, the latter most often the focus of L2 (rather than FL) projects. Others, so-called global simulations, are built around a set of problems, with "a reality of function in a simulated and structured environment" (Jones, 1984, cited by Levine, 2004, p. 27).

Some projects are highly structured by the teacher, whereas others are either semistructured (with details determined in part by the teacher and in part by students) or highly unstructured (giving students independence in defining the directions and goals of the project). Projects can involve face-to-face interviews, surveys, library or Internet searches, snail mail written correspondence, e-mail exchanges, and/or field trips; almost all projects expose students to language by means of authentic information sources. Some projects result in theatrical performances, the formation of a club, or a fund-raising event (Gaer & McClintick, 1995); others conclude with formal written reports, posters, bulletin board displays, booklets, debates, class newspapers, oral presentations supported by graphic displays, multimedia presentations, videos, portfolios, and so forth. Final outcomes such as these can be directed toward authentic audiences (e.g., a letter to a governmental official, a pin-and-string display in a railroad station, a Web site for tourists, a multimedia presentation for new students), while others are presented to simulated audiences made up of classmates and the teacher.

In some settings, project-based learning is a natural extension, or an enhancement, of what is already taking place in class. For example, a thematic unit on animal communication in an intensive English program might be structured to engage students in a project that lasts for the duration of the instructional unit, culminating with written reports that oblige students to integrate information from the teacher-orchestrated portion of the unit with their own project-based research. In other contexts, projects are incorporated into instruction to shift students' attention away from the standard curriculum, thereby adding some degree of novelty to the students' educational experience. In either case, projects usually extend instruction beyond the four walls of the traditional classroom, taking students into the community (and/or onto the World Wide Web), giving them access to new information sources, and creating genuine opportunities for communication. Project work has also been integrated into teacher-training curricula, not only to model an approach that teachers in training may subsequently use with language learners later in their careers (Levy, 1997), but also to reinforce the content of the teacher-training curriculum. Despite these varied conceptions, project work is viewed by most of its advocates "not as a replacement for other teaching methods," but rather as "an approach to learning which complements mainstream methods" (Haines, 1989, p. 1).

That project-based learning has been translated into practice in so many different ways may be due, in part, to the particularities of different instructional settings (defined by diverse student populations, instructional objectives, institutional constraints, and available resources). Its various configurations also reveal the flexibility of the approach. Despite these variations, common themes run across reports of successful project-based learning. The following quotations capture some of the principal characteristics of project-based learning:

> Projects are multi-skill activities focusing on topics or themes rather than on specific language targets....Because specific language aims are not prescribed, and because students concentrate their efforts and attention on reaching an agreed goal, project work provides students with opportunities to recycle known language and skills in a relatively natural context. (Haines, 1989, p. 1)

> Project work is a "versatile vehicle for fully integrated language and content learning." (Stoller, 1997, p. 3)

> [P]roject work enables the gradual development of autonomy with progressively greater responsibility being taken by learners.... [Project work] is an excellent structure for preparing learners to approach learning in their own way, suitable to their own abilities, styles, and preferences. (Skehan, 1998, p. 273)

> Since the mid-1970s, as ELT [English language teaching] has come to espouse principles of learner-centred teaching, learner autonomy, collaborative learning, and learning through tasks, English language teachers have explored and exploited the tradition of project work.... [Project work] has been promoted in ELT for a number of reasons: for example, learners' use of language as they negotiate plans, and analyse and discuss information and ideas, is determined by genuine communicative needs. With younger learners, project work encourages imagination and creativity, self-discipline and responsibility, collaboration, research and study skills, and cross-curricular work through exploitation of knowledge gained in other subjects. (Hedge, 2000, pp. 362, 364)

> Project work: The quintessential experiential language learning approach... in terms of its view of learning, power relations, teacher and learner roles, view of knowledge, view of curriculum, learning experiences, control of process, motivation, and evaluation. (Eyring, 2001, p. 336)

> Project work is student-centred and driven by the need to create an end-product. However, it is the route to achieving this end-product that makes project work so worthwhile. The route to the end-product brings opportunities for students to develop their confidence and independence and to work together in a real-world environment by collaborating on a task. (Fried-Booth, 2002, p. 6)

The versatility of project-based learning makes it difficult to articulate one single definition that takes into account the various ways in which the concept can be translated into practice. For the purposes of this chapter, a definition is attempted by specifying the numerous conditions that should be present for effective project-based learning to take place: Project-based learning should (a) have a process and product orientation; (b) be defined, at least in part, by students, to encourage student ownership in the project; (c) extend over a period of time (rather than a single class session); (d) encourage the natural integration of skills; (e) make a dual commitment to language and content learning; (f) oblige students to work in groups and on their own; (g) require students to take some responsibility for their own learning through the gathering, processing, and reporting of information from target language resources; (h) require teachers and students to assume new roles and responsibilities (Levy, 1997); (i) result in a tangible final product; and (j) conclude with student reflections on both the process and the product.

POSITIVE OUTCOMES OF PROJECT-BASED LEARNING

Practitioners report a host of benefits resulting from student engagement with project-based learning. An analysis of 16 publications covering different aspects of project-based learning in L2 and FL settings reveals eight commonly reported benefits (see Table 2.1).[1] The most commonly reported positive outcome of project work is linked to the authenticity of students' experiences and the language that they are exposed to and use. While engaged in project work, students partake in authentic tasks for authentic purposes—both conditions sadly absent from many language classrooms. For example, many projects oblige students to take notes (from books, newspaper articles, Web sites, informational pamphlets, interviews, etc.) and then consult and use the notes for meaningful purposes. In other projects, students conduct interviews, not for the sake of listening and speaking practice, but rather to gain access to information that can be used in meaningful ways to complete the project. Similarly, when students write letters as part of their projects, they expect actual responses from real people and real institutions. When students share the results of their projects, whatever they may be, with authentic audiences (e.g., the mayor's office, a school principal, their classmates), once again they are engaged in authentic tasks, using (and being exposed to) authentic language at the same time.

Another commonly reported benefit of project-based learning is the intensity of students' motivation, involvement, engagement, participation, and enjoyment. It is not clear from these reports what the relationship among these outcomes is. What comes first, motivation or involvement? Perhaps student motivation leads to more engagement (or involvement, or participation, or enjoyment); or possibly student engagement leads to

Table 2.1. Most Commonly Cited Benefits Attributed to Project Work in Second and Foreign Language Settings

Rank	Reported Benefits	A	B	C	D	E	F	G	H	I	J	K	L	M	N	O	P
																Publications About Project-Based Learning	
1	Authenticity of experience and language	✓		✓	✓	✓	✓	✓	✓	✓	✓	✓	✓	✓	✓	✓	✓
2	Intensity of motivation, involvement, engagement, participation, enjoyment, creativity			✓	✓	✓	✓	✓	✓	✓	✓	✓	✓	✓	✓	✓	✓
3	Enhanced language skills; repeated opportunities for output, modified input, and negotiated meaning; purposeful opportunities for an integrated focus on form and other aspects of language			✓	✓	✓	✓		✓	✓	✓	✓	✓	✓	✓	✓	✓
4	Improved abilities to function in a group (including social, cooperative, and collaborative skills)			✓				✓	✓	✓	✓	✓	✓	✓	✓		
5	Increased content knowledge	✓	✓	✓					✓	✓	✓	✓					✓
6	Improved confidence, sense of self, self-esteem, attitude toward learning, comfort using language, satisfaction with achievement		✓	✓			✓		✓	✓	✓	✓	✓	✓			
7	Increased autonomy, independence, self-initiation, and willingness to take responsibility for own learning			✓				✓	✓	✓	✓	✓	✓				
8	Improved abilities to make decisions, be analytical, think critically, solve problems	✓				✓	✓	✓								✓	

Key—A: Allen (2004); B: Carter and Thomas (1986); C: Coleman (1992); D: Ferragatti and Carminati (1984); E: Fried-Booth (1982); F: Gardner (1995); G: Gu (2002); H: Gu (2004) I: Ho (2003).; J: I. Lee (2002); K: Legutke (1984); L: Legutke (1985); M: Levine (2004); N: Padgett (1994); O: Sheppard and Stoller (1995); P: Stoller (1997).

increased student motivation. Whatever the cause-effect relationship is, the end result is reported to be positive.

Project-based learning is also said to inspire creativity, as students move away from mechanistic learning and toward endeavors that allow for and benefit from creativity. That projects do not usually have predetermined responses contributes to environments in which creativity pays off. In many projects, students are given a voice in defining both the process and the product of the project. It is possible that teacher-orchestrated efforts to engage students in project planning, in addition to the open-endedness of the project, stimulate creativity.

The third most commonly reported benefit of project work is students' enhanced language skills. Practitioners have reported improved reading, writing, speaking, listening, vocabulary, and grammar abilities, possibly due to the fact that project work facilitates repeated opportunities for interaction (output), modified input, and negotiated meaning. Because projects lend themselves naturally to integrated skills, we find that students are engaged in authentic tasks that require that they read to write, write to speak, listen to write, and so forth, leading to meaningful language use and the important recycling of vocabulary and grammar forms. Equally if not more important is the fact that projects oblige students to read to learn, listen to learn, and speak to learn, preparing them for lifelong learning. Fortunately, for students, project work also lends itself to opportunities for an explicit focus on form and other aspects of language, most easily accommodated and appreciated at three points in the development of a project, specifically just before the information-gathering, processing, and reporting phases of the project (see Alan & Stoller, 2005; Sheppard & Stoller, 1995; Stoller, 1997). It has been suggested that the tangible end product associated with project work, often shared with a real audience, leads students to take their "formal accuracy more seriously" (Skehan, 1998, p. 274).

Another reported benefit of project work is students' improved social, cooperative, and collaborative skills. These skills, easily transferable to other settings, develop over time as students work with classmates to gather, process, synthesize, and report information related to their projects. What often occurs, over the course of a project, is that students begin to "view each other as single links in a chain that merge through exchanges of information and negotiation of meaning, to produce a successful project outcome" (Alan & Stoller, 2005).

Because projects are planned around the gathering, processing, and reporting of "real" information related to the project theme, practitioners report that students complete their projects with increased content knowledge. Project work, in fact, is compatible with content-based instruction and its dual commitment to content and language learning (Stoller, 2004).

As students progress through the various phases of the project, the information that they themselves have collected, as well as the information compiled by classmates, is recycled and revisited in meaningful ways (see Stoller, 2002), thereby consolidating content learning.

Practitioners also report students' improved self-confidence, enhanced self-esteem, positive attitudes toward learning, comfort using the language, and satisfaction with personal achievements. That sound projects have easily identifiable stages (information collecting, processing, reporting, evaluating) and tangible final products makes it possible for students to track (or at least reflect on) their own progress. The final outcome of the project gives students a chance to view (and assess) the results of their hard work. Furthermore, the tangible outcome serves "as a sort of public record of the project" (Skehan, 1998, p. 274). When students receive constructive feedback about their progress over the course of the project, the end result can be improved self-concepts and confidence to use language more comfortably.

That students demonstrate increased autonomy, independence, self-initiation, and a willingness to take responsibility for their own learning as a result of project work represents another set of benefits touted in the literature. When projects are structured to engage students actively in early project planning (even if student contributions are small), students gradually develop a sense of ownership and pride in the project. When students are given choices throughout the project, including the chance to shape the project, they become more autonomous and independent (see Skehan, 1998). It is not surprising that projects stimulate student interest, lead to active student involvement, and nurture a willingness to take responsibility.

Finally, practitioners report that project work results in improved decision-making abilities, analytical and critical thinking skills, and problem solving. Interestingly, conditions for optimal learning, in general, are said to require challenge and opportunities for decision making, critical thinking, and problem solving (see Csikszentmihalyi, 1990, 1993; Csikszentmihalyi & Csikszentmihalyi, 1988; Egbert, 2003). Increased competence in such abilities may very well contribute to many of the other benefits mentioned here and in the literature.

INSIGHTS FROM THE LITERATURE THAT OFFER SUPPORT FOR PROJECT-BASED LEARNING

Only a few empirical studies have been conducted to evaluate the effects of project work on language learning. Nonetheless, numerous studies (from inside and outside the fields of L2 and FL learning) offer support for many of the positive outcomes attributed to project work. My original intention was to document support for each of the benefits introduced earlier (and listed in Table 2.1). However, that approach would have been artificial because of the extensive overlap among the benefits espoused by practitioners. That overlap can be seen clearly in discussions of motivation (the second benefit listed in Table 2.1), which touch upon almost all the other benefits mentioned by practitioners, including improved self-esteem, learner autonomy, and student-student cooperation. Thus, separating those commonly cited benefits, and others, from a broader discussion of motivation would have distorted the symbiotic relationships that seem to exist among the positive outcomes of project work. To capture these relationships and showcase the varying types and levels of support for project-based learning that exist in the professional literature, four broad areas of investigation are discussed: motivation, expertise, input/output, and learner centeredness. Together, they may contribute to the formation of a theoretical foundation for project-based instruction.

It should be noted here that the most commonly cited benefit of project-based learning—specifically the authenticity of experience and language—is a complex topic that provides no straightforward conclusion. The topic of authenticity has prompted spirited discussions among English for academic purposes (EAP) and English for specific purposes (ESP) materials writers, course developers, and curriculum designers. Explorations of gradations of authenticity of text, purpose, audience, and interaction between readers and text reflect many of the issues that EAP and ESP professionals discuss (Dudley-Evans & St. John, 1998; Flowerdew & Peacock, 2001; Jordan, 1997). Few, if any, of these discussions, however, offer direct support for project-based learning. (See van Lier, 1996; Widdowson, 2003, for additional discussions on authenticity and language teaching.)

Motivation

Many language professionals have pointed out that project-based learning has resulted in increased student motivation, in addition to common outcomes of motivation, including increased student autonomy, enhanced self-confidence and self-concept, and increased interest. What we cannot ascertain, partially because of the paucity of empirical studies on project work, is whether student motivation and associated outcomes stem from students' actual involvement in project work or if motivation leads to students' enthusiastic participation in project work. Most likely, the combination of the two perspectives is likely to play a role in project-based learning.

Research is extensive on motivation in general, and motivation to learn a L2 and FL more specifically (see Dörnyei, 2001a, 2001b). It is not the purpose of this chapter to provide a comprehensive summary of motivation research, yet some interesting observations about that research may reveal why project-based learning leads to increased student motivation, autonomy, interest, self-confidence, and self-concept. Particularly persuasive, with respect to project-based learning, are theories that suggest that humans are motivated when the following conditions exist, all possible (though not necessarily by default) in project-based learning: Individuals need to (a) feel competent, (b) be granted sufficient autonomy, (c) have the opportunity to set worthwhile goals (see Beckett & Slater, 2005), (d) receive feedback, and (e) be positively affirmed by others (see Walker & Symons, 1997, cited in Dörnyei, 2001b).

Furthermore, motivation usually results from situations in which learners are engaged in tasks that are neither too easy nor too difficult, but rather are characterized by just the right amount of challenge (see Csikszentmihalyi, 1990, 1993; Csikszentmihalyi & Csikszentmihalyi, 1988; Egbert, 2003). Moreover, motivation usually evolves gradually, as learners engage in complex sets of tasks that move them from planning, goal setting, and task implementation through outcome evaluation (see Dörnyei, 2001b). Such phases are standard features of many project-based frameworks (e.g., Alan & Stoller, 2005; Knutson, 2003; M. M. T. Lee et al., 1999; Stoller, 1997). Students are likely to be motivated when projects are structured to arouse student curiosity, provide opportunities to understand some phenomenon of interest, and set students up for success with tasks that are challenging but manageable.

Motivation and Learner Autonomy

There is evidence that motivation and learner autonomy go hand in hand (Benson, 2000). Project-based learning easily accommodates conditions necessary for learner autonomy, including real choices, opportunities to take on leadership roles, and responsibility for and sense of control over one's own learning. Another condition needed for enhanced motivation and a sense of autonomy is students' perception that successes (and failures) are attributable to one's own efforts and strategies rather than to factors outside one's control (Dickinson, 1995; Oxford & Shearin, 1994). Projects—whether they are structured by the instructor, semistructured, or unstructured—can be orchestrated to give students the chance to negotiate aspects of the project, including, but not limited to, the theme, tangible outcomes, procedures to attain outcomes, individual roles, and group responsibilities.

Motivation and Self-Confidence

Language professionals have reported that project work involvement leads to enhanced self-confidence, self-esteem, and self-concept. According to Dörnyei (2001b), self-confidence emerges when individuals perform tasks competently, produce results, and accomplish established goals. Project work, defined by a sequence of tasks that concludes with a tangible outcome and an opportunity to evaluate both the process and the product, allows students to judge whether they have performed tasks competently and accomplished their goals. In project work settings, student accomplishments (in terms of language learning, content learning, skill learning, strategy use, and final outcome) can be confirmed, explicitly and implicitly, by means of formative and summative feedback provided by peers and the instructor. Ongoing feedback makes it easier for students to reflect on their accomplishments, thereby contributing to potential growth in self-confidence, self-esteem, and self-concept.

Motivation and Interest

Research indicates that motivation and interest arise in part from the recognition that learning is indeed occurring and that the learning justifies the effort. Further, considerable research argues that students who are motivated, who develop an interest in curricular goals and activities, and who perceive themselves as both successful and capable are willing to work hard to process challenging materials, recall information, elaborate, learn more, and do better in school (e.g., Alexander, Kulikowich, & Jetton, 1994; Krapp, Hidi, & Renninger, 1992; Tobias, 1994; Turner, 1993). This intersection of motivation and interest provides a possible explanation for the relationships that exist between better learning and depth of processing (see Grabe & Stoller, 1997, for a review of related research). Project-based learning can easily build in these so-called conditions for improved motivation and interest.

Motivation and Cooperative Learning

Related to motivation is the role of cooperative learning, a generic term that refers to methods of organizing instructional activities to achieve mutual learning goals by means of shared, though not necessarily identical, responsibilities and cooperation. Project work is often structured around cooperative-learning activities that capitalize on the strengths of students in learning groups, with the ultimate aim of combining efforts to complete the project. Slavin's (1995) research, with more than 100 experimental studies, has demonstrated strong improvements in student learning when students work in groups that have structured objectives, have well-defined group goals and rewards, promote individual accountability, and provide each student in the group with equal opportunities for success. Slavin's research has indicated that cooperative learning leads to greater student cooperation, higher motivation for learning, more positive student attributions for learning success, better attitudes toward school and learning, and greater self-esteem.

Cooperative learning leads to more complex teacher and student roles, the result of a restructuring of traditional classroom paradigms. Cooperative-learning lessons, like many project work frameworks, call for negotiated syllabi, the teacher as facilitator (e.g., McDonell, 1992), student work groups, and various levels of interdependence among teacher and students. Project-based learning lends itself nicely to these conditions.

In line with cooperative learning are the principles of collaborative learning espoused and utilized by Wilhelm (1999) in the development and implementation of project-based classes. The principles of collaborative learning include cooperative learning, individualized instructional planning and feedback, student involvement in evaluation, teacher as facilitator, and learner and teacher reflection. When principles such as these are applied to project-based learning, Wilhelm reports enhanced critical thinking, investigative skill building, motivation, and communicative competence. (See Wilhelm, 1999, for the dos and don'ts of collaborative learning.)

Development of Expertise

Proponents of project-based learning often mention the content learning, problem-solving abilities, and critical-thinking skills that result from student involvement in projects. These same positive outcomes also surface in more general discussions of the development of expertise. Research on the nature of expertise provides support for many of the features of project-based learning. Bereiter and Scardamalia (1993) have outlined a theory of expertise in which they argue that expertise develops when learners reinvest their knowledge in a sequence of progressively more complex problem-solving activities. Expert-like learners look for increasing complexity in the tasks in which they engage; in the process, learning improves and motivation increases, in part because students recognize their growing expertise. In fact, the very nature of project work assists students in applying, developing, and extending subject-matter knowledge, adding to their growing expertise. Because most projects extend well beyond one lesson, students find themselves with multiple opportunities to connect new information with known information, thereby consolidating the learning of content information.

Extended engagement with subject matter, in addition to deliberate practice (i.e., activities designed specifically to improve performance), have been identified as necessary, though not sufficient, for building expertise (Ericsson, 2002). Deliberate practice, as described by Ericsson (2002), requires active learner concentration to go beyond current abilities, "consistent with the mental demands of problem solving and other types of learning" (p. 29). In project work settings where students are guided in the deliberate practice of skills and language required for the successful completion of the various project work stages (e.g., data collection, analysis, and presentation), students are likely to witness the gradual, but steady, development of expertise in the topic being explored. When project work is embedded in content-based curricula, with their dual commitment to language and content learning (e.g., Grabe & Stoller, 1997; Stoller, 2004), it has the real potential for leading to increased student expertise. In fact, motivation may stem from students' perceptions that a particular project is relevant to their language- and content-learning goals (Chambers, 1999; Dörnyei, 2001b).

Meaningful Input and Output

Many language professionals praise project-based learning because it creates purposeful opportunities for language input, language output, and explicit attention to language-related features (e.g., forms, vocabulary, skills, strategies). The need for comprehensible input, meaningful output, and explicit instruction on relevant and contextually appropriate language forms has been proposed by Swain (1985), as a result of extensive research on Canadian immersion programs. Swain's output hypothesis argues that input is a necessary but insufficient condition for language learning; students need opportunities for speaking and writing (i.e., output), and also active engagement in language-learning activities based on explicit instruction (see Mohan & Beckett, 2001, for an analysis of grammatical scaffolding used with students engaged in a project in a content-based class). Some project work frameworks (in particular Alan & Stoller, 2005; Stoller, 1997) argue for explicit attention to students' language and skill needs at various points in the project. For example, immediately preceding the stage in which students actually gather information for their project, the instructor prepares students for the language, skill, and strategy demands associated with information gathering. With student ability levels in mind, the instructor prepares activities for each of the information-gathering tasks. For instance, if students will conduct interviews to gather information, the instructor may plan activities (e.g., role plays) in which students have to form questions, ask follow-up questions, request clarification, and take notes. If students expect to write letters, the instructor might introduce (or review) the format and language of formal letters. If students intend to conduct an Internet search, the instructor may review search procedures and introduce useful note-taking strategies. A similar attention to forms, vocabulary, and skills is appropriate immediately preceding the information analysis and information-reporting stages.

Related to meaningful language input and output is the common claim that project-based learning lends itself to the natural integration of language skills (reading, writing, speaking, and listening), mirroring real-world language use where skills are rarely used in isolation. Project-based learning also lends itself to the integration of language- and content-learning objectives, as one might see in content-based classrooms (e.g., Stoller & Grabe, 1997).

Learner Centeredness

One might attribute the reported successes of project work to the fact that project-based learning has the potential to narrow the gap between traditional classrooms and more learner- and learning-centered settings (see Nunan, 1995). In many project work settings, students are given some control over their learning and granted some choices in defining (or possibly negotiating) goals, emphases, processes, and product, characteristics of more learner/learning-centered classrooms. The gap between teaching and learning is narrowed when certain conditions are met (see Table 2.2). Many of these conditions exist (or have the potential to exist) in project-based settings.

Table 2.2.   Conditions Needed in Learning- and Learner-Centered Curricula

The gap between teaching and learning is narrowed when conditions such as these are met:

- Instructional goals are made explicit to learners.
- Learners are involved in selecting, modifying, and/or adapting goals and content.
- Learners create their own goals and generate their own content.
- Active links are created between the content of the classroom and the world beyond the classroom.
- Learners are trained to identify the strategies underlying pedagogical tasks.
- Learners are encouraged to identify their own preferred learning styles and experiment with alternative styles.
- Learners are given space to make choices and select alternative learning pathways.
- Learners are given opportunities to modify, adapt, create, and evaluate pedagogical tasks and learning processes.
- Learners are encouraged to become their own teachers and researchers.
- Learners are given opportunities to explore . . . relationships between language forms and communicative functions.
- Classroom learning opportunities are created that enable learners to . . . articulate their understanding of how language works as well as put language to communicative use in real or simulated contexts.

Adapted from Nunan, 1995, p. 154

To nurture a more learner-centered curriculum and help students understand the value of project work (despite its departure from traditional classroom practices), Beckett and Slater (2005) advocate the incorporation of several of the conditions set forth in Table 2.2. For example, through the use of *planning graphics* and *project diaries* (together comprising a project framework), students engage in setting explicit goals; charting plans for meeting goals; and monitoring language, content, and skills learning. The use of the Project Framework is reported to result in students' heightened consciousness about a new way of learning language, increased motivation, and a greater appreciation for project work.

CONCLUSION

Project-based learning has earned the endorsement of many L2 and FL practitioners, largely because of its reported positive effects on students' motivation, language skills, ability to function in groups, content learning, self-confidence, autonomy, and decision-making abilities. Although teachers' anecdotal reports cannot be used by themselves to build a theoretical foundation for project-based learning, most teachers' assertions are supported by studies in areas related to motivation, the development of expertise, the role of input and output in language learning, and the value of learner centeredness in classroom instruction. Research in these areas suggests that the following conditions contribute to the positive outcomes so often associated with project-based learning:

(a) Projects should be content driven.
(b) Students need to be engaged in a complex set of manageable yet challenging tasks that are neither too easy nor too difficult. The tasks should be structured so that students have the opportunity to reinvest knowledge in progressively more complex problem-solving activities.
(c) Students must be given real choices, possibly through the negotiation of select aspects of the project (including goals, themes, procedures, outcomes).
(d) Projects must be defined and orchestrated to stimulate students' curiosity and interest.
(e) Student work groups should be formed to capitalize on the strengths of group members. Each group member should be given the opportunity to contribute meaningfully and successfully to group aims. Student group members should understand overall project objectives and the role of their individual contributions to the group effort.
(f) Students should be held accountable for their work.

(g) Students should be given the opportunity to engage in deliberate practice of the skills and language required for the successful completion of each stage of the project.
(h) Students must be given ongoing feedback, in the form of formative and summative assessment, so that they can evaluate their own learning, progress, and attainment of process- and product-oriented goals.

These features, along with the defining characteristics of project-based learning stated earlier in the chapter, may coalesce to form a defendable theoretical foundation for and practical orientation toward project-based learning.

Of course, this foundation could be much stronger if there were not such a paucity of empirical studies focusing on project-based learning in language-learning settings. There is a pressing need for more empirical research on project-based learning in the context of L2 and FL instruction, more generally, and on its various configurations and component parts (e.g., teachers, students, tasks, themes, process, product, procedures, assessment, and feedback), more specifically. Fruitful areas of investigation include, but are not limited to, the following:

- The role of formative and summative assessment in students' project work performance; methods of providing feedback to students at different project work stages
- The effective sequencing of manageable yet challenging tasks in light of project objectives
- The identification and implementation of deliberate practice in the skills and language needed for the successful completion of projects
- The effectiveness of project work implemented in different time frames
- The interface between content- and language-learning objectives in successful project-based learning
- Steps toward the development of expertise in the context of project-based learning
- Measures of improved language learning while students engage in various types of project work
- The definition and role of problem solving and critical thinking in project-based learning
- Reciprocal relationships between the process and product components of project-based learning
- Compatibility of different teacher-learner and learner-learner interaction patterns with the attainment of different learning goals
- Differences between students' language and content learning in project work environments and traditional classrooms

Investigations into topics such as these are needed to strengthen the theoretical foundation for project-based learning as proposed in this chapter. Moreover, insights from such studies could prove useful in informing the practices of teachers, curriculum and course designers, and materials developers, and in guiding formative and summative assessment. The result could be more effective approaches to project-based learning, the real beneficiaries being students who have real language- and content-learning needs.

NOTE

1.   The publications reviewed were not written specifically to espouse the benefits of project-based learning. Rather, it was *my* purpose, while reading the publications, to pull out the benefits that were explicitly or implicitly stated by the authors, regardless of the authors' original intentions.

REFERENCES

Alan, B., & Stoller, F. L. (2005). Maximizing the benefits of project work in foreign language classrooms. *English Teaching Forum, 43*(4), 10–21.

Alexander, P. A., Kulikowich, J. M., & Jetton, T. L. (1994). The role of subject-matter knowledge and interest in the processing of linear and nonlinear texts. *Review of Educational Research, 64*, 201–252.

Allen, L. Q. (2004). Implementing a culture portfolio project within a constructivist paradigm. *Foreign Language Annals, 37*, 232–239.

Beckett, G. H. (1999). *Project-based instruction in a Canadian secondary school's ESL classes: Goals and evaluations*. Unpublished doctoral dissertation, University of British Columbia, Vancouver.

Beckett, G. H. (2002). Teacher and student evaluations of project-based instruction. *TESL Canada Journal, 19*(2), 52–66.

Beckett, G. H. (2005). Academic language and literacy socialization through project-based instruction: ESL student perspectives and issues. *Journal of Asia Pacific Communication, 15*, 191–206.

Beckett, G. H., & Slater, T. (2005). The project framework: A tool for language and content integration. *English Language Teaching Journal, 59*, 108–116.

Benson, P. (2000). *Teaching and researching autonomy in language learning*. New York: Longman.

Bereiter, C., & Scardamalia, M. (1993). *Surpassing ourselves: An inquiry into the nature and implications of expertise*. Chicago: Open Court Press.

Carter, G., & Thomas, H. (1986). "Dear Brown Eyes": Experiential learning in a project-orientated approach. *English Language Teaching Journal, 40*, 196–204.

Chambers, G. N. (1999). *Motivating language learners*. Clevedon, UK: Multilingual Matters.

Coleman, J. A. (1992). Project-based learning, transferable skills, information technology and video. *Language Learning Journal, 5,* 35–37.

Csikszentmihalyi, M. (1990). *Flow: The psychology of optional experience.* New York: Harper & Row.

Csikszentmihalyi, M. (1993). *The evolving source: A psychology for the third millennium.* New York: HarperCollins.

Csikszentmihalyi, M., & Csikszentmihalyi, I. S. (1988). *Optimal experience: Psychological studies of flow in consciousness.* New York: Cambridge University Press.

Dickinson, L. (1995). Autonomy and motivation: A literature review. *System, 23,* 165–174.

Dörnyei, Z. (2001a). *Motivational strategies in the language classroom.* Cambridge, UK: Cambridge University Press.

Dörnyei, Z. (2001b). *Teaching and researching motivation.* New York: Longman.

Dudley-Evans, T., & St. John, M. J. (1998). *Developments in English for specific purposes: A multi-disciplinary approach.* Cambridge, UK: Cambridge University Press.

Egbert, J. (2003). A study of flow theory in the foreign language classroom. *The Modern Language Journal, 87,* 499–518.

Ericsson, K. A. (2002). Attaining excellence through deliberate practice: Insights from the study of expert performance. In M. Ferrari (Ed.), *The pursuit of excellence through education* (pp. 21–55). Mahwah, NJ: Erlbaum.

Eyring, J. L. (1989). *Teacher experience and student responses in ESL project work instruction: A case study.* Unpublished doctoral dissertation. University of California, Los Angeles.

Eyring, J. L. (1997). *Is project work worth it?* (ERIC Document Reproduction Service No. ED 407 838)

Eyring, J. L. (2001). Experiential and negotiated language learning. In M. Celce-Murcia (Ed.), *Teaching English as a second or foreign language* (3rd ed., pp. 333–344). Boston: Heinle & Heinle.

Ferragatti, M. L., & Carminati, E. (1984). Airport: An Italian version. *Modern English Teacher, 2*(4), 15–17.

Flowerdew, J., & Peacock, M. (2001). The EAP curriculum: Issues, methods, and challenges. In J. Flowerdew & M. Peacock (Eds.), *Research perspectives on English for academic purposes* (pp. 177–194). Cambridge, UK: Cambridge University Press.

Fried-Booth, D. L. (1982). Project work with advanced classes. *English Language Teaching Journal, 36,* 98–103.

Fried-Booth, D. L. (1986). *Project work.* New York: Oxford University Press.

Fried-Booth, D. L. (2002). *Project work* (2nd ed.). New York: Oxford University Press.

Gaer, S., & McClintick, L. (1995, April). *Project driven curriculum.* Paper presented at the annual meeting of Teachers of English to Speakers of Other Languages, Long Beach, CA.

Gardner, D. (1995). Student-produced video documentary provides a real reason for using the target language. *Language Learning Journal, 12,* 54–56.

Glick, C., Holst, M., & Tomei, J. (1998). Project work for select faculties. *Gengo Bunkabu Kiyo (Journal of the Department of Language and Culture), 34,* 41–53.

Grabe, W., & Stoller, F. L. (1997). Content-based instruction: Research foundations. In M. A. Snow & D. M. Brinton (Eds.), *The content-based classroom: Perspectives on integrating language and content* (pp. 5–21). New York: Longman.

Gu, P. (2002). Effects of project-based CALL on Chinese EFL learners. *Asian Journal of English Language Teaching, 12,* 195–210.

Gu, P. (2004). Tech view: Leaving the bathtub to make waves. *Essential Teacher, 1*(4), 32–35.

Haines, S. (1989). *Projects for the EFL classroom: Resource material for teachers.* Walton-on-Thames, UK: Nelson.

Hedge, T. (2000). *Teaching and learning in the language classroom.* Oxford: Oxford University Press.

Henry, J. (1994). *Teaching through projects.* London: Kogan Page.

Hilton-Jones, U. (1988). *Project-based learning for foreign students in an English-speaking environment.* (ERIC Document Reproduction Service No. ED 301 054)

Ho, R. (2003). *Project approach: Teaching* (2nd ed.). (ERIC Document Reproduction Service No. ED 478 224)

Jordan, R. R. (1997). *English for academic purposes: A guide and resource book for teachers.* Cambridge, UK: Cambridge University Press.

Kenny, B. (1993). Investigative research: How it changes learner status. *TESOL Quarterly, 27,* 217–231.

Knutson, S. (2003). Experiential learning in second-language classrooms. *TESL Canada Journal, 20*(2), 52–64.

Kogan, Y. (2003). A study of bones. *Early Childhood Research and Practice: An Internet Journal on the Development, Care, and Education of Young Children, 5*(1). Retrieved September 2, 2005, from http://ecrp.uiuc.edu/v5n1/kogan-thumb.html

Krapp, A., Hidi, S., & Renninger, K. A. (1992). Interest, learning, and development. In K. A. Renninger, S. Hidi, & A. Krapp (Eds.), *The role of interest in learning and development* (pp. 3–25). Hillsdale, NJ: Erlbaum.

Lee, I. (2002). Project work made easy in the English classroom. *Canadian Modern Language Review, 59,* 282–290.

Lee, M. M. T., Li, B. K. W., & Lee, I. K. B. (1999). *Project work: Practical guidelines.* Hong Kong: Hong Kong Institute of Education.

Legutke, M. (1984). Project Airport: Part 1. *Modern English Teacher, 11*(4), 10–14.

Legutke, M. (1985). Project Airport: Part 2. *Modern English Teacher, 12*(1), 28–31.

Legutke, M., & Thiel, W. (1983). *Airport: Ein Projekt für den Englischunterricht in Klasse 6* [Airport: A project for 6th-grade English instruction]. Wiesbaden, Germany: Hessisches Institut für Bildungsplanung und Schulentwicklung (HIBS).

Legutke, M., & Thomas, H. (1991). *Process and experience in the language classroom.* New York: Longman.

Levine, G. S. (2004). Global simulation: A student-centered, task-based format for intermediate foreign language courses. *Foreign Language Annals, 37,* 26–36.

Levis, J. M., & Levis, G. M. (2003). A project-based approach to teaching research writing to nonnative writers. *IEEE Transactions on Professional Communication, 46,* 210–221.

Levy, M. (1997). Project-based learning for language teachers: Reflecting on the process. In R. Debski, J. Gassin, & M. Smith (Eds.), *Language learning through social computing* (pp. 181–191). Melbourne: Applied Linguistic Association of Australia and Horwood Language Center.

McDonell, W. (1992). The role of the teacher in the cooperative learning class-room. In C. Kessler (Ed.), *Cooperative language learning: A teacher's resource book* (pp. 163–174). Englewood Cliffs, NJ: Prentice Hall Regents.

Mohan, B., & Beckett, G. H. (2001). A functional approach to research on content-based language learning: Recasts in causal explanations. *Canadian Modern Language Review, 58,* 133–155.

Moulton, M. R., & Holmes, V. L. (2000). An ESL capstone course: Integrating research tools, techniques, and technology. *TESOL Journal, 9*(2), 23–29.

Nunan, D. (1995). Closing the gap between learning and instruction. *TESOL Quarterly, 29,* 133–158.

Oxford, R. L., & Shearin, J. (1994). Language learning motivation: Expanding the theoretical framework. *Modern Language Journal, 78,* 12–28.

Padgett, G. S. (1994). An experiential approach: Field trips, book publication, video production. *TESOL Journal, 3*(3), 8–11.

Papandreou, A. P. (1994). An application of the projects approach to EFL. *English Teaching Forum, 32*(3), 41–42.

Phillips, D., Burwood, S., & Dunford, H. (1999). *Projects with young learners.* Oxford: Oxford University Press.

Savoie, J. M., & Hughes, A. S. (1994). Problem-based learning as classroom solution. *Educational Leadership, 52*(3), 54–57.

Sheppard, K., & Stoller, F. L. (1995). Guidelines for the integration of student projects in ESP classrooms. *English Teaching Forum, 33*(2), 10–15.

Skehan, P. (1995). A framework for the implementation of task-based instruction. *Applied Linguistics, 16,* 542–566.

Skehan, P. (1998). *A cognitive approach to language learning.* Oxford: Oxford University Press.

Slavin, R. E. (1995). *Cooperative learning* (2nd ed.). Boston: Allyn & Bacon.

Stoller, F. L. (1997). Project work: A means to promote language and content. *English Teaching Forum, 35*(4), 2–9, 37.

Stoller, F. L. (2002). Promoting the acquisition of knowledge in a content-based course. In J. Crandall & D. Kaufman (Eds.), *Content-based instruction in higher education settings* (pp. 109–123). Alexandria, VA: TESOL.

Stoller, F. L. (2004). Content-based instruction: Perspectives on curriculum planning. In M. McGroarty (Ed.), *Annual Review of Applied Linguistics* (pp. 261–283). New York: Cambridge University Press.

Stoller, F. L., & Grabe, W. (1997). A six-T's approach to content-based instruction. In M. A. Snow & D. M. Brinton (Eds.), *The content-based classroom: Perspectives on integrating language and content* (pp. 78–94). New York: Longman.

Swain, M. (1985). Communicative competence: Some roles of comprehensible input and comprehensible output in its development. In S. Gass & C. Madden (Eds.), *Input in second language acquisition* (pp. 235–253). Rowley, MA: Newbury House.

Tobias, S. (1994). Interest, prior knowledge, and learning. *Review of Educational Research, 64*(1), 37–54.

Tomei, J., Glick, C., & Holst, M. (1999). Project work in the Japanese university classroom. *The Language Teacher, 23*(3), 5–8.

Turner, J. C. (1993). A motivational perspective on literacy instruction. In D. J. Leu & C. K. Kinzer (Eds.), *Examining central issues in literacy research, theory, and practice* (pp. 153–161). Chicago: National Reading Conference.

van Lier, F. (1996). *Interaction in the language curriculum: Awareness, autonomy, and authenticity.* New York: Longman.

Ward, G. (1988). *I've got a project on...* Rozelle, Australia: Primary English Teaching Association.

Wicks, M. (2000). *Imaginative projects: A resource book of project work for young students.* Cambridge, UK: Cambridge University Press.

Widdowson, H. G. (2003). *Defining issues in English language teaching.* Oxford: Oxford University Press.

Wilhelm, K. H. (1999). Collaborative dos and dont's. *TESOL Journal, 8,* 14–19.

Willis, J. (1996). *A framework for task-based learning.* Essex, UK: Longman.

Wood, A., & Head, M. (2004). "Just what the doctor ordered": The application of problem-based learning to EAP. *English for Specific Purposes, 23,* 3–17.

CHAPTER 3

PHOTOVOICE AND FREIREAN CRITICAL PEDAGOGY

Providing a Liberatory Theoretical Framework to Project-Based Learning in Second Language Education

Mary Brydon-Miller
University of Cincinnati

I can see validity only in a literacy program in which men understand words in their true significance: as a force to transform the world.

—Freire, 1973, p. 81

The dedication in Paulo Freire's 1970 volume, *Pedagogy of the Oppressed*, reads, "To the oppressed, and to those who suffer with them and fight at their side" (2004 [1970]). From the outset, Freire demands that we understand the highly politicized nature of our role as educators and that we embrace the radical possibility of education as a force to challenge oppression. But as Darder, Baltodano, and Torres (2003) have observed, "each time a radical form threatens the integrity of the status quo, generally this element is appropriated, stripped of its transformative intent, and reified into a palatable form" (p. 14).

Project-Based Second and Foreign Language Education, pages 41–53
Copyright © 2006 by Information Age Publishing

Project-based learning has the potential to embody the kind of politically engaged, transformative approach to education envisioned by Freire and other critical educators, but it runs the very real risk of instead becoming simply another formula for reinforcing existing systems of oppression, especially among second language learners, so many of whom are already marginalized due to inequitable economic and social forces. In this chapter I reexamine the basic notions that underlie Freirean critical pedagogy and discuss the intersections between this perspective and project-based learning. I then suggest specific classroom practices that educators can use to incorporate Freirean approaches in project-based learning through the use of photovoice and other educational action research methods. Finally, I explore challenges faced by educators working within a critical pedagogical framework in promoting individual and community empowerment among second language learners and consider strategies for maintaining this liberatory focus in the face of current pressures to revert to more traditional approaches to education that fail to serve the true interests of our students.

FREIREAN CRITICAL PEDAGOGY

Freire first introduced the notions of problem-posing education and critical pedagogy by contrasting them to what he called the banking concept of education, in which "knowledge is a gift bestowed by those who consider themselves knowledgeable upon those whom they consider to know nothing" (2004 [1970], p. 72). The banking approach to education, which continues to typify educational practices in the United States at all levels, focuses on a unidirectional system in which the teacher deposits learning into the empty vessels who are the students, later withdrawing this learning in the form of testing. Standardized tests are thus the ultimate form of narrow-minded accountancy in the banking approach to education.

Project-based learning is more akin to Freire's notion of problem-posing education, an approach that "bases itself on creativity and stimulates true reflection and action upon reality, thereby responding to the vocation of persons as beings who are authentic only when engaged in inquiry and creative transformation" (2004 [1970], p. 84). By drawing on the knowledge and experience of learners, and by encouraging learners to engage in a dialectical process of action and reflection, that knowledge is transformed into critical consciousness in a process Freire refers to as *conscientization.* Freire (1983) links literacy and action by examining the relationship between the word and the world:

As an event calling forth the critical reflection of both the learners and educators, the literacy process must relate *speaking the word to transforming reality* (emphasis in original), and to man's[1] role in this transformation. Perceiving the significance of that relationship is indispensable for those learning to read and write if we are really committed to liberation. Such a perception will lead the learners to recognize a much greater right than that of being literate. They will ultimately recognize that, as men, they have the right to have a voice. (p. 13)

In Freire's mind, this process of critical reflection has an explicit and radical political agenda. "Whereas cultural action for freedom is characterized by dialogue, and its preeminent purpose is to conscientize the people, cultural action for domination is opposed to dialogue and serves to domesticate the people" (1983, pp. 46–47). This notion of dialogue is central to Freire's conceptualization of educational practice and is key in the struggle for political and social change. "Critical and liberating dialogue, which presupposes action, must be carried on with the oppressed at whatever the stage of their struggle for liberation" (2004 [1970], p. 65).

This focus on action is another key component of Freire's notion of liberatory educational practice. Through praxis, "reflection and action upon the world in order to transform it" (2004 [1970], p. 51), we come to develop a more critical understanding of the world and of our own ability, as individuals and as members of communities, to challenge inequality and to bring about positive social change.

PROJECT-BASED LEARNING AS A PROCESS OF CONSCIENTIZATION

There are two approaches to second language teaching and learning: the formal linguistics approach and the functional linguistics approach (see Chapter 4). The former, which is still the most prevalent approach in the United States, tends to replicate the banking model by focusing on vocabulary and grammar divorced from any relationship to the learners' own past experiences or current concerns. The latter, which is starting to gain popularity in the United States and around the world, calls for content-based language learning that incorporates project work. This latter approach challenges the banking model by locating learning within the lives of students and by providing opportunities to students to give voice to their own understanding of the world. To do this, however, teachers must learn to trust their students' knowledge and experience and must relinquish sole control of the educational process in order to engage in genuine dialogue. This begins by recognizing the political implications of all forms of educational practice and by acknowledging our complicity when working within existing structures of education in maintaining processes of domination. Linking Freire's work to that of Gramsci, Darder (2003) notes that Freire "exposed how even well-meaning teachers, through their lack of critical moral leadership, actually participate in disabling the heart, minds, and bodies of their students—an act that disconnects these students from the personal and social motivation required to transform their world and themselves" (p. 498). This warning has implications for those of us who are classroom teachers, as well as for the educators who prepare them, to be continually mindful of the ways in which our practice comes to support a confining status quo rather than the emancipatory interests of our students.

A reexamination of project-based learning from this perspective would begin by engaging learners in an exploration of the issues currently facing them, their families, and their communities. As Lankshear and McLaren have observed, "The world must be approached as an object to be understood and known by the efforts of learners themselves" (cited in McLaren, 2000, p. 162). Having identified areas of common community concern, educators and their students can work together to develop projects that provide opportunities for learners to develop a more critically informed understanding of the nature of these problems and possible strategies for addressing them. Stringer suggests ways in which educators can incorporate project-based learning in order to encourage the development of this kind of critical consciousness. "Even the poorest communities have a store of experience and local knowledge that can be incorporated into exciting and meaningful activities having the power to transform the education of people and children" (Stringer, 2004, p. 33). These activities need not be focused on addressing large-scale social problems. In fact, in my experience it is important to identify issues that can be successfully addressed by project participants if they are to begin to develop a sense of self-efficacy and confidence. But they should be meaningful to learners and should reflect our commitment to engaging our students as co-creators of knowledge and as individuals capable of taking action to address real issues of concern.

PHOTOVOICE AS AN APPROACH
TO PROJECT-BASED LEARNING

Project-based learning engages students in "creating knowledge in order to solve problems that arise while they are engaged in purposeful, real-world activities" (Beckett, 2002, p. 53). Photovoice, or photo novella as it has sometimes been called, is an approach to project-based learning that uses students' photography combined with their written accounts of the images and locates these activities within the context of specific social, economic, and political concerns identified by the learners themselves. Working to improve access to health care for women in rural China, Caroline Wang and her colleagues (Wang, 1999; Wang & Burris, 1994; Wang, Burris, & Ping, 1996) gave project participants cameras with which to record the effects that lack of adequate medical services had on families in their own communities. They then used these images and the women's descriptions of them to advocate with government representatives for reform. As Wang et al. (1996) observe, "photographs can communicate the voices of women who ordinarily would not be heard, and broadcast their voices to decision-makers" (p. 1396).

Similarly, Mayan women in rural Guatemala were able to use photovoice as a strategy for beginning to address their community's legacy of state-sponsored violence and continuing poverty and political disenfranchise-ment (Lykes, 2001; McIntyre & Lykes, 2004). As Lykes (2001) observes, "the visual image is quite unlike any other form of communication because it is universally apprehended and can be used to facilitate discussion, docu-mentation, and analysis of social issues by the photographer and by those who view the 'objects of her gaze'" (p. 191).

Kroeger has adapted the method of photovoice in his work with at-risk middle school students (Meyer, Hamilton, Kroeger, Stewart, & Brydon-Miller, 2004). In this project, which incorporated aspects of photovoice and teacher reflection, Kroeger and the other teachers on his team gained a deeper insight into both the lives of their students and their own motiva-tions for teaching. As Kroeger observes, "One of the greatest gains of our research was not the change we were making in our classrooms or even the gradual improvement of scores, but the deepening of our bonds with stu-dents who were at risk" (p. 562).

My own experience of using photovoice in my work with recently arrived refugees over the past 7 years reflects this same transformative power (Bry-don-Miller, 2001b). In general, these projects begin with the distribution of disposable cameras to a group of students and the generation of some gen-eral question or theme. After being trained in the use of the cameras, the students go out and take photographs of themselves, their families, homes, and communities and bring them back to the school where we collect and label them and have the film developed. The finished photographs are returned to the students who then select one or more images about which to write. Thus the process becomes a learner-centered literacy activity grounded in the student's own experience.

This focus on drawing literacy materials directly from the lives of learn-ers is based specifically in Paulo Freire's (1973) practice of critical peda-gogy and the use of language central to the student's own experience, what Freire called generative themes, to make learning more meaningful to stu-dents. As Wang and her colleagues note in describing their work, "just as

Freire developed word lists for literacy classes forged from the life experiences of his students, so photo novella's curriculum is the photographic image of daily life as depicted by the women" (Wang et al., 1996, p. 1392). These images can be incorporated into the development of improved teaching practice (Meyer et al., 2004), shared with public officials, as was the case in Wang's studies, or used within the community itself to encourage a shared process of reflection and to generate strategies for addressing common concerns as reflected in many of the projects Lykes has conducted in Mayan communities. As is the case with my own work with refugee communities, these images can also be displayed in settings such as schools, libraries, churches, or government offices, as a form of community education intended to raise awareness and to inform members of the public about the lives and concerns of these new members of their community.

These examples of photovoice all reflect the power of this approach to use project-based learning to promote critical consciousness and to reenvision education as a truly liberatory process for educators and learners alike. This is especially important in working with second language learners, particularly with recent immigrants and refugees, to whom education and opportunities for engagement in democratic processes may have been denied in the past. For these students this approach to project-based learning can afford a safe and secure environment within which to examine their own understanding of the world, and an opportunity to engage with others in identifying and addressing the issues that confront them. In this way project-based learning can reflect Freire's liberatory and democratic vision of education.

EDUCATIONAL ACTION RESEARCH
AND PROJECT-BASED LEARNING

Photovoice is just one approach used by practitioners conducting educational and community-based participatory action research. Action research has been defined as "a participatory, democratic process concerned with developing practical knowing in the pursuit of worthwhile human purposes" (Reason & Bradbury, 2001, p. 1). As this definition suggests, action research is an explicitly political practice whose practitioners share a commitment to collaborative practice and social justice. Action research rejects the notion that research must be objective and value neutral, insisting instead that all research is located within a larger social, political, and economic context and that our practice as researchers should involve challenging existing structures of oppression in order to bring about positive social change. As Noffke (1995) has observed, "this belief in the power of communities participating in social change is often regarded as a fundamental component of democratic living as well as of action research" (p. 6).

The legitimacy of action research as a valid form of inquiry draws upon Habermas' notion of critical science, that is, "knowledge born of social action that supports the emancipatory interests of humankind" (Brydon-Miller, 2001a, p. 79). As described by Comstock (1994), "a critical science must directly contribute to the revitalization of moral discourse and revolutionary action by engaging its subjects in a process of active self-understanding and collective self-formation" (p. 626). Within this framework knowledge generation is viewed as a collaborative process in which researchers and community participants work together to challenge oppression, a process in which research becomes a form of social action and the researcher a scholar/activist.

Action research combines aspects of popular education, collaborative research, and action for social change (Brydon-Miller, 2001a). It can include both quantitative (e.g., Minkler & Fuller-Thompson, 1999) and qualitative (e.g., Maguire, 1987; Piran, 2001) methods, but action researchers have also developed a variety of innovative approaches that include participatory theater (e.g., Lynd, 1992; Mienczakowski & Morgan, 2001), collage, and fiber and textile arts (e.g., Bastos & Brydon-Miller, 2004). These arts-based methods, including photography, engage participants and honor the artistic and expressive traditions of their own cultures and communities, making them particularly appropriate in work with second language learners. As Hall (2001) observes, "When looking for inspiration around methods of participatory research we need to take our clues from the creative and collectively constructed practices which abound in our societies and movements" (p. 174).

Action research focuses on the process as well the outcome of the work. The questions participants raise, the relationships that are formed within the community of researchers, the decision-making strategies adopted by participants, are all components of the research itself. In this regard the goals of action research can be seen to parallel those of project-based learning, in which the final product, while certainly of interest, is not as important as the learning that students engage in together as they take part in the process.

Interest in the application of action research in the field of education is evident by the number of recent texts published in this area (see, e.g., Holly, Arhar, & Kasten, 2005; Johnson, 2005; Meyers & Rust, 2003; Mills, 2003; Stringer, 2004; Tomal, 2003). At its best, such research engages teachers and their students in collaborative processes of knowledge generation aimed at deepening participants' shared understanding of the social, political, and economic forces that inform educational policy with the goal of improving educational practice. In some cases, however, this critical component seems to have been lost as teacher action research is deraci-nated and redirected toward the more narrow goals of raising test scores and improving student behavior. Integrating project-based learning and true educational action research will ensure that this practice continues to serve the interests of learners rather than those of policymakers whose main interest is in dictating uniform content in school curricula and stan-dardization of all aspects of the educational experience.

Bridging community and educational action research, a number of community literacy projects have also used a project-based learning approach. (For a general review of this literature, see Williams & Brydon-Miller, 2004.) These projects are exemplified by Samant's (2002) work with women in Bombay whose original interest in learning how to petition the police regarding illegal liquor sales eventually grew into an extended use of their growing literacy skills to a variety of other areas.

Given this focus on using literacy to address specific issues and to achieve social change, project-based learning is clearly already central to the practice of educational action research. A recent project connecting local fiber and textile artists with older Bosnian women refugees provides an example of how an arts-based action research process demonstrates project-based learning with second language learners. Recognizing that fiber and textile arts provide a sort of "common language" linking women from around the world, this project brought local women skilled in a vari-ety of textile arts together with a group of older Bosnian women who share an equally strong tradition in this area. Our meetings focused on sharing skills, demonstrating different techniques, and the creation of a collabora-tive quilt project featuring the fine crochet work of the Bosnian women. Learning the terms for the materials, the techniques, and the shared foods—and the general conversation around these activities—provided an opportunity for language learning embedded in a shared interest and an acknowledged area of expertise for the refugee women. The unveiling of the quilt at a recent World Refugee Day celebration, as well as plans to exhibit the quilt at a branch of the public library, provides opportunities for the women to gain public recognition for their skill and their artistic collaboration, while at the same time giving the broader public an oppor-tunity to learn more about the art and culture of the refugee community.

PROBLEMMATIZING FREIREAN
PROJECT-BASED LEARNING

The notion of providing opportunities to second language learners to give voice to their experiences through project-based learning experiences seems then, on the surface, a relatively straightforward process. It is important, however, to remain mindful of the many ways in which issues of power and privilege influence educational settings, even when we, as teachers and researchers, strive to honor the experience of our students and to encourage them in expressing their thoughts and feelings openly. Pratt (1991) has referred to such settings as contact zones, "the social spaces where cultures meet, clash and grapple with each other, often in contexts of highly asymmetrical relations of power, such as colonialism, slavery, or their aftermaths as they are lived out in many parts of the world today" (p. 35). Negotiating these "asymmetrical relations of power" requires us to step back from our own understandings and interpretations of events in order to allow our students' own stories to be heard.

Photovoice and other visual arts–based action research methods can provide an opportunity for this to happen, but I would challenge the claim that images are universally apprehended and suggest instead that our understanding of images or other forms of artistic expression can be as culturally biased as our interpretation of language. I recall looking at a collage created by a young Bosnian woman that included a photograph of the young Jackie and John F. Kennedy. The associations I have to this image— Camelot, the optimism of the Kennedy administration, my Irish American grandmother's devotion to JFK, the grief of his assassination—were all unknown to this young woman who told me she selected the picture because they were so attractive. Many of the other collages also provided a window into a very different understanding of our society. Some included images of clocks and watches, reflecting the artists' sense of American's obsession with time; cars because as one participant observed, "everybody drives"; and other images that reflected the consumer-based culture the women observed in the United States. Linking images and words provides the opportunity for those participating in photovoice projects to clarify their own interpretation of the world to their audience and in this way, to establish a sense of ownership and control over the learning process, while at the same time providing those of us who are their teachers with a unique, and sometimes challenging, view of our own culture.

And yet, even this more explicit process of interpretation does not guarantee a shared understanding. Bhabha (1994) discusses this slippage between the enunciation of a message and its reception, suggesting the challenge of developing shared meanings especially across cultural differences. It is important to understand in this instance that the teacher's understanding is not more accurate than the student's, nor is it the teacher's task to correct the student. Rather, through a dialogic process in which teacher and student jointly challenge their individual assumptions, actively reflect upon the other's point of view, and engage in an open process of shared meaning making, both may come to a more nuanced and contextualized understanding of the world. As Freire (2004 [1970]) puts it, "the requirement is seen not in terms of explaining to, but rather dialoguing with the people about their actions" (p. 53).

This notion of telling one's own story, particularly when that story challenges the dominant view of oneself and one's community in a process Delgado (2000) has labeled "counterstorytelling," is a key concept within critical race theory. He observes that,

> Most who write about storytelling focus on its community-building function: Stories build consensus, a common culture of shared understandings, and a deeper, more vital ethics. But stories and counterstories can serve an equally important destructive function. They can show that what we believe is ridiculous, self-serving, or cruel. They can show us the way out of the trap of unjustified exclusion. They can help us understand when it is time to reallocate power. They are the other half—the destructive half—of the creative dialectic. (p. 61)

This notion of voice, central to both postcolonial and critical race theory, is central to our understanding of a Freirean approach to project-based learning with refugees and other second language learners (Brydon-Miller, 2001b). A photovoice project conducted with young Sudanese refugees provides a particularly telling example. On the same day that this group of young men were given their cameras for the photovoice project, a television camera crew arrived to record them in their new home. But the constant flash from the disposable cameras made that task nearly impossible, as the young Sudanese men turned the tables on the reporters and began to create their own record of their lives, complete with the somewhat frustrated television cameramen! One image from this project is especially memorable for me. It was the image of the median strip outside the home of one of the young Sudanese men. It seemed at first glance completely unremarkable. But when I asked the photographer to describe the image, he explained that he had taken the picture because it was more grass than he had ever seen in one place in his life. I have to admit that I have been unable to look at a median strip in quite the same way since!

The majority of teachers, whether within the K–12 school system, higher education, or community-based English as a second language (ESL) programs, represent the dominant culture. To the extent that we can engage these counterstories as a means of confronting our own preconceptions and examining our own worldview more critically, we can become learners ourselves. As Delgado (2000) suggests, "stories may expand that empathic range if artfully crafted and told; that is their main virtue" (p. 70).

PROJECT-BASED LEARNING WITH SECOND LANGUAGE LEARNERS AND LIBERATORY EDUCATIONAL PRACTICE

"Speaking the word" and "transforming the world"—these must be the dual goals of all educators, but they are especially relevant for those of us working with second language learners, so many of whom have been denied the opportunity for educational and political engagement in the past. Project-based learning, with its focus on combining engaging educational processes and tangible, meaningful outcomes, provides an effective vehicle for achieving these goals. To do so, however, we must come to understand our students as individuals with a wealth of experience and wisdom, as members of communities dedicated to addressing issues of concern, and as political agents capable of articulating a vision of social justice and of acting on their convictions. Furthermore, we must commit to stand beside our students and to challenge educational structures that would limit their opportunities for learning, personal growth, and community development. As Ladson-Billings (1999) has suggested, "We may have to defend a radical approach to democracy that seriously undermines the privilege of those who have so skillfully carved that privilege into the foundation of the nation" (p. 27). We must, as a community of teachers, scholars, and students, see the "project" of project-based learning as the achievement of Freire's vision of liberatory education as a means of bringing about positive social change.

NOTE

1. Freire's use of masculine pronouns and other examples of what now would be considered sexist language reflect the conventions of the time in which he was writing. In later work Freire acknowledged this problem and addressed this issue in his writing.

REFERENCES

Bastos, F., & Brydon-Miller, M. (2004). Speaking through art: Subalternity and refugee women artists. In B. M. Lucas & A. B. Lopez (Eds.), *Global neo-imperialism and national resistance: Approaches from postcolonial studies* (pp. 107–118). Vigo, Spain: Universidade de Vigo.

Beckett, G. H. (2002). Teacher and student evaluations of project-based instruction. *TESL Canada Journal, 19*(2), 52–66.

Bhabha, H. (1994). *The location of culture.* London: Routledge.

Brydon-Miller, M. (2001a). Education, research and action: Theory and methods of participatory action research. In D. L. Tolman & M. Brydon-Miller (Eds.), *From subjects to subjectivities: A handbook of interpretive and participatory methods* (pp. 76–89). New York: New York University Press.

Brydon-Miller, M. (2001b). A glimpse of a lighthouse: Participatory action research, postcolonial theory, and work in refugee communities. *Committee on refugees and immigration selected papers, 9,* 254–276.

Comstock, D. E. (1994). A method of critical research. In M. Martin & L. C. McIntyre (Eds.), *Readings in the philosophy of social science* (pp. 625–639). Cambridge, MA: MIT Press.

Darder, A. (2003). Teaching as an act of love: Reflections on Paulo Freire and his contributions to our lives and our work. In A. Darder, M. Baltodano, & R. D. Torres (Eds.), *The critical pedagogy reader* (pp. 497–510). New York: RoutledgeFalmer.

Darder, A., Baltodano, M., & Torres, R. D. (2003). Critical pedagogy: An introduction. In A. Darder, M. Baltodano, & R. D. Torres (Eds.), *The critical pedagogy reader* (pp. 1–21). New York: RoutledgeFalmer.

Delgado, R. (2000). Storytelling for oppositionists and others: A plea for narrative. In R. Delgado & J. Stefancic (Eds.), *Critical race theory: The cutting edge* (pp. 60–70). Philadelphia: Temple University Press.

Freire, P. (1973). *Education for critical consciousness.* New York: Continuum.

Freire, P. (1983). *Cultural action for freedom.* Cambridge, MA: Harvard Educational Review.

Freire, P. (2004 [1970]). *Pedagogy of the oppressed.* New York: Continuum.

Hall, B. (2001). I wish this were a poem of practices of participatory research. In P. Reason & H. Bradbury (Eds.), *The handbook of action research: Participative inquiry and practice* (pp. 171–178). London: Sage.

Holly, M. L., Arhar, J., & Kasten, W. (2005). *Action research for teachers: Traveling the yellow brick road* (2nd ed.). Upper Saddle River, NJ: Pearson Merrill Prentice Hall.

Johnson, A. P. (2005). *A short guide to action research* (2nd ed.). Boston: Pearson Allyn & Bacon.

Ladson-Billings, G. (1999). Just what is critical race theory, and what's it doing in a *nice* field like education? In L. Parker, D. Deyhle, & S. Villenas (Eds.), *Race is...race isn't: Critical race theory and qualitative studies in education* (pp. 7–30). Boulder, CO: Westview Press.

Lynd, M. (1992, Winter). Creating knowledge through theater: A case study with developmentally disabled adults. *The American Sociologist,* 100–115.

Lykes, M. B. (2001). Activist participatory research and the arts with rural Mayan women: Interculturality and situated meaning making. In D. Tolman & M. Brydon-Miller (Eds.), *From subjects to subjectivities: A handbook of interpretive and participatory methods* (pp. 183–199). New York: New York University Press.

Maguire, P. (1987). *Doing participatory research: A feminist approach.* Amherst: Center for International Education, University of Massachusetts.

McIntyre, A., & Lykes, B. (2004). Weaving words and pictures in/through feminist participatory action research. In M. Brydon-Miller, P. Maguire, & A. McIntyre (Eds.), *Traveling companions: Feminism, teaching, and action research* (pp. 57– 77). Westport, CT: Praeger.

McLaren, P. (2000). *Che Guevara, Paulo Freire, and the pedagogy of revolution.* Lanham, MD: Rowman & Littlefield.

Meyer, H., Hamilton, B., Kroeger, S., Stewart, S., & Brydon-Miller, M. (2004). The unexpected journey: Renewing our commitment to students through educational action research. *Educational Action Research, 12*(4), 557–573.

Meyers, E., & Rust, F. (Eds.). (2003). *Taking action with teacher research.* Portsmouth, NH: Heinemann.

Mienczakowski, J., & Morgan, S. (2001). Ethnodrama: Constructing participatory, experiential and compelling action research through performance. In P. Reason & H. Bradbury (Eds.), *The handbook of action research: Participative inquiry and practice* (pp. 219–227). London: Sage.

Mills, G. E. (2003). *Action research: A guide for the teacher researcher* (2nd ed.). Upper Saddle River, NJ: Pearson Merrill Prentice Hall.

Minkler, M., & Fuller-Thompson, E. (1999). The health of grandparents raising grandchildren: Results of a national study. *American Journal of Public Health, 89,* 1384–1389.

Noffke, S. (1995). Action research and democratic schooling. In S. Noffke & R. B. Stevenson (Eds.), *Educational action research: Becoming practically critical* (pp. 1–10). New York: Teachers College Press.

Piran, N. (2001). Re-inhabiting the body from the inside out: Girls transform their school environment. In D. L. Tolman & M. Brydon-Miller (Eds.), *From subjects to subjectivities: A handbook of interpretive and participatory methods* (pp. 218–238). New York: New York University Press.

Pratt, M. L. (1991). Arts of the contact zone. *Profession, 91,* 33–40.

Reason, P., & Bradbury, H. (2001). Introduction: Inquiry and participation in search of a world worthy of human aspiration. In P. Reason & H. Bradbury (Eds.), *The handbook of action research: Participative inquiry and practice* (pp. 1–14). London: Sage.

Samant, U. (2002). Literacy and social change: From a woman's perspective. *Proceedings of the 1996 World Conference on Literacy.* Retrieved February 2, 2002, from http://listserver.literacy.upenn.edu/products/ili/pdf.ilprocus.pdf

Stringer, E. (2004). *Action research in education.* Upper Saddle River, NJ: Pearson Merrill Prentice Hall.

Tomal, D. R. (2003). *Action research for educators.* Lanham, MD: Scarecrow Press.

Wang, C. (1999). Photovoice: A participatory action research strategy applied to women's health. *Journal of Women's Health, 8*(2), 185–192.

Wang, C., & Burris, M. A. (1994). Empowerment through photonovella: Portraits of participation. *Health Education Quarterly, 21*(2), 171–186.

Wang, C., Burris, M. A., & Ping, X. Y. (1996). Chinese village women and visual anthropologists: A participatory approach to reaching policymakers. *Social Science and Medicine, 42*(10), 1391–1400.

Williams, B., & Brydon-Miller, M. (2004). Changing directions: Participatory action research, agency, and representation. In S. G. Brown & S. Dobrin (Eds.), *Ethnography unbound: From theory shock to critical praxis* (pp. 241–257). Albany: State University of New York Press.

CHAPTER 4

BEYOND SECOND LANGUAGE ACQUISITION

Secondary School ESL Teacher Goals and Actions for Project-Based Instruction

Gulbahar H. Beckett
University of Cincinnati

BACKGROUND

Project-based instruction as an educational activity originates from Dewey's work (Brubacher, 1947) and was introduced to English as a second language (ESL) education as an approach to implement student-centered learning principles (Hedge, 1993). Project-based instruction is becoming increasingly popular in various contexts. Many project-based second and foreign language education centers have been established (see Beckett, 2005, for a discussion of this topic; see also Chapter 2), and various instructional and assessment materials have been written (e.g., Alan & Stoller, 2005; Fried-Booth, 2002; Stoller, 1997; see also Chapter 15). Numerous successful applications of project-based instruction have been reported (e.g., Alan & Stoller, 2005; Hilton-Jones, 1988; Tomei, Glick, & Holst, 1999). An increasing number of empirical research studies that investigate project-

Project-Based Second and Foreign Language Education, pages 55–70
Copyright © 2006 by Information Age Publishing

based teaching/learning in second and foreign language education are also emerging (e.g., Beckett, 2005; Beckett & Slater, 2005; Eyring, 1989; Fang & Warschauer, 2004; Gu, 2002; Kobayashi, 2003, 2004; Mohan & Beckett, 2003; see also Chapters 5, 6, and 7).

However, most of the existing studies in second language education were conducted in postsecondary contexts. Furthermore, second language acquisition literature shows gaps in its goals for project-based instruction, particularly when they are compared to the goals reported in general education literature (see Beckett, 2002). This chapter bridges these gaps in the research literature by presenting a part of the findings of a large study conducted in Vancouver, Canada, to understand the language socialization (Ochs, 1988) of immigrant ESL students in a secondary school. The part of the study discussed in this chapter focuses on ESL teachers' goals for project-based instruction and their actions in achieving their goals. It addresses two central questions: (1) What are ESL teachers' goals for project-based instruction for ESL learners? (2) How do ESL teachers achieve their goals?

STUDIES ON TEACHER GOALS AND ACTIONS

Goals and Actions for Project-Based Instruction in SLA

As I have pointed out elsewhere (Beckett, 1999), project-based instruction is exploratory in nature. What students learn during their project work cannot always be anticipated in advance. Nevertheless, there are many goals in general and second language education that proponents believe can be achieved through project-based instruction. The major goal reported in early second language acquisition (SLA) literature is comprehensible output, that is, providing opportunities for second language learners to practice the four skills of the target language (Brumfit, 1984; Candlin, Carter, Legutke, Semuda, & Hanson, 1988; Eyring, 1989; Fried-Booth, 1986; Hilton-Jones, 1988). A second related goal is providing students opportunities to "recycle known language and skills" in natural contexts (Haines, 1989, p. 1). These project goals were achieved through short projects such as getting-to-know-each-other multicultural parties (see Eyring, 1989, and Fried-Booth, 2002, for a detailed discussion of such projects). There has also been occasional mention of the goal of developing analytical skills (Gardner, 1995), time management skills (Coleman, 1992), and responsibility (Fried-Booth, 1986; Hilton-Jones, 1988). Teachers achieved these goals by organizing video-making and learning-about-other-cultures projects where students were responsible for topic identification, time management, and analyzing and presenting information orally and visually.

A review of more recent literature indicates that second language instructors have begun to include other goals such as promoting learner autonomy and independence (Fried-Booth, 2002; Hedge, 2000; Skehan, 1998); fostering collaborative learning, creativity, and responsibility (Hedge, 2000); and developing critical thinking skills (Beckett, 2005; Kobayashi, 2004). Other goals in recent work include teaching discipline-specific ESL writing (e.g., Levis & Levis, 2003), academic discourse (language and literacy) socialization (Beckett, 2005; Mohan & Beckett, 2003; see also Chapter 5), content-based language teaching (Stoller, 1997), and alternative assessment of language and content learning (Beckett & Slater, 2005; see also Chapter 15). These goals were achieved through long-term (several weeks to several months), real-world projects that required students to identify topics and to carry out their projects by making choices and decisions and reporting them orally and in writing. Examples of real-world projects include research projects on the aging process and the human brain (see Mohan & Beckett, 2003) and an investigation of identity issues among some First Nations Canadian youth (see Kobayashi, 2004).

Goals and Actions for Project-Based Instruction in General Education

Most of the goals discussed previously were set for and achieved in post-secondary contexts. Little is known about the goals secondary school ESL teachers have for project-based instruction and how they achieve those goals. The few studies that explore the implementation of project-based instruction at lower levels seem to be in the general education literature. The general education literature reports the goals for project-based instruction to be, among others, fostering problem solving, developing independent and cooperative working skills and critical thinking and decision-making skills, and promoting in-depth learning of subject matter (Barron, 1998; Barrow & Milburn, 1990; Blumenfeld et al., 1991; Breault & Breault, 2005; Dewey, 1924). It is also believed that by engaging in group projects, students learn to discuss alternative strategies, debate critical issues, and make judgments, all of which leads to the consolidation of knowledge (Barrow & Milburn, 1990; Dewey, 1924; Holt, 1994; Kilpatrick, 1918).

Additional goals such as intrinsically motivating students to learn, teaching students to see the connection between theoretical and practical knowledge, and in-depth learning of subject matter content are also reported in the general education literature (Berliner, 1992; Krajcik, Blumenfeld, Marx, & Soloway, 1994; Ladewski, Krajcik, & Harvey, 1994).

According to Berliner (1992), for example, project-based instruction can intrinsically motivate students to learn by giving them ownership of their learning (Kilpatrick, 1925) and by allowing them to apply theoretical knowledge in practice (Dewey, 1931; Hoyt, 1997). It is also believed that students gain deeper understanding of a topic when they are asked to choose, conceptualize, research, and reflect on their own projects. In doing so, they become familiar with the facts and viewpoints related to a topic; with the methodologies and analytical tools of the subjects in which the topic arises; and with the constraints of time, resources, and labor that researchers face when working on a topic (Krajcik et al., 1994; Ladewski et al., 1994).

THEORETICAL FRAMEWORK

The present study takes a functional perspective that views language as a resource within a particular sociocultural context (Halliday, 1994; Mohan, 1986, 1989). This view of language is related to the *socialization* approach of language learning. In contrast to the view that language learning is a matter of learning a set of rules, the language socialization view holds that language learning is the acquisition of linguistic as well as sociocultural knowledge. In this view, language is a medium of "socialization through the use of language and socialization to use language" (Schieffelin, 1990, p. 14). This view is a useful theoretical framework for the present study because, as pointed out by Schieffelin and Ochs (1986), it treats language as a focus of study as well as a medium of studying. By taking the language socialization approach from a sociohistorical perspective, the present study sees project-based instruction as an activity or a sociocultural context that provides opportunities for ESL teachers to teach the English language, school and social cultures, curriculum content, and various skills. It is also an activity or context in which ESL teachers teach the English language functionally by requiring students to listen, speak, read, and write in English to learn content material (Dewey, 1926; Dewey & Dewey, 1915; Mohan, 1986) and to learn how to learn in Canadian schools and how to survive in Canadian society.

RESEARCH SITE, PARTICIPANTS, AND DATA COLLECTION AND ANALYSIS PROCEDURES

The study was conducted at Carlton High (pseudonym) in Vancouver, British Columbia, Canada. The school had a large ESL student population (62% of the students spoke languages other than English at home; Vancouver School Board, 1994) and was actively involved in ESL research through its collaboration with a major research university. The participants in the larger study included 3 teachers and 73 Chinese ESL students (from Hong Kong, Taiwan, and the People's Republic of China) from grades 8–12. For the purpose of this chapter, data obtained from the two teachers who volunteered to participate in the study (hereafter Ms. Jones and Ms. Brown) and observations of two projects will be presented. At the time of data collection, Ms. Jones taught transitional social studies and English language center (ELC) courses and Ms. Brown taught ESL writing. Both were experienced teachers with an interest and expertise in research. They were interviewed and observed for the study as they led their students through their project work.

The data were analyzed inductively (McMillan & Schumacher, 1993) using Strauss and Corbin's (1990) coding system, Spradley's (1980) ethnographic microanalysis, and Patton's (1990) key events, processes, and issues analysis. Interview data were analyzed to identify recurring themes and patterns (Spradley, 1980). The key issues and events analysis suggested by Patton (1990) was applied for the analysis of documents. Data relevant to the key issues or major themes were presented in synthesis with the interview data. Transcribed data were then categorized in synthesis with the field notes according to the key events, key processes, and key issues relevant to the major themes and categories that emerged from the interview data. Key events here refer to the events that were of critical importance to the study.

FINDINGS

Teachers' Goals for Project-Based Instruction

The ESL teachers who participated in the present study reported their goals for project-based instruction to be: to foster lifelong learning by the language socialization of ESL students into Canadian school and social cultures; to challenge students' creativity and resourcefulness; to foster independence; to teach decision-making, critical thinking, and cooperative learning skills; and to teach students how to learn. This section presents and discusses these findings. Teaching language in context, that is, teaching ESL through subject matter content, was reported to be another major goal teachers had for project-based instruction. For a discussion of these goals, see Beckett and Mohan (2005).

Lifelong Learning and Language Socialization into School and Social Cultures

Ms. Jones and Ms. Brown reported that their goals for project-based instruction were to foster ESL students' lifelong learning and "language socialize" them into Canadian school and social cultures. During interviews, Ms. Brown reflected on how she prepared her students for the future by teaching them lifelong learning skills through project work, while Ms. Jones said:

> . . . some of the underlying principles that I embrace also have to do with the life long learning. If I don't think something's going to be useful, I won't do it. Hence the spanking thing [referring to the project topic], because I feel somewhere along the way, Canadian society will benefit from their [students'] having thought or had the opportunity to think about how to grow up and whether they were doing things differently.

Analysis of Carlton High's ESL department policies revealed that Ms. Brown's and Ms. Jones' goals for lifelong learning were consistent with their departmental policies as prescribed in their school's ESL handbook. The ESL teachers' goal of lifelong learning also seems to be consistent with the goals of project-based instruction in general education. As discussed earlier, instilling lifelong learning has been a major goal of the activity since it was first developed (see Kilpatrick, 1918). This goal, however, is not given as a goal of project-based instruction in the SLA literature.

The teachers reported that one of their goals for project-based instruction was language socialization of ESL students into Canadian school culture. In fact, project work itself was seen as an example of Canadian school culture. Ms. Brown said that projects can serve as an excellent activity in the language socialization of ESL students:

> Socializing them [ESL students] into the school culture here is naturally the major goal. As I said, it's not just the language they need to learn. A lot of other things are foreign to them, including how the schools operate here. Projects are an excellent way for them to find out how things work.

Ms. Jones added that project work is a feature of Canadian school culture that immigrant students have to learn:

> Project [work] is something that our kids do for six years here [in Canada] before they come to us [in secondary school]. They know how to do this stuff. But immigrant students have said that they had not done projects before. So, we need to show them how to do it. That's why I do a lot of projects. Group projects and individual projects.

In fact, Carlton High's ESL Department Handbook lists projects as one of the features of Canadian school cultures (see Beckett, 1999, for a more detailed discussion of this topic). Language socialization of ESL students into a different school culture is not mentioned as a goal for project-based instruction in either the early SLA or in the general education literature. But this finding is consistent with reports of more recent SLA literature that have begun to list academic discourse socialization as one of the goals for project-based instruction (see Beckett, 2005; Levis & Levis, 2003; Mohan & Beckett, 2003; see also Chapter 5).

Ms. Jones and Ms. Brown reported that another important goal for their project-based instruction was the language socialization of ESL students into Canadian social cultures. Ms. Jones designed projects to help her students learn about Canadian social history:

> Yes, introducing them [ESL students] into Canadian social culture is my goal, too. We do lots of projects on cultures and cultures of Canada. As you saw from their [project] evaluation, students enjoyed doing projects on Chinese immigrant contribution to the country's rail-way industry. They learned that Chinese people and their culture are an important part of our [Canadian] society and culture. It's important for them to know those facts, especially the stuff that they can relate to.

Ms. Brown reiterated this goal by telling the researcher how she takes her students downtown and to libraries and museums to explore Canadian social cultures as part of project assignments. This goal, too, seems to be consistent with their departmental policy articulated to students in the departmental handbook and to parents at one of the Parents' Night meetings held at the school (see Beckett, 1999, for a discussion of these topics).

Language socialization of students into social cultures is an important goal for all students, and as Ms. Brown and Ms. Jones pointed out, project-based instruction may be an excellent means of doing this. However, this goal is not mentioned in the general education literature as a goal for project-based instruction, although it seems it could easily have been. The SLA literature mentions it either as a minor goal (Hilton-Jones, 1988) or as an implied one (e.g., Kobayashi, 2004). Since schools are becoming increasingly multicultural, both general education and SLA researchers need to examine how project-based instruction can serve as the goal for "language socializing" students to facilitate an easier transition into target school and social cultures.

Creativity, Independence, Critical Thinking, and Cooperative Work Skills

Both teachers reported that challenging students' creativity and foster-ing independence, critical thinking skills, and cooperative work skills are also among their goals for project-based instruction. They stated that they believe the open-ended nature of project-based instruction is conducive to achieving these goals. According to Ms. Jones,

> It [project work] calls on their independence and creativity because there is no end to what they can do. So, it challenges all of their...creativity.... Project is open. They can hang themselves by working 12 hours a day...

The teachers' goal of fostering creativity through project-based instruction seems to be consistent with SLA goals (Hedge, 2000) as well as with general education goals (Kimbrough, 1995) for project-based instruction.

Ms. Jones and Ms. Brown also said that fostering student independence is a complicated but necessary process that needs to be taught and rein-forced constantly. According to Ms. Brown,

> I want them (ESL students) to learn how to do things on their own. That's one of the things they need training in. They can get very dependent, you know. I train them by organizing projects. It's perfect for doing that kind of thing, because I'm not going to do their research for them. They have to do it by themselves. You know what I mean? That's how they learn to be inde-pendent.

Ms. Jones agreed:

> To be independent and to learn those skills themselves is not an easy trick. You have to be on that stuff every exercise you do.... That's what I did with the projects you saw.

This finding, fostering learner independence or autonomy, is consistent with goals listed for project-based instruction in some SLA literature (Fried-Booth, 2002; Hedge, 2000; Skehan, 1998) as well as in some general education literature (Barron, 1998; Barrow & Milburn, 1990; Blumenfeld et al., 1991; Breault & Breault, 2005; Dewey, 1924).

Critical thinking is another important goal that the two teachers reported having for project-based instruction. They emphasized critical thinking because, they felt, their ESL students were not used to it. Ms. Brown, for instance, encouraged critical thinking by having students discuss controversial issues that arose in movies, in poetry, and in their projects:

Critical thinking is another thing that I do with projects. It's important. These students are not used to that. You saw me doing it. It's always part of everything I do. I show them movies, read them poetry, and organize projects. We discuss controversial issues. They (the students) hear people say different things about it. There. You have critical thinking going. I mean not all students get it. But, most of them do. As I said, the purpose was to get them to use the different facilities, and to get them to think differently.

Fostering students' critical thinking was also Carlton High ESL department's policy. This finding seems to be consistent with the goals reported in the general education literature (e.g., Blumenfeld et al., 1991; Breault & Breault, 2005; Dewey, 1924) and in recent SLA literature for project-based instruction (Beckett, 2005; Kobayashi, 2004).

While Ms. Jones and Ms. Brown said that enhancing independence, individual creativity, and critical thinking were important goals, they emphasized that it was equally important to foster group or cooperative work skills. They believed that both sets of skills had to be learned if ESL students were to be successful in their new country. To achieve the latter goal, the teachers organized group projects that called for the students to exercise cooperative work and communication skills. Ms. Jones talked about the importance of fostering these skills:

They [projects] are important to me for many reasons. For group projects, students have to work together. They have to use group skills. They have to do division of labor. They have to allocate. They learn many many skills when they do group projects. They have to be mainstreamed. When they do, they need to know these things. They have to know how to work in groups and make decisions. They have to know how to communicate. All these can happen in projects.

In most SLA literature, with the exception of Hedge (2000), group or cooperative learning is seen as a means to SLA, rather than a skill that needs fostering through project work. Therefore, this finding of the current study adds to the SLA literature on project-based instruction by confirming Hedge and reports in the general education literature that see project-based instruction as conducive to group or cooperative work because it can create opportunities for students to learn from each other through discussions and debates over critical issues (Barrow & Milburn, 1990; Dewey, 1924; Holt, 1994).

Implementing the Goals

To understand if and how the goals reported by teachers were implemented, the researcher observed two projects. One project (hereafter

Project I) was called *Child Abuse* and was implemented by Ms. Jones in her two transitional social studies and two ELC classes. The other project (hereafter Project II) was called *Search a Word* and was implemented by Ms. Brown in four of her ESL writing classes.

In Project I, students worked on developing interview questions in groups of four, researching the issue of child abuse. The research involved reading newspaper articles (either brought to class by the teacher or found by students outside class) and listening to the radio and watching television. Before starting their interviews, each group was asked to submit a list of their research questions, participants, sample size, hypotheses, and methods and to share them with the class, explaining the reasons for their choices. The students were asked to share their research design with the class and then to conduct their interviews as homework. After completing their interviews, students were expected to analyze and report their findings in the form of an in-class oral presentation. With an occasional reminder from the teacher to make eye contact, students presented their research impressively. They compared and contrasted their findings with what they had read and provided their own viewpoints about issues with supporting arguments.

Project II included mostly individual word projects. Its purpose was to help students learn through learning how to use the research facilities in school, community, and city libraries. The project began with the whole class brainstorming for suitable words such as happy, hot, and joyful. After that, students were asked to choose a word that they wanted to research for the next 2 weeks and to tell the class the reasons they had for choosing one word over the others. The students were then given a color-coded instruction sheet they were required to follow in order to complete the project. According to the instructions, the students were to take notes of everything they read so that they could write about the most interesting things they discovered about their words. The students were also asked to write about how they liked this method of learning (i.e., project-based learning). In addition to the written instructions, the teacher and a teacher librarian, as well as librarians at the community and city libraries, assisted the students throughout their research to encourage successful completion of the project. The researcher's analyses of the students' portfolios, which recorded the process of their work for the project, showed that they remarkably achieved all the goals their teacher set for this project and more.

What is the significance of the researcher's observations? For the researcher herself, the observations confirmed the teachers' view that project-based instruction is an activity that can provide contexts for students to learn many things. They provided firsthand opportunities to witness how teachers achieved the goals stated during the interview. For instance, during the two projects observed for this study, the researcher saw students learning Canadian school and social cultures as well as learning and using the discourse of research (e.g., participants, hypotheses, interviews, findings, and discussions). The students worked cooperatively, made decisions, and learned how to conduct research through interviews and library document analysis. They also learned social studies and writing curriculum content, and they learned how to use research facilities and equipment such as computers, card catalogs, and microfiche. The researcher's observations revealed that the students did an excellent job of not only learning what the teachers intended for them but also presenting their work orally and in writing.

DISCUSSION AND IMPLICATIONS

The findings of the current study show that the teachers had many more goals than those stressed for project-based instruction in the early SLA literature and mentioned in the recent SLA literature for project-based instruction implemented in postsecondary contexts. They also had two goals that are not even included in the general education literature, namely, language socialization of ESL students into school and social cultures and teaching language in context, which was one of the early goals for project-based instruction (Dewey, 1926; Dewey & Dewey, 1915). Teachers achieved their goals through purposefully designed and carefully and systematically implemented projects. This suggests that, like their general education and postsecondary counterparts, secondary school ESL teachers perceive project-based instruction to be an activity conducive to achieving many goals with their ESL students. The findings of the current study also indicate that the teachers held and implemented a broad, integrated conception of project-based instruction that includes a functional view of language that is consistent with the language socialization theoretical perspective (Ochs, 1988; Schieffelin, 1990; Schieffelin & Ochs, 1986) discussed earlier in the chapter. This is reflected in goals such as fostering life-long learning through the language socialization of ESL students into Canadian school and social cultures; challenging students' creativity and resourcefulness; fostering independence; teaching decision-making, critical thinking, and cooperative learning skills; and teaching language in context. It is also reflected in how these teachers implemented project work to achieve their goals. It is important to point out that this goes beyond the comprehensible output (i.e., providing second language learners extensive exposure to the target language; Brumfit, 1984; Candlin et al., 1988; Eyring, 1989; Fried-Booth, 1986; Hilton-Jones, 1988) that is listed as the major goal for project-based instruction in the early SLA literature. It is also consistent with goals reported in more recent SLA literature (e.g., Beckett, 2005; Beckett & Slater, 2005; Fried-Booth, 2002; Hedge, 2000; Kobayashi, 2004; Levis & Levis, 2003; Mohan & Beckett, 2003; Skehan, 1998; Stoller, 1997; see also Chapters 5 and 15).

The discussion of the existing literature and findings of the current study also show that there are additional goals such as intrinsically motivating students to learn (Kilpatrick, 1925; Wolk, 1994), teaching students to see the connection between theoretical and practical knowledge (Dewey, 1931; Hoyt, 1997), and in-depth learning of subject matter content that is also reported in the general education literature (Berliner, 1992; Krajcik et al., 1994; Ladewski et al., 1994). However, these are neither discussed in the SLA literature nor reported by the teachers who participated in the current study.

A few points need to be made regarding the goals for project-based instruction in SLA and general education. First, the general education literature lists more goals for project-based instruction when compared to the SLA literature. Clearly, second language education, as it is presented in the literature, is not utilizing project-based instruction to its fullest potential. Researchers need to reexamine the general literature, as well as more SLA practice, to find out if and how general education goals may be imported into SLA education. Skills such as problem solving, critical thinking, decision making, independent and cooperative working, and in-depth learning of subject matter should be developed across all curricula. However, this cannot be done if the major goal of project-based instruction for SLA education is comprehensible output, that is, practicing the four language skills (e.g., Eyring, 1989; Fried-Booth, 1986, 2002). More research needs to be conducted to see if and how the goals discussed in more recent SLA literature, such as the ones discussed in this chapter, may be implemented in other contexts such as lower level ESL classes as well as what other goals may be set and implemented.

Second, SLA researchers have paid insufficient attention to the development of learning skills and content knowledge by focusing mainly on language or discourse, and have neglected intrinsic motivation (Kilpatrick, 1925; Wolk, 1994), theory practice connection (Dewey, 1931; Hoyt, 1997), and in-depth learning of subject matter content (Berliner, 1992; Krajcik et al., 1994; Ladewski et al., 1994). General education researchers seem to have neglected the development of language or discourse by focusing solely on learning skills and content knowledge. Inclusion of discourse development in the goals for project-based instruction is important because as Dewey (1926) and Mohan (1986) point out, human thought is dependent on participation in forms of culture as well as in factual discourse, which is an organic constituent of practical thought (Tiles, 1988). Therefore, general education researchers should explore the goals and practices of project-based instruction in second language education to find out if and how they can establish language socialization of students into school and social cultures as well as academic discourse development as goals for project-based instruction. Although these goals may seem more suited to second language research and practice, as the learners in this context may need them more, general education students can benefit from and also need to have and achieve these goals. These students include mainstreamed ESL students who still need help and African American students who also need help in language socialization into school cultures as they come from home and community discourses (languages and cultures) that are different from that of their schools. Further studies should also investigate what goals, if any, ESL and general education students may have for project-based learning and how they may achieve those goals.

Third, the findings of this study suggest that second language teachers need to realize that project-based instruction has a great potential for teaching languages meaningfully. It can be applied to teach not only language but also various skills such as the ones discussed in this chapter, keeping in mind that, as active agents, students may have different goals for project-based instruction. Such differences may result in frustrations, dilemmas, and conflicts that need to be and can be managed (see Beckett, 2002, 2005; Beckett & Slater, 2005).

REFERENCES

Alan, B., & Stoller, F. L. (2005). Maximizing the benefits of project work in foreign language classrooms. *English Teaching Forum, 43*(4), 10–21.

Barron, B. J. S. (1998). Doing with understanding: Lessons from research on problem- and project-based learning. *Journal of the Learning Sciences, 7,* 271–311.

Barrow, R., & Milburn, G. (1990). *A critical dictionary of educational concepts: An appraisal of selected ideas and issues in educational theory and practice.* New York: Harvester Wheatsheaf Books.

Beckett, G. H. (1999). Project-based instruction in Canadian school's ESL classes: Goals and evaluations. Unpublished doctoral dissertation, University of British Columbia, Vancouver.

Beckett, G. H. (2002). Teacher and student evaluations of project-based instruction. *TESL Canada Journal, 19,* 52–66.

Beckett, G. H. (2005). Academic language and literacy socialization through project based instruction: ESL student perspectives and issues. *Journal of Asian Pacific Communication, 15,* 191–206.

Beckett, G. H., & Mohan, B. (2005). *Content-based ESL instruction through projects.* Unpublished manuscript.

Beckett, G. H., & Slater, T. (2005). The project framework: A tool for language and content integration. *English Language Teaching Journal, 59,* 108–116.

Berliner, D. C. (1992). Redesigning classroom activities for the future. *Educational Technology, 32*(10), 7–13.

Blumenfeld, P. C., Soloway, E., Max, R. W., Krajcik, J., Guzdial, M., & Palincsar, A. (1991). Motivating project-based learning: Sustaining the doing, supporting the learning. *Educational Psychologist, 26,* 369–398.

Breault, D., & Breault, R. (Eds.). (2005). *Experiencing Dewey: Insights for today's classroom.* Indianapolis: Kappa Delta Pi.

Brubacher, J. S. (1947). *The history of the problems of education.* New York: McGraw-Hill.

Brumfit, C. (1984). *Communicative methodology in language teaching.* London: Cambridge University Press.

Candlin, C., Carter, G., Legutke, M., Semuda, V., & Hanson, S. (1988, March). Experiential learning: Theory into practice. *TESOL Colloquium,* Chicago.

Coleman, J. A. (1992). Project-based learning, transferable skills, information technology and video. *Language Learning Journal, 5,* 35–37.

Dewey, J. (1924). *The school and society.* Chicago: University of Chicago Press.

Dewey, J. (1926). *Democracy and education: An introduction to the philosophy of education.* New York: Macmillan.

Dewey, J. (1931). *The way out of educational confusion.* Cambridge, MA: Harvard University Press.

Dewey, J., & Dewey, E. (1915). *Schools of to-morrow.* London: J. M. Dent & Sons.

Eyring, J. L. (1989). *Teacher experience and student responses in ESL project work instruction: A case study.* Unpublished doctoral dissertation, University of California, Los Angeles.

Fang, X., & Warschauer, M. (2004). Technology and curriculum reform in China: A case study. *TESOL Quarterly, 38,* 301–323.

Fried-Booth, D. L. (1986). *Project work.* New York: Oxford University Press.

Fried-Booth, D. L. (2002). *Project work* (2nd ed.). New York: Oxford University Press.

Gardner, D. (1995). Student produced video documentary provides a real reason for using the target language. *Language Learning Journal, 12,* 54–56.

Gu, P. (2002). Effects of project-based CALL on Chinese EFL learners. *Asian Journal of English Language Teaching, 12,* 195–210.

Haines, S. (1989). *Projects for the EFL classroom: Resource material for teachers.* Walton-on-Thames, UK: Nelson.

Halliday, M. A. K. (1994). *An introduction to functional grammar* (2nd ed.). London: Edward Arnold.

Hedge, T. (1993). Project work. *English Language Teaching Journal, 47*(3), 276–277.

Hedge, T. (2000). *Teaching and learning in the language classroom.* Oxford: Oxford University Press.

Hilton-Jones, U. (1988). *Project-based learning for foreign students in an English-speaking environment* (Report No. FL017682). Washington, DC: U.S. Department of Education. (ERIC Document Reproduction Service No. ED 301 054)

Holt, M. (1994). Dewey and the "cult of efficiency": Competing ideologies in collaborative pedagogies of the 1920s. *Journal of Advanced Composition, 14*(1), 73–92.

Hoyt, B. R. (1997). *Design and implement custom electronic performance support system(EPSS) for training in project-based classes* (Report No. IR018487). Washington, DC: U.S. Department of Education. (ERIC Document Reproduction Service No. ED 410 925)

Kilpatrick, W. H. (1918). The project method. *Teachers College Record, 19*(4), 319–335.

Kilpatrick, W. H. (1925). *Foundations of method: Informal talks on teaching.* New York: Macmillan.

Kimbrough, D. R. (1995). Project design factors that affect student perception of the success of a science research project. *Journal of Research in Science Teaching, 32*(2), 157–175.

Kobayashi, M. (2003). The role of peer support in ESL students' accomplishment of oral academic tasks. *Canadian Modern Language Review, 59,* 337–368.

Kobayashi, M. (2004). *A sociocultural study of second language tasks: Activity, agency, and language socialization.* Unpublished doctoral dissertation, University of British Columbia, Vancouver.

Krajcik, J. S., Blumenfeld, P. C., Marx, R. W., & Soloway, E. (1994). A collaborative model for helping middle grade science teachers learn project-based instruction. *The Elementary School Journal, 94*(5), 483–497.

Ladewski, B. G., Krajcik, J. S., & Harvey, C. L. (1994). A middle grade science teacher's emerging understanding of project-based instruction. *The Elementary School Journal, 94*(5), 499–515.

Levis, J. M., & Levis, G. M. (2003). A project-based approach to teaching research writing to nonnative writers. *IEEE Transactions on Professional Communication, 46,* 210–221.

McMillan, J. H. & Schumacher, S. (1993). *Research in education: A conceptual introduction* (3rd ed.). New York: Harper Collins.

Mohan, B. (1986). *Language and content.* Reading, MA: Addison-Wesley.

Mohan, B. (1989). Knowledge structures and academic discourse. *Word, 40*(1–2), 99–114.

Mohan, B., & Beckett, G. H. (2003). Functional approach to content-based language learning: Recasts in causal explanations. *Modern Language Journal, 87,* 421–432.

Ochs, E. (1988). *Culture and language development: Language acquisition and language socialization in a Samoan village.* Cambridge, UK: Cambridge University Press.

Patton, M. Q. (1990). *Qualitative evaluation and research methods* (2nd ed.). Newbury Park, CA: Sage.

Schieffelin, B. B. (1990). *The give and take of everyday life: Language socialization of Kaluli children.* New York: Cambridge University Press.

Schieffelin, B., & Ochs, E. (1986). *Language socialization across cultures.* Cambridge, UK: Cambridge University Press.

Skehan, P. (1998). *A cognitive approach to language learning.* Oxford: Oxford University Press.

Spradley, J. (1980). *Participant observation.* New York: Holt, Rinehart, & Winston.

Stoller, F. L. (1997). Project work: A means to promote language and content. *English Teaching Forum, 35*(4), 2–9, 37.

Strauss, A., & Corbin, J. (1990). *Basics of qualitative research: Grounded theory procedures and techniques.* Newbury Park, CA: Sage.

Tiles, J. E. (1988). *Dewey.* London: Routledge.

Tomei, J., Glick, C., & Holst, M. (1999). Project work in the Japanese university classroom. *The Language Teacher, 23,* 5–8.

Vancouver School Board. (1994). *Multi-level ESL Program*. Vancouver: Author.

Wolk, S. (1994). Project-based learning: Pursuits with a purpose. *Educational Leadership, 52*(3), 42–45.

CHAPTER 5

SECOND LANGUAGE SOCIALIZATION THROUGH AN ORAL PROJECT PRESENTATION

Japanese University Students' Experience

Masaki Kobayashi
Rikkyo University

INTRODUCTION

This chapter examines the second language (L2) socialization of three Japanese undergraduate students through their project work by focusing on their oral presentation. According to Henry (1994), although there is no generalized definition of the term "project," many educators and scholars agree that a project lasts over an extended period, allows students to select their topics and locate their own source materials, and provides them with opportunities to conduct an independent piece of work either individually or in groups under the guidance of their teacher and to present an end product including written reports and oral presentations.

Project-Based Second and Foreign Language Education, pages 71–93
Copyright © 2006 by Information Age Publishing

Potential values of project work include integrating the four language skills, integrating language and content learning, developing problem-solving and decision-making skills, cultivating students' interests, fostering student autonomy and self-determination, and promoting cooperation (Beckett, 2002; Fried-Booth, 2002; Haines, 1989; Henry, 1994; Jordan, 1997; van Lier, 1996; Wray, 1999; see also Chapter 2). As we will see later, the three focal students in the present study carried out a group research project as a major assignment for their sheltered content-based course on intercultural communication in an English as a second language (ESL) context. Bygate (1999) suggests that projects provide learners with opportunities to use an L2 for a wide range of purposes, which include "planning and organizing of roles and tasks; the organization and preparation of information and opinions; the organization of running of small and large group sessions, and the communication of information and negotiation of meaning that this involves" (p. 674). Furthermore, Jordan (1997) states that one advantage of project work is that it can overcome the possible difficulty of teaching study skills since it allows students to cope with particular problems—language or skills—as they arise in the context of a meaningful activity (see also Wray, 1999). In fact, many of the benefits mentioned previously were the goals of the examined course and its project work.

EMPIRICAL STUDIES ON L2 PROJECT WORK

Despite the pedagogical and psycholinguistic rationales discussed previously, only a few empirical studies have examined project work in the context of L2 teaching and learning. These include Eyring's (1989) study on the implementation of project-based instruction in ESL classes at an American university and students' responses to this instruction, Beckett's (1999) ethnographic study on the implementation of project-based instruction for ESL students in a Canadian high school context, Turnbull's (1999) case study on the effectiveness of multidimensional project-based teaching in core French classes at Canadian schools, and Leki's (2001) longitudinal qualitative study on the experiences of two L2 undergraduate students doing a group project with their L1 peers. Kobayashi (2003) documents the ways in which a group of Japanese undergraduate ESL students engaged primarily outside of class to prepare for the oral presentation of their project work. In other words, the focus was the process of their preparation for a *target task* (Legutke & Thomas, 1991) or "the route to the end product" (Fried-Booth, 2002, p. 6). This analysis suggests that students' task preparation was an important context for joint meaning making or data processing (see also Kobayashi, 2004).

Perhaps of the greatest relevance to the present study is Mohan and Beckett's (2001) study. By conducting a functional analysis, the researchers examined how their teacher-participant scaffolded her students' causal discourse production through her use of functional recasts during their oral presentation on the human brain, shedding important light on the vital role of the teacher in apprenticing the students into academic content and discourse. The present chapter seeks to contribute to this body of literature by examining students' meaning-making efforts through their oral presentation and other project-related activities such as journal writing.

THEORETICAL FRAMEWORK AND RESEARCH QUESTIONS

This study draws upon several sociocultural theories, including language socialization theory, which hold that children and other newcomers to a community learn both language and culture as they participate in language-mediated interaction with more experienced members of that community (Duff, 1995; Halliday, 1978; Mohan, 1987; Schieffelin & Ochs, 1996; Wertsch, 1991). According to Mohan (1987),

> Language socialisation means not only socialisation in the ways of talk, but socialisation through language. Language is a major source for learning about and expressing what one must say, know, value and do in order to participate in sociocultural situations of society. (p. 507)

Thus, language is considered to be both a major object and a medium of learning and socialization. Grounded in this line of work, this chapter recognizes the situated nature of activity and the integrity of language learning and culture/subject matter learning. Language learning is viewed as the process of expanding one's linguistic and interactional repertoire through participation in socioculturally valued activities (Mohan, 1986). The major intent of the present study was to better understand L2 students' learning of language and culture/content through their participation in a project presentation. The investigation was guided by the following questions: (1) What is the nature of the academic discourse and practices of oral presentations into which L2 students are socialized in a university content course? (2) How do students realize their meaning in the L2 oral presentations of their projects?

METHODOLOGY

Participants and Setting

The data to be examined in this chapter were collected in the context of a larger study (Kobayashi, 2004) involving a group of Japanese undergraduate students from Keishin University[1] who were studying at a large research university in Canada. In the first semester, most of the students were enrolled in Language Fieldwork A, a 3-credit, sheltered-content course designed for Keishin students. The instructor of the course was Dr. Izzat Mukkammal, who specialized in the integration of language and content through project-based instruction.

This chapter focuses on the oral presentation given by a group of three female students, Ringo, Fuyumi, and Tamiko. This particular group was *purposefully* selected as they were deemed to be an *information-rich* case (Patton, 2002) that would provide us with illuminating insights about the valued practices of oral presentations in the focal community. In fact, they received an A+ for their task performance. Ringo was a 20-year-old sophomore in an interdisciplinary program in human science at Keishin University. Fuyumi and Tamiko were also second-year students, but they majored in international relations. All the three students were considered by Izzat to be active participants in classroom activities. The average score of their on-arrival TOEFL was 507.

The Curricular Context

Language Fieldwork A, which dealt with intercultural communication, was one of the first courses that most of the Keishin students took in Canada. In her course outline, Izzat wrote that this was "a theoretical as well as practical course that takes place through lectures, seminars, and computer lab work, and field research" (course outline, p. 1). Like other Keishin courses, this course consisted of one 90-minute lecture, one 90-minute-seminar, and one 90-minute laboratory session per week, all of which were intended to complement and reinforce one another. Lectures and lab sessions were taught by the course instructor, whereas the seminar was taught by her teaching assistant, Mr. Abraham Simons. For the lectures, students were required to read chapters of Fred Jandt's (1998) *Intercultural Communication: An Introduction* (2nd ed.). This textbook embraced a variety of topics, such as a dispute over the definition of culture, comparative cultural patterns, language as a barrier, and improving intercultural communication. Most of the lab time was allocated for students' volunteer work and oral presentations.

Language Fieldwork A was organized in such a way that the instructor's lectures focused primarily on students' development of background knowledge about intercultural communication through exposition and reflection, whereas Abraham's lessons focused primarily on students' development of practical understanding of the same subject matter through hands-on awareness-raising activities. According to Izzat and Abraham, the former teacher's lessons dealt mainly with the "theory" of intercultural communication, whereas the latter teacher's lessons dealt mainly with the "practice" of it. Moreover, Izzat often explained the rationales for and requirements of the course assignments in her class, and Abraham instructed the students how to do the same assignments by providing models and explanations. For example, in mid-October, the TA gave a model presentation upon Izzat's request. Thus, the instructor focused mainly on the "what and why" of the tasks, and the TA focused mainly on the "how" of the tasks.

The Focal Project

As the course title indicates, one major component of the course was fieldwork. Izzat's students were required to undertake at least 10 hours of volunteer work at their chosen places. For example, 16 of her 60 students worked at either daycare centers or preschools. Six students volunteered at senior centers and 11 in Japanese language classes at the Canadian university. This was a research project in that students were required to make observations about cultural actions and events at their chosen sites and to consider how these observations might relate to the subject matter of the course. While in the field, the students were required to keep a journal, which was to be submitted for evaluation and feedback three times over the course of the semester. Moreover, the project entailed two major end products: an oral presentation to be made in pairs or groups of three (worth 10%) and a research paper to be written alone (15%).

For the fieldwork requirement of the project, Ringo chose to work at a senior center. However, being the only one in her class working at that particular center, she decided in October to work on the oral presentation with Fuyumi and Tamiko who volunteered at a different but similar place. Thus, their target task was to reflect orally on their experiences as volunteers at senior centers in Canada.

Data Collection

According to Schieffelin and Ochs (1996), one important goal of language socialization research is to link the microanalysis of participants' discourse to more macrolevel, ethnographic accounts of cultural values, roles, and practices of communities into which participants are being socialized. To make this link, I employed an ethnographic case study approach (Merriam, 1998), triangulating multiple sources of data: namely, audiorecorded observations of students' project-related activities in and out of class (e.g., lectures, group meetings); collections of relevant documents and products such as course outlines, student journals, and written reports; and in-depth, semistructured audio-recorded interviews with students and teachers. Ringo, Fuyumi, and Tamiko were observed and audio-recorded as they prepared for their presentation.

Data Analysis

The major analytical unit in this study was students' oral presentations of their fieldwork (see also Kobayashi, 2003, 2004). Audio-recorded discourse, including the focal group's presentation and their interactions during their out-of-class group meetings, was transcribed (see the Appendix for the transcription convention). To strengthen the *trustworthiness* of the study (Lincoln & Guba, 1985; Merriam, 1998), the focal students were invited to check the accuracy of the transcripts and offer comments. All the other audio-recorded data, including the interviews, were also transcribed and analyzed, together with the collected documents, through constant comparisons, which resulted in categories and subcategories (Lincoln & Guba, 1985).

Verified by Ringo, Fuyumi, and Tamiko, the transcribed discourse of their presentation was examined by using Mohan's (1986, 1987, in press) social practice theory analysis (see also Slater, 2004, for its application). According to Mohan (in press), a social practice is a cultural unit that consists of cultural knowledge and cultural action in a theory/practice, reflection/action connection (see also Mohan, 1986). For instance, the social practice of a parliamentary meeting involves background knowledge about its rules and procedure and actual participation in the meeting (Mohan, 1987). The former component includes the knowledge structures of classification, principles, and values, whereas the latter includes the knowledge structures of description, sequence, and choice. Mohan (1998) states that knowledge structures are enacted not only as structures of discourse as people participate in social activities but are also as "structures in the mind that people use to process discourse" (p. 175). The background knowledge structures correspond to theoretical discourse, whereas the action knowledge structures correspond to practical discourse. One major difference between these two types of discourse lies in whether the subject of the verb is general or specific (Mohan, in press).

This analysis method draws upon the perspective of Hallidayan systemic functional linguistics (SFL), on which Mohan's social practice theory is based. Halliday (1978) identified three metafunctions of language: ideational (experiential and logical), interpersonal, and textual. The ideational function enables us to make sense of our experiences and to describe how things are related. Halliday (1978) describes this function as "expressing the speaker's experience of the external world, and his own internal world, that of his own consciousness" (p. 45). The interpersonal function encodes relationships among people in social situations. Language is a major means through which individuals take part in the world, interact with others, negotiate roles and identities, and establish and maintain rapport (Derewianka, 1999; Eggins & Slade, 1997). Finally, the textual function allows us to organize ideational and interpersonal meanings into a coherent text (Butt, Fahey, Feez, Spinks, & Yallop, 2000). Ideational meanings realize *field*, interpersonal meanings realize *tenor*, and textual meanings realize *mode*. These three parameters together constitute the "register" of a text—both spoken and written—and define the context of situation (Halliday & Hasan, 1985). Mohan's social practice analysis foregrounds "the *field* of activity and the subject matter with which the text is concerned ('what's going on, and what is it about?')" (Halliday & Matthiessen, 1999, p. 320, emphasis in original) while keeping track of mode and tenor in the background (Mohan, 1987, in press). Slater (2004) conducted a social practice theory analysis to examine how teachers and students in different science lessons constructed causal explanations through classroom discourse. Likewise, the present study transformed selected discourse into four-column charts to illustrate how students drew a connection between theory and practice or between general knowledge and specific experience (Figure 5.1).

Speaker	Specific Reflection	General Reflection	Other

Figure 5.1.   Mohan's Social Practice Analysis

As we will see later, the OTHER column differs from the two REFLECTION columns (i.e., Specific Reflection and General Reflection) in that the former is based on what the speaker is doing (e.g., interaction with the audience, managing discourse), whereas the latter are based on what the speaker is talking about. Students' utterances in the OTHER column were analyzed drawing on the SFL work of Eggins and Slade (1997). Moreover, where relevant, selected discourse will be analyzed for the knowledge structure of choice. According to Mohan (1986),

> Human choice is central to action situations.... Talk about choice is talk which
> goes beyond the limits of the immediate situation and calls for a wider lan-
> guage potential. From the decision-making view, a person in an action situa-
> tion is making reasoned choices about what to say and what to do. Language
> learning in action situations is therefore more than learning to speak appropri-
> ately. It includes talking about and learning about reasons for acting. (p. 55)

As will be reported later, Izzat encouraged her students to talk about their
choice of volunteer positions. Thus, talking about one's choice was an important part of their language socialization. As Mohan (1986) suggests, the
knowledge structure of choice involves options, decisions, and reasons, which
cannot be captured in a general/specific difference alone. However, the
above-mentioned difference between the OTHER column and the remaining
columns applies to the choice data (Excerpt 2) as well (Figure 5.2).

Speaker	Options	Decisions and Reasons	Other

Figure 5.2.   Mohan's Social Practice Analysis of a Decision-Making Situation

FINDINGS

Ringo, Fuyumi, and Tamiko's presentation was scheduled for the last day for
the student presentations. To prepare for this public, in-class task, the three
students held five out-of-class group meetings in their dorm rooms, each of
which lasted 2 to 4 hours. In these meetings, they decided to divide their presentation into four major parts: (1) their volunteer work settings, (2) their
choice of volunteer work, (3) their volunteer activities, and (4) their learning from their respective experiences. In each of these parts, the students
spoke in turns. In her group's rehearsals and the actual presentation, Ringo
used a manuscript that was proofread by a native speaker of English.

Talking About Volunteer Work Settings

Excerpt 1 is the very beginning of the group's approximately 23-minute
presentation. As can be seen, Ringo started by greeting the class ("Hello
everyone"), introducing the group members ("I'm Ringo Kanda."), and
informing the audience of their topic. These utterances were categorized as
other since they were not made to reflect on the group's field experience, but
to perform the speech acts of greeting, introducing, and informing. Interestingly, most groups included the introduction of the group members in their
presentations although they knew each other fairly well by that time.

Excerpt 1

Speaker	Specific Reflection	General Reflection	Other
Ringo			Hello, everyone. I'm Ringo Kanda. This is Fuyumi Akiba, and this is – Tamiko Tomizawa. Today, we'd like to talk about our volunteer experience at the senior – center – senior center.
	Umm I work at uh South Senior Center A. These are the pictures – of – of Senior Center A. And Fuyumi and Tamiko worked at – Senior Center B. –		
			First, I'm going to talk about Senior Center A.
	Senior Center A is a nonprofit organization. So – it is run by external funding. – And it is managed by only four staff members and a lot of – a lot of volunteers. And the purpose of the senior center is to provide seniors programs and courses – umm to promote seniors' umm health and an independent life style . . .		
			Umm – could you look at the handouts? This side of handouts? Umm here umm here special events on Fridays.
	They had Thanksgiving lunch, or – and some lectures. – And – they – they also provide lunch to seniors with low costs umm once a month. And – sometimes uh the senior center – senior center help – umm concerns of seniors.		
			Next – Fuyumi is going to talk about Senior Center B.

In Excerpt 1, Ringo had two major responsibilities: to tell the audience where her group members worked and to describe her volunteer work setting. As such, her utterances made specific reference to the site ("they," "the purpose of the senior center") as subjects, thus falling into the category of specific reflection. About half of the verbs used in these utterances were relational verbs (e.g., "is," "is managed"), which refer to processes of being in which two pieces of information are linked, and about half of them were action verbs (e.g., "provide," "help"), which refer to processes of doing and happening (Halliday, 1994). Thus, the students primarily described in this section what their work places were and what these places did as institutions. Ringo's utterances in the OTHER column included a command ("Could you look at the handouts?") and a statement ("I am going to talk about..." and "Fuyumi is going to..."). The former performs the function of interacting with the audience, whereas the latter performed the function of organizing and managing the discourse of the group presentation.

Talking About Choice

About 8 minutes into their presentation, the focal group started to talk about their choice of volunteer work. As briefly mentioned earlier, this was one of the practices that Izzat encouraged her students to do. In fact, none of the three students explained their choice in the first set of journal entries; however, having received written feedback from Izzat and having observed other groups' presentations, they decided to talk about their choice for the group presentation. In Excerpt 2, Fuyumi, who has just finished describing her volunteer site and activities, informs the audience that Ringo will tell them why she chose to work at the senior center. Ringo then responds with an okay and a smile and takes over the floor. Fuyumi's utterance seems to be fulfilling two functions: to state their speech plan and to hand over the floor.

Excerpt 2

Speaker	Options	Decisions and Reasons	Other
Fuyumi			Okay – now Ringo is gonna talk – why she worked at the senior center.
Ringo			Okay. ((smiles))
	Umm actually I applied for Maple Tree Art Gallery to do volunteering – with Mina and – Yuri.		
		But umm – however, they didn't accept me – all of us. So – umm as a result, I had to find another volunteering.	

Excerpt 2 (Cont.)

Speaker	Options	Decisions and Reasons	Other
	And uh the information which Sally gave me is on uh SPCA.[2] And Child Care Center, <u>and</u> this – umm Senior Center.		
		Umm – unfortunately, I don't like to take care of children. [And –	
Class			[((laugh))
Ringo		[And =	
Izzat		= It's a lot of work. Children – especially little ones – require a lot of attention and care.	
Ringo		Yeah. ((laughing)) It's a lot of work. ((back in normal voice)) And I'm – allergic to cats, so: I chose this volunteering.	
			Next, Tamiko is going to talk about – uh why she chose – this volunteering.

Here, Ringo is not only talking about her options and decisions, but she is also giving her reasons for having chosen a senior center over other places. Notice that the subjects of most of her utterances are particular nouns (i.e., "I," "the information Sandy gave me"). As such, most of the utterances can be classified as specific reflection. This is not surprising, given that Ringo is talking about her decision making. The exceptions are Izzat's contributions in the DECISIONS AND REASONS column. Having heard Ringo say, "I don't like to take care of children," which simply refers to her personal preference, Izzat goes further to provide a possible reason for Ringo's not liking to take care of children. The subject of Izzat's first utterance is a generic noun, which refers to taking care of children, and the subject of the second one is also a generic noun (i.e., children). In her next turn, Ringo agrees ("Yeah."), repeating part of Izzat's contribution ("It's lot of work."). In short, Ringo and Izzat jointly constructed the knowledge structure of choice through L2 oral discourse. Importantly, Ringo later commented in her reflective interview that she thought that Izzat wanted her to realize the importance of going beyond mere expressions of personal likes and dislikes in academic activities. Table 5.1 summarizes the linguistic features of the focal group's choice discourse.

Table 5.1.   Major Linguistic Features of Students' Choice Discourse

Subjects	I, they [the art gallery], the information which Sandy gave me, Yuko, she (Sandy), it [working at Senior Center B], one of the reasons why I applied for a volunteer work at the senior center
Sensing verbs	I **don't like** to take care of children, I **thought** it's interesting, I **chose** this volunteering, I was **thinking** [of] volunteer work, I **decided** to work at senior center, I **like** to work, I **wanted** to **know**
Other verb groups showing reasons	I **had to find** another volunteering, I thought I **might be able to listen**, I couldn't find
Evaluation lexis (appraisals[3])	interested, interesting, **better** for me
Connectives showing reasons	so, as a result, therefore, then,
Conjunctions showing reasons	because

Talking About Volunteer Activities

In their third section, the three students talked about their respective volunteer activities. Thus, their discourse included many action verbs. For example, Ringo used "did," "doing," "setting," and "cleaned" in Excerpt 3. This is not surprising, given their intent to talk about their activities as volunteers. The rest of the verbs are relational ("is," "was," and "have"). For example, the relational verb "is" in Ringo's third utterance was used to list some of her actions, thus providing information about her volunteer activities, and the remaining relational verbs were used to describe her state and feelings.

Excerpt 3

Speaker	Specific Reflection	General Reflection	Other
Ringo			Now I'm going to talk about what – what I **did** at the Senior Center.
	Umm what I usually **did** at the senior center is – **doing** chores. Like **setting** tables and chairs, **serving** some tea and cookies, and **doing** the dishes. And also, I **cleaned** up the kitchen after party. – And – I was very busy – umm that I **spend** most of the time – in a kitchen during **working**. So: I didn't have enough time to talk with seniors. I was a little disappointed.		

The analysis has indicated that the focal group's discourse has remained mostly descriptive. However, as mentioned earlier, the instructor expected her students to go beyond mere descriptions of their experiences or observed events and demonstrate their reasoning. As the preceding analysis suggests, the students demonstrated some reasoning through their talk about choice of volunteer work; however, they were required to demonstrate their learning from the course by relating their subject matter and fieldwork, or to borrow Wallace's (1991) terms, their *received knowledge* and *experiential knowledge*. In the next section, we will examine how Ringo dealt with this task requirement.

Reflecting on Learning From the Fieldwork

In their final section, Ringo, Fuyumi, and Tamiko reflected on their learning from the fieldwork. For this reason, their discourse included many mental verbs/verb groups such as "learned," "noticed," and "couldn't help realizing." In Excerpt 4, after making a statement to inform the audience of her speech plan ("I'd like to..."), Ringo says, "I learned that there is a similarity between Canadian seniors and Japanese seniors." Note her use of the present-tense form of *to be*, "is," which constructs an existential process with the *there* in the *that*-clause. Interestingly, Ringo later said in her interview that she had chosen the present tense "is," rather than the past tense "was," because she believed the statement to be "true." She added that she had learned this exception to the tense agreement rule in her high school grammar classes. In short, it was a deliberate choice that Ringo made to claim the trueness of her statement. To support her general statement, Ringo then starts to talk about a particular event about a South Korean form of healing, which she observed at the senior center. Her use of past-tense verbs (e.g., "had," "understood," "dealt") suggests that her utterances in the third row can be classified as specific reflection.

Excerpt 4

Speaker	Specific Reflection	General Reflection	Other
Ringo			Okay, I'd like to talk about what I learned and noticed – through my volunteer experience at the senior center.
		I learned that there is a similarity between Canadian seniors and Japanese seniors.	

Excerpt 4 (Cont.)

Speaker	Specific Reflection	General Reflection	Other
	Canadian seniors understood Oriental idea despite of the fact that Canadian had umm Western concepts through uh South Korean form of healing. One day umm the senior center invited an expert of a South Korean form of healing. She had lecture which dealt with umm powerful energy called *Ki* in Japanese.		

After Ringo's speech in Excerpt 4, Ringo and Tamiko provided a brief demonstration with the former presenter playing the role of the healer and the latter playing the role of a senior at the center. This demonstration was followed by Excerpt 5 in which Ringo compared Canadian seniors and Japanese seniors. Once again, Ringo starts her speech by informing the audience about what she is going to talk next. She then makes a general statement about Japanese seniors' ways of thinking and provides an example of her own grandmother. Ringo's argument is as follows: Many of the Canadian senior citizens at the center seemed to believe in the power of a South Korean healer, which is arguably part of so-called Eastern culture. She is certain that, as an Asian, her own grandmother would believe in the power as well. Therefore, it can be concluded that Canadian seniors and Japanese seniors have similarities (as well as differences) in their way of thinking.

Excerpt 5

Speaker	Specific Reflection	General Reflection	Other
Ringo			Umm umm let me compare – umm the Canadian seniors with Japanese seniors.
		Uh I think Japanese seniors feel almost the same as umm the – the Canadian seniors feel.	
	Umm for example if my grandmother umm take – take a massage with a		

Excerpt 5 (Cont.)

Speaker	Specific Reflection	General Reflection	Other
	power from the experts she must believe. Umm like the Canadian believed the – this power.		
		Umm it is because *Ki* is widely known to Japanese and other oriental people. So I have no doubt, umm many Japanese seniors don't question the power of the healing. Umm according to the textbook of intercultural communication, "members of a culture share similar thoughts and experiences." Umm in general – Canadian culture is regarded as – Western culture. On the other hand Japanese culture is uh is regarded as part of – Oriental culture...	
	I found that similarity.		
			Like here. ((points to the screen))
		Umm it seems that two cultures are completely different –	
	but I found similarities.		
			Umm – Finally, I'd like to mention what's – what's significance umm what's significance this learning will have my future.
		Umm I'm assured that – more similarity – uh there – there're more similarities uh among different cultures.	
	Umm my – my experience makes it possible to prevent – communication problems occurring communication barriers –		

Excerpt 5 (Cont.)

Speaker	Specific Reflection	General Reflection	Other
	barriers and having ste-reotypes about different cultures and communi-ties. This volunteer enables to me have a broader umm view – point of view.		
			Next, Tamiko is – talk about uh what's – what she learned.

What is particularly important about this excerpt is that Ringo moves back and forth between specific reflection and general reflection, thus demonstrating that she is going beyond mere descriptions of her observed events. She said in her interviews and group meetings that her main goal was to draw a clear connection between her field experience and the course content. This is indicated by her moves between theory and practice as well as by her use of the key terms "stereotypes" and "communication barriers" and a quotation from the course textbook.

In the ninth row, Ringo announces that she will discuss what significance her volunteer experience will have for her future, which was another requirement of the task. Given this focus on the connection between her own past and future, it is not surprising that most of Ringo's utterances fall into the category of specific reflection, as evidenced by her use of the first-person singular pronouns (i.e., my, me). It should be noted here, however, that this speech differed from those of several other groups. Several students said in their presentations that they were glad that they had had an opportunity to do volunteer work that had a direct bearing on their desired future careers. Considering such a conclusion to be somewhat uncritical, Ringo and her partners chose to discuss instead how their respective experiences would help them in the future.

After her group's presentation, Ringo said in her audio-journal entry:

> I think our presentation was a success. We were able to deliver what we had prepared. And judging from her comments, Izzat seemed to have liked it. But it leaves a lot of room for improvement. Our focus was to connect our volunteer work with the content of intercultural communication. We focused on this aspect so much that we couldn't afford to care about our audience's comprehension. And I was nervous. So I read my manuscript or said what I had remembered. Next time, I want to improve this aspect. . . . I think our content was good. But I liked Otome and Noriko's presentation better because they made good use of the textbook knowledge and questionnaires.

It was great that they made those visuals [diagrams]. I think I need to do some more research and interviews for the paper. (Audio-journal, November 22, 2000, the researcher's translation)

As this comment suggests, Ringo was reasonably satisfied with her group's task performance. However, she thought that she would need to be more considerate of her audience's comprehension. To improve this aspect, she made comprehension checks (e.g., "Okay?" Do you know what I mean?") in the next presentation that she made with another classmate in the second semester. As the social practice analysis has indicated, this type of utterance was absent from Ringo's speech given in the first semester. Moreover, having observed her classmates' presentations and Izzat's responses to them, Ringo felt it necessary to draw a stronger connection to the subject matter of the course in her written report. Subsequently, she went to the WPU library to look for references, discussed her ideas with her classmates and teachers, and conducted an interview with her Canadian friend.

DISCUSSION

Informed by several sociocultural theories, this chapter has explored the L2 socialization of Japanese undergraduate students through their project work in a sheltered-content course on intercultural communication. The focus was students' oral presentations of their volunteer experiences. The analysis of the data (including classroom discourse, interviews, and relevant documents) has suggested that connecting theory (i.e., background knowledge gained through exposition) and practice (i.e., experiential knowledge and insights gained through fieldwork) was one of the most valued practices in the focal classroom community. Throughout the half-year course, the instructor encouraged her students to go beyond mere descriptions of their experiences in their project-related tasks, including the oral presentation, by providing explicit explanations in her course outline and classes and by asking questions as part of her feedback to her students' journal entries. Another valued practice was collaboration. In fact, the instructor expected and advised her students to work in pairs or groups of three for their presentation.

This study conducted a social practice theory analysis and an SFL analysis to examine how a particular group of Japanese students realized meaning in their L2 oral presentation. This presentation received one of the best evaluations from the instructor. Because of this, the analysis of its discourse was deemed to provide revealing insights about what constituted the practices of a valued oral presentation in the classroom community.

In their group meetings, the focal group decided to include four major sections in their presentation: (1) volunteer work settings, (2) choice of volunteer work, (3) volunteer activities, and (4) learning from their volunteer experiences. Consequently, the students drew on different sets of linguistic resources in each section. For example, in the first section, they mainly used relational verbs and action verbs to describe their work settings; in the second section, they constructed the knowledge structure of choice by using a variety of resources to show options, reasons, and decisions; and, in the third section, they mainly used action verbs to describe their volunteer activities while using some relational and sensing verbs to describe their thoughts and feelings. While these sections dealt with some of the reasoning in which the students engaged, they were mostly descriptions of their experiences and observed events. However, the students did not stop there; they went beyond the descriptive level in their final section. The social practice theory analysis has visually indicated that Ringo related the course content and her own field experience by moving back and forth between specific reflection and general reflection in her final turn. The discourse of these students involved a number of sensing verbs. Moreover, the three students used a variety of linguistic resources to manage their discourse and interact with their audience throughout their presentation (see Table 5.2). For example, they managed their discourse by announcing their speech plan. In many cases, it was the current speaker who made such an announcement for the next speaker. As Izzat said in her class, this brief transitional sequence seemed to indicate that the speakers had actually collaborated not only in their actual performance in class but also in other situations since it required some group planning.

The present study offers several major implications for L2 pedagogy. First, not all groups performed their presentations as successfully as the focal group. Despite the teacher's guidance, some groups talked mainly about their fieldwork and failed to refer to the course content while others talked about various issues of intercultural communication without reflecting very much on their field experiences. What can be done to help students to relate theory and practice in their courses? One way to do this would be to give them opportunities to share their journal entries in class. Another way would be to give students class time to list their experiences and observations and discuss in groups how they may relate to issues and topics covered in the textbook and lectures. In fact, these were what several of the key student groups did in their group meetings (see Kobayashi, 2004).

The second implication has to do with the language side of the presentation task. As mentioned earlier, one important goal of the language fieldwork course was for students to understand their experience in terms of the theory of intercultural communication and vice versa. As such, students were expected to make generalizations from their experiences and

Table 5.2.   Major Speech Functions in the Focal Group's OTHER Column

Speech Functions	Speech Sample	Clause Mood
Greeting	Hello, everyone.	Formulaic
Introduction of members	**I'm** Ringo Kanda. **This is** Fuyumi Akiba, and **this is** – Tamiko Tomizawa.	Declarative
Statement of speech plan and handover	R: Today, we'**d like to talk** about our volunteer experience at the senior – center – senior center.	Modulated declarative
	R: First, **I'm going to talk** about Senior Center A.	Declarative
	R: Umm umm **let me compare** – umm the Canadian seniors with Japanese seniors.	Imperative
Compliance	F: Okay – now Ringo is gonna talk – why she worked at the senior center.	
	R: **Okay.** ((smiles))	Minor clause and nonverbal
Command (demanding an action)	R: Umm – **could you look** at the handouts?	Modulated interrogative
Question (demanding an answer)	F: **Can you guess** what these – names mean?	Modulated interrogative
	(X): Street? Is that names of street?	
(checking the audience's comprehension)	F: **Do you know** what – I'm spe – I'm speak-ing about?	Interrogative
Appreciation	F: Thank you. ((to the audience)	Formulaic
	R: Thank you. ((to the audience))	

observations. My analysis suggests that some students made statements that seemed a little too strong (see Schleppegrell, 2002, for a relevant discussion). As a matter of fact, the instructor, who noticed this tendency, introduced expressions to hedge, such as "it seems that" and "this may be because" at the beginning of the second semester. Another possible way is to have students read the transcripts of well-performed presentations or other kinds of well-written texts (e.g., research articles) and examine how general statements are constructed. Perhaps underlining or taking notes of all hedging expressions would help heighten students' language awareness (van Lier, 1996). This activity can certainly be applied to help students become aware of other aspects of a "good" presentation, including linguistic resources to manage discourse and interact with their audience.

In conclusion, this study indicates the usefulness of conducting a social practice analysis coupled with an SFL analysis to examine L2 students' academic language socialization through oral project presentations and related tasks. The research focused on the reporting stage of the project work. Future research could examine other phases of an L2 project such as planning and data analysis by using these analytical tools with the goal of yielding a better understanding of how L2 students learn to make choices about their projects and related tasks while engaged in the discourse of choice (Mohan, 1986). Future research could also examine students' learning across their presentations. Longitudinal research involving an SFL analysis could reveal how students expand their linguistic repertoire over time through their repeated participation in these types of project activities.

ACKNOWLEDGMENTS

This chapter comes from my doctoral dissertation, which was financially supported by the International Academic Relations Division of the Department of Foreign Affairs and International Trade Canada and the University of British Columbia. I am grateful to these organizations for their generous support. My greatest debt of thanks goes to my research supervisor Patricia Duff, who provided me with invaluable guidance, insights, and support throughout the study. I would like to thank Gulbahar Beckett, Margaret Early, Emi Kobayashi, and Tammy Slater for their unwavering support over the years. A special word of thanks is due to Bernard Mohan for his insights, generosity, and support. I would also like to thank the editors and anonymous reviewers for their helpful comments. Last but not least, I would like to extend my heartfelt gratitude to all of the participants, including Ringo, Fuyumi, Tamiko, Abraham, and Izzat for their long-term cooperation and commitment.

NOTES

1.   Pseudonyms were used for all the names of participants and institutions.
2.   This stands for the Society for the Prevention of Cruelty to Animals.
3.   According to Eggins and Slade (1997), "Appraisal refers to the attitudinal coloring of talk along a range of dimensions including: certainty, emotional response, social evaluation, and intensity. . . . Appraisal is mainly realized lexically although it can be realized by whole clauses" (p. 124).

REFERENCES

Beckett, G. H. (1999). *Project-based instruction in a Canadian secondary school's ESL classes: Goals and evaluations.* Unpublished doctoral dissertation, University of British Columbia, Vancouver.

Beckett, G. H. (2002). Teacher and student evaluations of project-based instruction. *TESL Canada Journal, 19,* 52–66.

Butt, D., Fahey, R., Feez, S., Spinks, S., & Yallop, C. (2000). *Using functional grammar: An explorer's guide.* Sydney: National Centre for English Language Teaching and Research, Macquarie University.

Bygate, M. (1999). Speaking: Second language pedagogy. In B. Spolsky (Ed.), *Concise encyclopedia of educational linguistics* (pp. 668–675). Oxford: Elsevier.

Derewianka, B. (1999). *Introduction to systemic functional linguistics.* Singapore: RELC.

Duff, P. A. (1995). An ethnography of communication in immersion classrooms in Hungary. *TESOL Quarterly, 29,* 505–537.

Eggins, S., & Slade, D. (1997). *Analysing casual conversation.* London: Cassell.

Eyring, J. L. (1989). *Teaching experiences and student responses in ESL project work instruction: A case study.* Unpublished doctoral dissertation, University of California, Los Angeles.

Fried-Booth, D. L. (2002). *Project work* (2nd ed.). Oxford: Oxford University Press.

Haines, S. (1989). *Projects for the EFL classroom: Resource material for teachers.* Walton-on-Thames, UK: Nelson.

Halliday, M. A. K. (1978). *Language as social semiotic: The social interpretation of language and meaning.* London: Edward Arnold.

Halliday, M. A. K. (1994). *An introduction to functional grammar* (2nd ed.). London: Edward Arnold.

Halliday, M. A. K., & Hasan, R. (1985). *Language, context, and text: Aspects of language on a social semiotic perspective.* Oxford: Oxford University Press.

Halliday, M. A. K., & Matthiessen, C. M. I. M. (1999). *Constructing experience through meaning: A language-based approach to cognition.* London: Cassell.

Henry, J. (1994). *Teaching through projects.* London: Kogan Page.

Jandt, F. E. (1998). *Intercultural communication: An introduction* (2nd ed.). Thousand Oaks, CA: Sage.

Jordan, R. R. (1997). *English for academic purposes: A guide and resource book for teachers.* Cambridge, UK: Cambridge University Press.

Kobayashi, M. (2003). The role of peer support in ESL students' accomplishment of oral academic tasks. *Canadian Modern Language Review, 59,* 337–368.

Kobayashi, M. (2004). *A sociocultural study of second language tasks: Activity, agency, and language socialization.* Unpublished doctoral dissertation, University of British Columbia, Vancouver.

Legutke, M., & Thomas, H. (1991). *Process and experience in the language classroom.* Harlow, UK: Longman.

Leki, I. (2001). "A narrow thinking system": Nonnative-English-speaking students in group projects across the curriculum. *TESOL Quarterly, 35,* 39–67.

Lincoln, Y. S., & Guba, E. G. (1985). *Naturalistic inquiry.* Newbury Park, CA: Sage.

Merriam, S. B. (1998). *Qualitative research and case study applications in education.* San Francisco: Jossey-Bass.

Mohan, B. A. (1986). *Language and content.* Reading, MA: Addison-Wesley.

Mohan, B. A. (1987). The structures of situations and the analysis of text. In R. Steel & T. Threadgold (Eds.), *Language topics: Essays in honour of Michael Halliday* (pp. 507–522). Amsterdam: John Benjamins.

Mohan, B. A. (1998). Knowledge structures in oral proficiency interviews for international teaching assistants. In R. Young & A. W. He (Eds.), *Talking and testing: Discourse approaches to the assessment of oral proficiency* (pp. 173–204). Amsterdam: John Benjamins.

Mohan, B. A. (in press). Knowledge structures in social practice. In J. Cummins & C. Davison (Eds.), *International handbook of English language teaching.* Dordrecht: Kluwer.

Mohan, B., & Beckett, G. H. (2001). A functional approach to research on content-based language learning: Recasts in causal explanations. *Canadian Modern Language Review, 58,* 133–155.

Patton, M. Q. (2002). *Qualitative research and evaluation methods* (3rd ed.). Thousand Oaks, CA: Sage.

Schieffelin, B. B., & Ochs, E. (1996). The microgenesis of competence: Methodology in language socialization. In D. I. Slobin, J. Gerhardt, A. Kyratzis, & J. Guo (Eds.), *Social interaction, social context, and language* (pp. 251–263). Mahwah, NJ: Erlbaum.

Schleppegrell, M. J. (2002). Challenges of the science register for ESL students: Errors and meaning-making. In M. J. Schleppegrell & M. C. Colombi (Eds.), *Developing advanced literacy in first and second languages* (pp. 119–142). Mahwah, NJ: Erlbaum.

Slater, T. (2004). *The discourse of causal explanations in school science.* Unpublished doctoral dissertation, University of British Columbia, Vancouver.

Stoller, F. L. (2001). Project work: A means to promote language and content. In J. C. Richards & W. A. Renandya (Eds.), *Methodology in language teaching: An anthology of current practice* (pp. 107–119). Cambridge, UK: Cambridge University Press.

Turnbull, M. S. (1999). Multidimensional project-based teaching in French second language (FSL): A process-product case study. *Modern Language Journal, 83,* 548–568.

van Lier, L. (1996). *Interaction in the language curriculum: Awareness, autonomy, and authenticity.* Harlow, UK: Longman.

Wallace, M. (1991). *Training foreign language teachers: A reflective approach.* Cambridge, UK: Cambridge University Press.

Wertsch, J. V. (1991). *Voices of the mind: A sociocultural approach to mediated action.* Cambridge, MA: Harvard University Press.

Wray, D. (1999). *Inquiry in the classroom: Creating it, encouraging it, and enjoying it.* Toronto: Pippin Publishing.

APPENDIX
Transcription Conventions

=	Speech that comes immediately after another person's (i.e., latched utterances), shown for both speakers
(words)	Words not clearly heard: (x), an unclear word; (xx), two unclear words; (xxx), three or more unclear words
((comments))	Comments or relevant details pertaining to interaction
:	Unusually lengthened sound or syllable
.	Terminal falling intonation
,	Rising, continuing intonation
?	High rising intonation, not necessarily at the end of a sentence
–	(unattached) brief, untimed pause
x-	(attached on one side) cutoff often accompanied by a glottal stop (e.g., self-correction)
"utterances/ sentences"	Attempts to reconstruct others' language (oral or written)
underlining	Spoken with emphasis

Adapted from Duff (1995).

CHAPTER 6

INSTRUCTOR EXPERIENCES WITH PROJECT WORK IN THE ADULT ESL CLASSROOM

A Case Study

Doreen Doherty
North Orange County Community College

Janet Eyring
California State University, Fullerton

BACKGROUND

Stoller (see Chapter 2) has aptly presented the confusing array of terms used in the literature to describe project-based learning: "experiential and negotiated language learning," "investigative research," problem-based learning," "project approach," and "project-based approach." Projects have been used from the elementary level to the university level in different types of English as a second language (ESL) and English as a foreign language (EFL) programs (see Eyring, 2001, for a summary of such projects). They may last from one day to a full school term and incorporate varying

Project-Based Second and Foreign Language Education, pages 95–122
Copyright © 2006 by Information Age Publishing
All rights of reproduction in any form reserved.

levels of teacher input—from being fully structured where the instructor plans all phases of a project to semistructured, where substantial student input is elicited during project phases, to highly unstructured where a teacher may or may not be present (Henry, 1994).

Understandably, the teacher's role will become most transformed during a long-term, semistructured project. In a structured project, processes will largely be teacher-controlled and the teacher's role will not vary much from teaching in a nonproject classroom. Likewise, in an unstructured project, processes will largely be student controlled and there will be little or no need for an instructor at all. However, in the semistructured project, especially the long-term one in which the whole class is working on a common outcome and accountability is important, the teacher will be called on to demonstrate new types of skills that may inspire, challenge, or frustrate him or her.

Translated into practice, classroom planning may need to be more flexible and allow more time for students to get acquainted, negotiate project topics, and organize project activities; to do in-depth research of topics which may or may not be familiar to the instructor; and to include more opportunities for formative assessment to help keep the project on track. The teacher may also need to create different types of learning and assessment materials tailored to the types of students in the class and different phases of the project. Because of the complexity of the tasks involved in a long-term project, he or she must also learn to manage cooperative groups, which may contain learners with different aptitudes, cognitive maturity, learning styles, ethnicities, and even motivation to do project work.

Since this research seeks to illuminate teacher experiences during project work in an adult ESL setting, this study will describe instructor experience while implementing a semistructured project. Like similar adult ESL projects described in the literature (Cray, 1988; Fried-Booth, 2002; Gaer, 1995, 1998; Lawrence, 1997; Legutke & Thomas, 1991; McGrath, 2003; Moss, 1997; Terrill, 2002; Wrigley, 1998), this project will incorporate student input, derive its content from the real second language world, integrate language skills, and extend over a fairly long time.

RESEARCH ON INSTRUCTOR EXPERIENCES WITH PROJECT WORK

Much of the theoretical or empirical literature about teacher experience during project work, project-like, or cooperative learning activities deals with the changed, more complex role of teachers. It is often associated with the restructuring of power in the classroom, which results from increased peer input and interaction (Breen, 1985; Gremmo & Abe, 1985;

Kramsch, 1985; Willet & Jeannot, 1993). In most cases, the process of change is not viewed neutrally but as a difficult process that involves the changing of fundamental attitudes about teacher/student relationships and the learning of new skills in management, materials development, methodology, assessment, and so forth (Abe, Duda, & Henner-Stanchina, 1985; Cohen, 1994; Fleischman, 2001; Fried-Booth, 2002; Henry, 1994; McGrath, 2003; Nunan, 1995). This process does not usually occur automatically but must be supported by extended teaching training (Krajcik, Blumenfeld, Marx, & Soloway, 1994) unless the teacher perchance intuitively understands the project work setting (Legutke & Thomas, 1991).

Until now, only one empirical study has focused on teacher experiences while implementing the project work approach in an adult setting. Eyring (1989, 1997) investigated a teacher implementing project work for the first time in an intermediate ESL multiskills classroom at a large metropolitan university. She collected qualitative and quantitative data in order to compare the project work teacher with a control group teacher over a period of one school term. Results showed that the project work teacher spent more time on planning, researching, and assessing activities than the control group teacher. Student input in negotiating the curriculum took much longer in the project work classroom. For example, 10.47 hours or about 21% of class time was spent on planning and organizing what to do versus 35 minutes or about 1.1% of class time for presenting and explaining the course syllabus. Teacher satisfaction with students making their own plans over the course of the term decreased over time. The project work teacher spent about the same amount of time on planning as the control group teacher, but it was more stressful and she stated that it required more "brainwork." At one point, the project work teacher was impelled to change plans when she perceived that her students' lack of enthusiasm reflected upon her own competence and professionalism. To address this concern, plans were dramatically altered to include traditional teacher-directed activities. Nothing similar to this occurred in the control class.

While facilitating the extended project, the project work instructor created activities and materials in response to student need that she observed during group work sessions. In the control class, learning activities were more predictable, followed a step-by-step organization, and did not incorporate group work to the same extent. In the project work class, the teacher's facilitator stance inspired some students but signaled to others an opportunity to "lay back" or not attend class. No similar negative attitude or attendance problem appeared in response to teacher behavior in the nonproject class.

Regarding evaluation, more time was spent on assessment activities in the project work classroom, but the power of the teacher in evaluation was lessened by the structuring of tasks to be evaluated and the means by which they were evaluated. Peers provided increased input and feedback in learning tasks and the teacher integrated more subjective, flexible grading in the evaluation process. The assignment of grades was different but was not more threatening than it was in the control class. However, teacher worry about how and when to correct during classwork was more evident.

This theoretical and empirical review provides a backdrop for a qualitative study of instructor experiences with project work instruction that will illuminate issues surrounding the implementation of this approach in the adult ESL context.

OVERVIEW AND RESEARCH QUESTIONS

In this case study of teacher experiences with project work, "project work" is operationally defined as a teaching approach that has three distinguishing features (a student-negotiated curriculum, extended research of one topic, and collaborative assessment) that vary on two parameters (more time being spent in the classroom in open negotiation of what is to be learned, how it is to be learned, and how it is to be assessed; and more student influence in class decision-making processes related to planning, research, and evaluation).

A university professor, a graduate student, and an adult ESL teacher collaboratively taught a multiskills project in an adult ESL setting. The ESL students researched the effects of the "post-911" attack on the United States, an event that was particularly germane to the political climate of the time because the class coincided with the U.S. war in Iraq. The adult ESL students selected the topic, collected data for the project, and evaluated themselves and the project. Ultimately, they produced a poster that included brief written texts with accompanying pictures about the impact of "9/11" on their lives.

The instructors documented their experiences while implementing project work activities. They focused on typical activities of project work from beginning to end and investigated several main questions:

  (a) How are lesson plans adjusted or abandoned for these and other activities inside and outside the classroom in the adult ESL classroom?
  (b) How are teaching and evaluation adjusted for project work activities in the adult ESL classroom?
  (c) What are the values and beliefs of these teachers during these activities and do they change throughout the term in the adult ESL classroom?

METHOD

Setting

The students in this study were enrolled in an advanced ESL writing and grammar course in an adult continuing education program in Southern California. The class lasted 90 minutes on Fridays and was listed in the schedule of classes as a specialty class designed to "enrich" content for the advanced-level student. It was an open-entry/open-exit class and was situated in a comfortable downtown center. The no-cost, no-credit aspect of the class lent itself well to a relaxed and casual atmosphere. The regular curriculum in this class centered on providing practice in writing lengthier pieces on individual topics, using more advanced English grammar, and refining mechanics. Students had been introduced to the writing process (prewriting, writing, and revising) several weeks prior to the beginning of the project.

The Students

Although listed as an advanced-level class per the California ESL Model Standards for Adult Education (California Department of Education, 1992), the students actually ranged from intermediate to advanced proficiency and had differing levels of ability in oral/aural and reading/writing skills. Ethnicities represented were Japanese, Chinese, Vietnamese, Korean, Mexican, and Costa Rican. Twenty-five students were enrolled in the course, and weekly attendance ranged from eight to twenty students with a core group of about five who attended every week. Ten students were in attendance on the last day of the class. Students were 20 to 45 years old and all had attended primary schools in their native countries. Others had attended previous adult ESL classes in the United States or had learned English naturally in the community. At the other end of the spectrum, a few students held postsecondary degrees or professional certifications from their native countries.

The Latin American students were long-term immigrants and had an average length of residence in the United States of 11 years (with a range of 1 to 28 years). The Asian students were short-term immigrants and had an average length of U.S. residence of 1.31 years (with a range of $\frac{1}{2}$ to 2 years). Most students possessed a degree of computer literacy in their first language. Some students hoped to pursue university-level work in English either in the United States or abroad, while others sought to improve their vocational English or simply learn English to function better in American society.

The Instructors

One instructor, Professor (P), was a TESOL teacher trainer at a large Southern California university. Her dissertation topic was on the project work approach, and she has trained hundreds of teachers for ESL work in the past 24 years. She was funded by a service-learning grant provided by her local university to collaborate in this project. As the project work expert, she took the lead in classroom planning.

The second instructor, Student (S), was a graduate student enrolled in the previously mentioned TESOL teacher-training program. As part of a graduate-course service-learning requirement, he assisted with teaching the class and preparing materials.

The third instructor, the instructor of record for the class, Teacher (T), employed by a continuing education program in a local community college district, was an alumnus from the previously mentioned TESOL teacher-training program at a large Southern California university. She had taught ESL at this site for the past 7 years. She was also funded by a service-learning grant provided by the local university to collaborate. She taught her class during the first few weeks of the school term and polled her students to see if they were interested in engaging in project work instruction with P and S from the university. Given a positive response, P and S prepared materials and taught the class during the latter 5 weeks of the school term. T mainly assisted as a monitor during group work activities.

The researchers collected several sources of data as both researchers and participants in the study. Using action research methodology (Wallace, 1998), the researchers were not only observers but also participants in classroom processes. They collected and analyzed the data using an ethnographic approach. Planning data consisted of lesson plans that were drafted by P, the project work expert, and shared with S (see Appendix A). T was sometimes informed via e-mail before the Friday session or after a session when input for the following week was solicited. To obtain data on the project itself, all three instructors took notes during class on such features as the number of students in attendance, relevant quotes from students, principles observed, group work dynamics, and final outcomes. Everyone also took notes during 10- to 30-minute discussions that took place after class during "debriefing" periods and again after the project was over. Finally, thoughts on teaching and assessing were exchanged through e-mail during the week by all three instructors (see Appendix B). Student questionnaires and checklists provided additional means of obtaining student response to the approach and their evaluation of the project as a whole (see Appendixes C, D, and E). This mutual collaboration and reflection allowed for the triangulation of perspectives on the three main research questions.

RESULTS

All three instructors enthusiastically began the project with the same research questions but different motivations in mind. At the outset, P and S assumed the role of instructor of the project work class and T the role of observer. P wanted to know if relatively novice project work teachers would encounter difficulties as they orchestrated a project. T wanted to know how her students could apply her lessons on pre-writing, composing, editing, and proofing to a self-chosen project. S wanted to know how theories he had been studying at the university would relate to a real-life setting. The sharing of perspectives and priorities surfaced throughout the 5-week period, while creating lesson plans and guiding and assessing the project.

Lesson Plans

The three teachers had somewhat different impressions about the efficacy of lesson plans during the project work course. In general, T felt that lessons were viable but were presented prematurely. P and S noted that lesson plans were not completed as originally designed. More often than not, certain activities had to be slowed down because of lack of student comprehension. For the same reason, other activities were eliminated altogether. Appendix F describes the actual sequence of activities followed throughout the project. In this section, deviations and revisions of those plans will be discussed.

On the first day, students seemed challenged by the initial project idea worksheet (Appendix G) and the handout with authentic environmental protection texts (e.g., letters, summaries, reports, newspaper articles) that had been provided as models of what they might produce. Both P and S were surprised for different reasons by the uneven proficiency of the students in an "advanced" class per the California ESL Model Standards for Adult Education (California Department of Education, 1992). P had not taught an adult ESL class for more than 19 years, and S had had little experience in this setting. T did not view this as a problem because she was accustomed to teaching to a variety of student proficiencies.

On the second day, P and S again encountered a mismatch between the materials introduced (an article on post-911 racial profiling obtained from the Internet [Kinsley, 2001]) and the students' ability to comprehend the material. To read and comprehend the entire article may have taken 30 to 45 minutes in an advanced class, but in this class, students as a whole were barely able to comprehend the first paragraph, even with the assistance of S clarifying vocabulary and main ideas.

S learned that authentic texts may be at an inappropriate level for a project work class and lessons may need to be adapted on the spot when he stated:

> The real lesson, for me as the instructor, was that lesson plans must be rapidly adapted and transformed if one hits a roadblock. The instructor must always be sensitive to the mood of the class and adapt accordingly. I realized that students had definite opinions about racial profiling, but I also realized that the text was perhaps too demanding for the students' reading level. (S Notes 5/30/03)

At the end of this second session, T requested that she be allowed 20 minutes at the beginning of each subsequent class to introduce the students to abridged versions of her writing process lessons (e.g., brainstorming, clustering, outlining). This was not part of the original plan but T felt they needed additional strategies to independently formulate and discuss ideas and readings relevant to the project. As a result, from the third lesson forward, T began giving these lessons during the first 20 minutes of the class.

On the third day, when the proficiency level seemed more clear to the instructors from the university, students had an easier time brainstorming a cluster for their final articles but had difficulty distinguishing main and supporting ideas (e.g., "anxiety" as a main topic for several related subtopics such as post-911 fears of flying, fear of Middle Eastern immigrants, economic concerns, etc.). As P and S expected, the instructors had to increase interaction with the students to assist them in teasing apart different ideas that related to "anxiety" in society. They noted that two original handouts were not even used because not enough students had mastered the earlier cluster tasks. T had to resist the desire to assist the students too much because she was uncomfortable watching them struggle.

On the fourth day, P and S noted that a few students had neglected to do their homework, while others had expanded and elaborated their homework, and still others appeared for the first time and did not know what was going on. S was intrigued by the process by which students had moved the topic from the abstract to the concrete. P was surprised that within small groups, students had abandoned the more sophisticated ideas obtained in the larger group discussion and settled on the cognitively less demanding topic of the personal effect of war on people—their families and their daily living. T was not surprised at all by the variety of student commitment to completing the homework assignment. These discussions left no time for another handout that had been prepared on "Planning the Argumentative Essay."

By the fifth day, the lesson plan was executed much as expected (without the stops and starts of earlier sessions). Students accepted the seriousness of collaboratively completing a final product within a time period. In fact, one student, echoing the instructors' beliefs about the group nature of the project, stated, "It's a team" as she and others were highly motivated to divide up the necessary tasks to complete the final product. Certain individuals who had taken a role in writing some of the original drafts deferred to other, more capable writers who could do the writing and editing faster. Still others assumed the role as artistic directors as they arranged the final drafts of the articles on the posters, cut and pasted related photos from magazines and newspapers, and finally posted the end product on the back wall of the classroom. The final few minutes of class were reserved for a pizza party as students reviewed and admired their posters and were photographed in front of their work.

In sum, implementing project work required a flexible attitude toward plans on the part of the instructors. Materials that were presented before students had been prepared to access them at a more demanding level usually had to be deferred, abandoned, or at least adapted, a situation not surprising for experienced teachers but more surprising for novice teachers or teachers who had been out of the classroom for some time. Supplementary materials also had to be designed to support their progress toward their goals. In most cases, the class activities did not correspond much to the written plans, except on the last day when students were motivated to complete their projects after so much planning in the previous weeks. T was decidedly more in tune with her students and thus more bothered by the struggles they were having with the lessons planned by P and S.

Teaching Adjustments

Negotiating the Curriculum

T was more concerned than P and S about the amount of time it took for learners to decide on what kind of project they would do and how they would complete it. This was evidenced in the previous discussion when T felt compelled to remind students of important brainstorming strategies when they appeared to be floundering for ideas. P and S also were observing some of the same behavior but interpreted this struggle as normal for students engaged with each other in the negotiation stage. All agreed, however, that the topic choices should be narrowed so that students could enter into a more formal organization stage of ideas. At this point, students were encouraged to select a favored topic around which they could provide supporting ideas and the topic was negotiated.

T noted her frustration with this stage of the negotiation process:

> I was uncomfortable watching students struggle with conceptualizing what it was they were going to do and felt responsible for enough guidance and support for the students to arrive at a point where they could apply their language skills to something. Ultimately, I felt that some imposed structure was required in order for them to function. (T Notes 5/30/03)

T was less comfortable than P and S with the amount of time and quality of interaction during the negotiation stage but all agreed that the time constraints of the class made it necessary for them to encourage students to make a decision about their topic and move on.

Facilitating a Long-Term Project

While facilitating the project, all three instructors gained greater awareness of the kind of metacognitive and research support needed for students to make progress on their projects. P and S also learned about the special challenges of implementing projects in an open-entry, open-exit, mixed-ethnicity adult class.

As mentioned earlier, the actual research and writing of the poster product began during the third day of instruction after the "Effects of 911" topic had been negotiated. The instructors' decision to encourage students to decide on a topic was later followed by another decision to encourage students to clarify the subcomponents of their topics and generate sufficient support needed to write articles for their posters. For example, in the second session students were sharing their ideas about rising gas prices, increased security in airports, and F1 visa problems. S served as scribe for these ideas and while doing so noticed that all of these topics related to repercussions of September 11. To put the ideas in some kind of order, he drew a circle with spokes in preparation for a cluster diagram. T reminded students that this was the same kind of process they had seen before in their class when they were selecting ideas for essay writing. S continued by labeling the center bubble "Effects of 911" and then inserted other ideas in the branching bubbles from the center. S noted the great benefits of this type of modeling to help students develop their ideas on new and challenging topics. While doing so, he made reference to theoreticians he had been reading about in his graduate studies:

> Students not only acquire a good pre-writing skill, but they are actively engaged in the process of linking their ideas and forming a descriptive if not an explanatory structure for these ideas. These are the foundations of what would naturally develop as theory building (Strauss & Corbin, 1990). It is no doubt a leap to make this claim, but nevertheless a well-modeled clustering activity can provide a foundation for subsequent research and critical thinking skills for students. (S Notes, 5/24/03)

All three instructors realized that the open-entry, open-exit nature of the class made it necessary for much review and recycling of material from one session to the next. New students appeared and old students never returned. To familiarize new students with the other students and with the goals of the project and the importance of participating with others in group work, the instructors instituted a short period of introductions near the beginning of each class. S began to coin this "elevator speech," based on his past sales experience when he had to pitch products and services in a short amount of time, such as in an elevator ride. Students who consistently attended the class became well versed in introducing new students into the fold, so to speak, by delivering these quick summaries of the project.

P presumed from past experience and cooperative learning research (Johnson & Johnson, 1994; Slavin, 1990) that every attempt should be made to mix nationalities during small group work to increase opportunities for English use. In this class, Latin American students and Asian students entered the classroom and automatically sat in the same place each week—the Latin American students on the teacher's right and the Asian students on the teacher's left. With the exception of a few assigned pair work tasks, both groups of students preferred to sit with students from their own ethnic background and even ignored or resisted P and S's attempts to mix them for small group discussions.

On the third day of the project, certain distinctive behaviors began occurring in the "Asian" and "Latin American" groups. The Asian group, when asked to write their ideas on paper, was on task, where each student worked on some aspect of post-911 effects. In the Latin American group, however, one student who had developed an extensive outline of an article and could have easily written up an article of her own insisted on having the whole group collaborate on writing the article, each person taking turns one by one in adding ideas. P noted:

> I was disappointed at how bogged down this group became when they had the potential of writing a very well supported article on the effects of 911 enhanced by Maria's research she had done for homework as well as her careful outline. Instead, Maria ignored her own work and waited patiently while a lower proficiency student served as scribe for the other students' ideas, which frankly were much weaker and less well articulated than the ones I could see clearly written on her homework paper. (P Notes 6/18/03)

Throughout the project, S and P did a great deal of research outside of class. S searched the Internet for at least 7 hours to locate articles on post-911 events, airport security, and driver's licenses. P and S prepared several original handouts on reading selections, model articles, rhetorical organization, grammar, and error detection. Students seemed to respond well to materials tailored to their interests and the topics they had selected. They also made some effort themselves to bring in related pictures and articles. Many of these were used in creating the final posters on the last day of class.

Assessment Adjustments

According to T, assessment in an adult ESL specialty writing class is normally limited to qualitative comments on student work. There are no tests, but T draws "happy faces" or writes "good" on individual pieces of writing to inform students they are on track. Different quantities of writing are accepted from different students, depending on their proficiency level. One student might produce a paragraph and another a full essay. As long as students are making progress in the writing process, they will receive a positive evaluation. Little, if any, collaborative evaluation is used.

On the other hand, collaborative assessment took several forms in this project work class, from questionnaires to oral and written feedback. Key to many expository writing classes is peer feedback (Ferris & Hedgcock, 1998); the project work course was no different. During the last session, P guided students in peer feedback and peer editing of their drafts. After a discussion of subject-verb agreement, students began assisting each other in finding faulty verbs as well as correcting other grammatical errors. S realized that this activity, which is often met with resistance in more advanced writing classes, was actually quite pleasurable. He states:

> We structured the class in a group-oriented framework from the beginning, so that collaboration, feedback, and debate became the norm rather than the exception. Students developed their ideas within a group ethic, so that when it came time to have their written product reviewed by peers, there was no threat to the face of any student. (S Notes 5/23/03)

Several measures were utilized to provide students with an opportunity to collaboratively evaluate their strengths and progress in the project work classroom. Patterned after a skills assessment instrument in a previous study of project work (Eyring, 1989), the instructors administered a Project Work Skills Assessment (Appendix C) to the students who enrolled on the first day. Twelve students completed the questionnaire. Eleven students indicated they had lived in the area from 1 week to 25 years, with an average of 6.14 years. They spoke Korean, Spanish, Japanese, and Cantonese and had such diverse skills as typing, word processing, artistic ability, photography, library research, good at talking to strangers, organizing ideas in logical order, proofreading, and editing. Others indicated they had access to cameras, cars, personal computers, the Internet, and tape recorders. Seventy-five percent of the group indicated that they had extra time they could work outside of class. All instructors gleaned useful information from this initial survey, but because the group changed from week to week, it was very difficult to keep track of who was there each time and what talents, skills, and equipment they had brought with them. This would have especially been useful information on the last day of the project when students were making posters, where good word processing and art skills were needed.

In addition, Kagan's (1992) Did I Help? group work evaluation was administered during the third day of the project at P's insistence. S and T, lacking experience in the methodology, were less attuned to the so-called theoretical importance of obtaining formative feedback from students about their group processes. Ten students answered questions about oral interaction strategies within the group. Seven females and three males indicated on a 3-point scale of "often, sometimes, or never" that they sometimes or often checked to make sure everyone understood what they did, answered any questions that were asked, gave explanations whenever they could, asked specific questions about what they didn't understand, when they had difficulty, got extra practice or help, and paraphrased what others said.

Eight of the ten students also provided written comments about the class up to that point. All comments were positive and indicated such sentiments as they loved the class, liked working in groups, liked learning more about their classmates, and wanted to do more projects like this. One comment, written in Spanish, indicated that the student liked projects but there were so many new words to learn that she was not able to understand everything. All three teachers felt that this commercially published questionnaire did not fit the task exactly and a customized questionnaire would have been more effective. However, all instructors agreed that the written comments showed a positive response to the approach during the middle stages of the project, at least from those present on the day it was administered.

Finally, an end-of-project questionnaire was administered to allow students to reflect on the project activities. In response to whether or not the students liked the project, all 10 students said "yes." One student did not respond because this was the first time he had attended the class. Four expressed confusion in the beginning but developed an increased understanding and appreciation for the project as the weeks went by. Five said that they liked the project when it started 4 weeks ago. One Japanese student stated, "First time I was ashamed to say what I thought. But everyone helped me. And even after I missed the class, I could join the class." When asked if they had any suggestions for improvement, six students said they had none, and three students, all Latin American, suggested that more organization be given, more time be given, and that more students have an opportunity to share ideas in English in small groups. When prompted to identify whether this project helped them with English, all said "yes," except one Korean nonresponder who only responded to the first question. The Japanese student added that she didn't have enough time to produce her own writing. When asked for further suggestions, five Latin American respondents thanked the instructors and all Asian respondents left this space blank.

Where assessment had largely been one way, from teacher to student, in the non-project writing classroom, in the project work classroom students had an opportunity to evaluate their own abilities, the abilities of their classmates, and the classroom experience as a whole.

DISCUSSION

As predicted by the literature, instructors assumed changed roles during the project. As planners, P, T, and S (experienced to novice teachers) felt disconcerted about the amount of adjustment needed in planning for projects in the adult school setting, where population changed daily, students consistently did not complete homework assignments, and mixed proficiency levels required multilevel planning. Certain plans, which would have been executed with some adjustment in a nonproject classroom, actually had to be abandoned or supplemented based on student input. Instructors found themselves in a constant state of fine-tuning and invented "elevator speech" to update newcomers to project progress.

The advantages of project work became immediately apparent to the instructors as the choice of project topic was directly affected by political events during the negotiation of topic stage. Allowing extended time to discuss a topic provided a window into the interests, biases, and motivations of the learners. With this information, teachers were better able to select materials, guide discussion, and encourage learning about a very relevant topic.

Also predicted by the literature for these types of projects, the instructors focused more on the process than on the product of learning during the project (Kramsch, 1985; Nunan, 1995). One of several examples of this occurred when the teachers felt they had used their best scaffolding to assist the class in producing a very sophisticated cluster diagram about the effects of war. Moving from this prewriting stage to writing, students showed very little memory or comprehension of this diagram when they produced their final products, short paragraphs describing the personal effects of 911 in their lives. However, this disconnect between sophisticated teacher-guided discussion and simplistic written description was not bothersome to the instructors who understood that project work is a student-centered approach that readily adapts to student level and motivation.

The instructors also realized that the demands of an authentic task in project work seemed to encourage a preference for working with classmates from similar backgrounds and with similar learning styles and motivations for learning (Reid, 1995). The Latin American groups, who were generally longer term immigrants, were primarily led by their interest in practical applications of English at work and home, and second by a desire to participate in academic settings. The groups tended to be more vocal, social, and cooperative in the distribution of tasks, assigning nonwriting tasks to some individuals and writing assignments to others. The Asian students were more focused on academic and professional applications, and they spent a lot of time practicing individual writing tasks. They talked less and digressed less during discussions. They spent much of their group time engaged in writing individual reports about their group subject and collecting graphics and materials on their own.

Finally, through collaborative evaluation, the instructors received insights about student progress and satisfaction with the project. As found earlier in Eyring (1989), students often feel satisfaction with projects that are theirs but may not be necessarily of a high quality. Students on the last day of the project enthusiastically applauded the use of projects because of the extensive input they had had in selecting and producing them. Yet, the poster end product did not aptly reflect the degree of reflection the students had engaged in during the previous sessions.

CONCLUSION

Project work is a dynamic approach that requires even experienced instructors like T to adjust their roles when they attempt it. This may be more challenging for T than for P or S. T, who is accountable to the students and to her district, understandably feels more wary of such innovations as lesson plans organically emerging out of project work's twists and turns, student-controlled discussions, and self-assessment than P and S, who are much more concerned about pedagogical theory and its impact on classroom culture and overall language acquisition through a process-based approach.

Based on the experiences of the three instructors in this study, the following suggestions for future implementations of project work in the adult ESL setting are given.

1. *Assess the true proficiency level of students.* Students labeled as "advanced" in an adult ESL classroom may actually perform at a lower level of proficiency according to model standards. Determine the true level of students before they engage in a project, since the teacher can waste a great deal of effort locating authentic materials and creating original exercises, which later need to be abandoned because the proficiency level was not accurately identified.

2. *Do flexible lesson planning.* Come to class with plans but be prepared to adjust these plans more dramatically than in a nonproject classroom when student interest or motivation draws the project in an unantici- pated direction. In some cases, be prepared to abandon plans alto- gether based on student input.

3. *Stand back.* Be prepared to restrain yourself from interfering excessively during the negotiation of curriculum stage. Student struggle often pre- cedes important student decision making and problem solving.

4. *Encourage good attendance.* During project work, remind students to make more effort to attend class every day of the project. Attendance is important in nonproject classes, but in project work classes, other students are even more dependent on their peers' work and if some- one is missing, the project may become bogged down.

5. *Provide methods of review.* If students miss class, provide plenty of review but also institute a buddy system where one student orients the new student to what has been going on in the ongoing project. The students and instructor may develop a short-hand method of doing this—such as by using "elevator speech" in this study.

6. *Help students identify and schedule subtasks.* Involve students in discuss- ing the subtasks they will need to do to complete their projects on time. A calendar may be used to help students identify what will need to be done each day and to encourage accountability to goals.

7. *Provide scaffolding.* Scaffold instruction to the needs of varying levels of students in whole-class and group work activities. Provide struc- ture if needed for less advanced students. Provide sufficient chal- lenge for more advanced students.

8. *Respect students' cultural needs.* Be prepared to acknowledge and appreciate students whose learning styles and preferred learning strategies may be different from your own or from other students in the class. Encourage different ethnic groups to work together but do not require it. Motivational benefits from working on a difficult task with students from the same background may outweigh the second language acquisition benefits of mixed groups.

9. *Do research.* Be a co-learner with students as they explore new topics. Search for a variety of materials and encourage learners to do so as well.

10. *Incorporate more process forms of evaluation.* Use process forms of evalua- tion such as checklists and questionnaires to obtain feedback from students about different phases of the project. Be sure to customize all instruments for project activities and, when appropriate, allow students to read each other's responses on these instruments so that all classroom participants may be informed of the status and success of project activities.

It was apparent very early in the project that all three instructors shared the desire to implement project work in the adult ESL setting. The classroom teacher wanted the research to broaden her repertoire of effective teaching tools. The professor and student wanted to know how theories of project work translated into the classroom. The triangulation of perspectives of the three instructors shed light on important pedagogical techniques and cultural implications of applying this method in a natural classroom setting. Discussion and collaboration also helped instructors to move through and solve problems in a more productive and positive way than had been the case in the ESL university project documented in Eyring (1989). More case studies of this kind will enable researchers and classroom instructors to help each other and to help new teachers who wish to implement project work in the adult ESL classroom.

REFERENCES

Abe, D., Duda, R., & Henner-Stanchina, C. (1985). A specialist? What specialist? In P. Riles (Ed.), *Discourse and learning*. London: Longman.

Breen, M. P. (1985). The social context for language learning—a neglected situation? *Studies in Second Language Acquisition, 7,* 135–158.

California Department of Education. (1992). *California ESL model standard for adult education.*

Cohen, E. (1994). *Designing groupwork* (2nd ed.). New York: Teachers College Press.

Cray, E. (1988). Why teachers should develop their own materials. *TESL Talk, 18*(1), 69–81.

Eyring, J. (1989). *Teacher experiences and student responses in ESL project work instruction: A case study.* Unpublished doctoral dissertation, University of California, Los Angeles.

Eyring, J. (1997). *Is project work worth it?* (ERIC Document Reproduction Service No. ED 407 838)

Eyring, J. (2001). Experiential and negotiated language learning. In M. Celce-Murcia (Ed.), *Teaching English as a second or foreign language* (3rd ed., pp. 333–344). Boston: Heinle & Heinle.

Ferris, D., & Hedgcock, J. (1998). *Teaching ESL composition: Purpose, process, and practice.* Mahwah, NJ: Erlbaum.

Fleischman, J. (2001). Approaches and strategies for assessment: Project-based learning using technology. *Converge, 4*(2), 38–40.

Fried-Booth, D. (1986). *Project work.* Oxford: Oxford University Press.

Fried-Booth, D. L. (2002). *Project work* (2nd ed.). New York: Oxford University Press.

Gaer, S. (1995). Cookbook project. In M. Warschauer (Ed.), *Virtual connections.* Honolulu: University of Hawaii Press.

Gaer, S. (1998). Less teaching and more learning. *Focus on Basics, 2.* Retrieved September 1, 2005, from http://www.ncsall.net/index.php?id=385

Gremmo, M.-J., & Abe, D. (1985). Teaching learning: Redefining the teacher's role. In P. Riley (Ed.), *Discourse and learning*. London: Longman.

Henry, J. (1994). *Teaching through projects*. London: Kogan Page.

Johnson, D. W., and Johnson, R. T. (1994). *Learning together and alone: Cooperative, competitive, and individualistic learning*. Boston: Allyn & Bacon.

Kagan, S. (1992). *Cooperative learning*. San Juan Capistrano, CA: Kagan Cooperative Learning.

Kinsley, M. (2001, September 28). Racial profiling at the airport: Discrimination we're afraid to be against. *Slate*. Retrieved September 28, 2005, from http://slate.msn.com/id/116347/

Krajcik, J. S., Blumenfeld, P. C., Marx, R., & Soloway, E. (1994). A collaborative model for helping middle grade science teachers learn project-based instruction. *The Elementary School Journal, 95*(5), 483–497.

Kramsch, C. (1985). Classroom interaction and discourse options. *Studies in Second Language Acquisition, 7,* 169–183.

Lawrence, A. (1997). Expanding capacity in ESOL programs (EXCAP): Using projects to enhance instruction. *Literacy Harvest: The Journal of the Literacy Assistance Center, 6*(1), 1–9.

Legutke, M., & Thomas, H. (1991). *Process and experience in the language classroom*. Harlow, UK: Longman.

McGrath, D. (2003). Rubrics, portfolios, and tests, Oh My! Assessing understanding in project-based learning. *Learning and Leading with Technology, 30*(8), 42–45.

Moss, D. (1997). *Project based learning and assessment: A resource manual for teachers*. Arlington, VA: Arlington Education and Employment Program (REEP). (ERIC Document Reproduction Service No. ED 442 306)

Nunan, D. (1995). Closing the gap between learning and instruction. *TESOL Quarterly, 29*(1),133–158.

O'Malley, J. M., & Chamot, A. U. (1990). *Learning strategies in second language acquisition*. New York: Cambridge University Press.

Reid, J. (Ed.). (1995). *Learning styles in the ESL/EFL classroom*. New York: Heinle & Heinle.

Slavin, R. E. (1990). *Cooperative learning: Theory, research and practice*. Englewood Cliffs, NJ: Prentice Hall.

Strauss, A., & Corbin, J. (1990). *Basics of qualitative research: Grounded theory procedures and techniques*. Newbury Park, CA: Sage.

Terrill, L. (2002). Q&A: Civics education for adult English language learners. National Center for ESL Literacy Education. Retrieved January 20, 2005, from http://www.cal.org/ncle/digests/civics.htm

Wallace, M. J. (1998). *Action research for language teachers*. Cambridge, UK: Cambridge University Press.

Willett, J., & Jeannot, M. (1993). On resistance to taking a critical stance. *TESOL Quarterly, 27*(3), 477–495.

Wrigley, H. S. (1998). Knowledge in action: The promise of project-based learning. *Focus on Basics, 2*. Retrieved September 1, 2005, from http://www.ncsall.net/index.php?id=384

APPENDIX A

2/27/03

Lesson Plan for Day 1

1. Pass out professor's card and write graduate student's name on board with e-mail.

   Project work: To learn language we need to use it for real purposes. To have opportunities to agree and disagree, persuade, support arguments, compare, contrast, and evaluate ideas, express opinions, order and prioritize, ask questions, read analytically, listen for details, take notes, summarize ideas, share ideas, draft and revise ideas, give speeches, present research, etc.

2. Get acquainted game: What are questions? Negotiate which ones?

Questions	Names	Names	Names	Names

3. Negotiate a project topic.

   Handout: Go through environmental project on BB.

4. Look at options. Argue and discuss. Teachers stand back.

5. Project work skills assessment.

APPENDIX B

Sample E-Mail Correspondence Among the Three Instructors

-----Original Message-----
From: Student
Sent: Sun 3/2/2003 12:03 PM
To: Teacher; Professor
Subject: Project Work Session 1...Some thoughts...
Dr. P and T,

I just wanted to share my thoughts with both of you about what we did on Friday. Overall, I think our first session was a success. I think that the articulated purpose of that first meeting was to pique student interest in something, anything, that would get them thinking about deeper issues. I think the pair work (personal interview) worked very well, and it helped to loosen up the students. However, I do have a couple of observations for us to think about in terms of improvement...

...I still have a nagging feeling that we might have "pushed" the students into making a choice. But then again, we didn't have all day to sit and debate either. I'm trying to think more deeply about the process by which we split the students into groups to brainstorm project ideas....I think that part of the session overwhelmed the students, and many felt out of their element, to a small degree. But, then again, that is perhaps the challenge of Project Work; we are pushing students to go a bit deeper than they have in previous course work.

Overall, I'm excited about next week and in getting on with our project.

Dr. E - I'm sure we'll talk on Tuesday, but, before then, I will gather newspaper articles and any other type of information about immigrant discrimination or hardship post 9-11. I'll bring some of it to class so we can glance through it quickly.

See you both soon!
S

-----Original Message-----
From: Professor
Sent: Tue 3/4/2003 7:12 AM
To: Student; Teacher
Subject: RE: Project Work Session 1...Some thoughts...
Hi S and T,

I had some of the same thoughts. I hope that students will begin to understand the purpose more as they take the idea sheet home and reflect on more ideas...I suggest that we work with what the students came up with and perhaps one more idea that occurs next Friday, when students return and a few new students arrive.

S, could you find one positive and one negative article on each of the two following topics? They can be from the internet (try to find reliable sources) or from a magazine article (again reliable source):

–Treatment of immigrants after 911 (in different cities, perhaps one on greater screening at airports and another of a city where people rallied around/defended immigrants)

–Immigrants and driving (in different cities, perhaps one on assistance to immigrants to get driver's licenses and another on police stopping immigrants in a discriminating way)

Next time, let's think about:

1. More negotiation of topic (perhaps one additional topic for the new people)
2. Selection of groups (two) and decision on final written product (poster, brochure, argumentation essay)
3. Prereading activity with articles (S, we'll need to develop this)
4. Jigsaw reading activity with the articles (and this)
5. Comprehension activity with the articles (perhaps half the class summarizes topic of two articles and the other half summarizes topic of the other two articles in writing. Then students present orally.)
6. Homework: Each person finds one more article related to topics

Let's also try to work on a process evaluation measure at the end of the class to find out how much the students are learning/enjoying the project. (I'll bring this)

Back to you both,

P

-----Original Message-----
From: Teacher
Sent: Wed 3/5/2003 5:19 PM
To: Student
Subject: RE: Project Work Session 2
Hi S-

I'm just catching up on my emails. I'm in the process of moving and my computer isn't hooked up to the DSL yet. I'll be back "in the loop" in another day or so. Meanwhile, I agree with both you and Dr. P about the first session. My only thoughts that are different are that I am not so worried about the students having grasped the idea of our project. Some get, some don't, but everyone who participates WILL. A lot of the students need to process through a challenge and they figure it out as they go. Fun to watch! The only thing that is going to be hard to manage is bringing new students up to speed if they have erratic attendance. We may have to give them structured tasks that support the project. Oh, I don't know... We'll talk more later. See you Friday.

T

APPENDIX C

Project Work—Skills Assessment

Name: _____

Phone Number: _____

Address: _____

_____

Length of Time in XXX County: _____

Which languages do you know?_____

What are your skills?

- ❑ Typing
- ❑ Word processing (Microsoft Word)
- ❑ Artistic ability (drawing, painting)
- ❑ Good at talking to strangers
- ❑ Fast reader
- ❑ Photography
- ❑ Proofreading/editing
- ❑ Organizing ideas in logical order
- ❑ Library research

Other skills: _____

Which of the following do you have or have access to?

- ❑ Camera
- ❑ Digital camera
- ❑ Car
- ❑ Video cassette recorder
- ❑ Personal computer
- ❑ Internet
- ❑ Tape recorder

Are you willing to work outside of class to prepare information and collect data for our project? Please share your thoughts below:

APPENDIX D

Evaluation of Post-911 Project

Name (Last/First): _____

Native Country: _____

Languages: _____

Number of years of English language study: _____

Number of years in the U.S. _____

1. Do you like the project we are doing? Please explain why or why not.

2. How did you feel about the project when we started four weeks ago? If you have not been in the class for that long, please share how you felt during your first class.

3. Do you have any suggestions for improvement?

4. Does this project help you with learning English?

5. If you have anything else you want to tell us, please write in the space below:

APPENDIX E

Did I Help?

Name _____   Group Name _____

Date _____

	Often	Sometimes	Never
1. I checked to make sure everyone understood what I did.	☐	☐	☐
2. I answered any questions that were asked.	☐	☐	☐
3. I gave explanations whenever I could.	☐	☐	☐
4. I asked specific questions about what I didn't understand.	☐	☐	☐
5. When I had difficulty, I got extra practice or help.	☐	☐	☐
6. I paraphrased what others said to be sure I understood.	☐	☐	☐

How can I be more helpful?

_____

_____

_____

_____

_____

_____

APPENDIX F

Project Overview

Before the project began, P had negotiated with T to allow her and S to guide the students through the project, with her assistance when needed. P had a clear concept of the stages of project work from her previous research and experience. S had studied these stages through academic reading. T had been incorporating authentic writing tasks in her instruction but had not done "project work" per se.

> **Day 1—February 28**
> Introductions of new instructors
> Introduction game for students
> Introduction to integrated projects
> Handout on project options
> Handout on sample texts for projects
> Small groupwork selecting project topics
> Discussion of preliminary project topics
> Handout on skills assessment
> HW: Reread materials and select a topic and final project

Sample Class Description
On the first day of instruction, P led off by introducing herself and S, by giving the students their contact numbers and e-mail addresses, and explaining the integrated nature of projects. Because of the importance of group solidarity and cooperation in the project learning experience, the students then played a get-acquainted game where they brainstormed ideas for questions they could ask each other to learn more about their classmates. Out of six options, the students finally settled on three questions: what their hobbies were, what their language and culture was, and what their opinion of the potential war in Iraq was. S then distributed a handout that introduced five different topics to the students: participating in city improvement, doing tutoring or working, creating a presentation about their homelands, designing a language-learning manual or guide, or developing a guidebook to recreational opportunities in their county.

To provide an example of the first type of project, participating in city improvement, P distributed and discussed a handout that included various texts related to saving a wilderness area inside of the city's limits. The handout had articles from the local newspaper, reports from city council meetings, letters to the editor, announcements about promotional hikes with other like-minded conservationists in the wilderness area. In small groups the students then discussed their preferences for doing each type of project.

At the end of the class, they indicated a preference for selecting a project directly related to immigrant treatment after 911 and immigrant drivers being stopped by police. Finally, they were asked to fill out a skills assessment form in which they identified their contact information, the length of time they had lived in the area, the languages they spoke, their skills (e.g., typing, artistic ability, photography, etc.), equipment they had (e.g., camera, car, Internet, etc.), and an open-ended question about whether or not they were willing to work outside of class to prepare information and collect data for their projects. For homework, they were asked to review all of the distributed materials and think about what they would most like to research in the coming weeks.

Day 2—March 7
Introductions
Narrow topics—immigrant issues
Distinguish racial profiling from racial discrimination
Prereading discussion questions
Review new vocabulary for first paragraph in article "Racial Profiling at the Airport"
Discuss first paragraph and assign the rest of the article for homework
Brainstorm important cultural characteristics of civilizations: Western, Latin American, etc.
Determine final product—poster
HW: Read and comprehend racial profiling article

Day 3—March 14
Sloppy copy—introduction to the writing process
Introduction of new students
Discuss racial profiling article
Develop cluster on anxiety: security, after 911 attack, economy, war, immigration
Discuss Homeland Security sample article for poster
Brainstorm specific ideas for each spoke of cluster and outline them
Evaluate group process
HW: Continue clustering and outlining, bring pictures for poster

Day 4—March 21
Sloppy copy—more on the writing process
Introduction of new students
Share clusters and freewrites about topics
Discuss organization. Both groups decide to write about the
    effects of war on people.
Write drafts
Pass out local newspaper for ideas for formatting articles
HW: Bring final drafts, pictures

Day 5—March 28
Sloppy copy—more on the writing process
Work on final drafts
Grammar Guidelines for Subject/Verb Agreement
Error detection on post-911 paragraph
Analyzing paragraph structure
Continue work on final drafts, peer edit.
Celebratory lunch
Evaluation of final project

APPENDIX G

Project Ideas*

Civic Involvement

1. Participate in city improvement.

   We could research a controversial topic in your city such as whether or not to save a wildlife area. We could read articles, interview residents, have debates, write letters to the editor, and voice our opinion at a city council meeting about the issue.

2. Do tutoring or working.

   We could work with a community center or after-school program and tutor elementary or junior high students. We could find students who speak our first languages and help tutor them in English and act as bilingual tutors. We would keep a journal to record our experiences and reflect on our service. Other potential ideas include working at a homeless shelter, joining a beach clean-up effort, or painting over graffiti.

Academic

3. Create a presentation about our homelands.

   We could research information about our homelands using written and Internet sources. We could interview friends and family about their experiences and then write and edit a report. We could also make a poster and give an oral presentation to another class at our school about our native countries.

4. Design a short ESL manual or guide.

   We could research different approaches to effective language learning. We could share methods and techniques that work for us and combine them into a short manual or guide to help other learners. We could design "how to" posters, helpful lists, strategy instructions, good conversation sites in the community, and helpful Web sites on the Internet.

Social/Recreation

5. XXX County Guidebook

   We could design a guidebook that features cultural "hotspots" for incoming ESL students. We could pool our knowledge of the XXX County area and design a short booklet or large poster that features cultural attractions, restaurants, and nightspots.

---

* Please remember that these are only ideas. You may talk to us about any kind of project you want to do. The above projects are only suggestions to get us thinking about potential project types.

CHAPTER 7

PROJECT WORK AS A CONDUIT FOR CHANGE IN THE NEWCOMERS CLASSROOM

Rod Case
University of Nevada, Reno

INTRODUCTION

Much of the scholarship addressing project work focuses on how it can be conducted in the classroom and its theoretical basis (Case, 2000; Cuthbert, 1995; Polman, 2000). Although this is valuable, scholarship that addresses the role that project work should play in the newcomers classroom—middle or high school English as a second language (ESL) students with less than 3 years of formal schooling in their native country—is quite limited. In one of the few accounts of project work in the newcomers classroom, Case (2000) details the planning, implementation, and assessment of a 12-week science unit on plant life in and around Midtown, Missouri. Case coaches the teacher, Ms. Smith, in her first attempt at using project work in her classroom. Excerpts from Ms. Smith's instruction and examples of student work in the form of journals, drawings, and written work show that project work was successfully adapted for the newcomers classroom. The

Project-Based Second and Foreign Language Education, pages 123–141
Copyright © 2006 by Information Age Publishing
All rights of reproduction in any form reserved.

clear direction that the different stages of project work offered and the emphasis on student-centered instruction provided a strong basis for students who had had limited schooling and achieved minimal literacy in English or their native languages.

An extension of Case's work is the equally interesting question of how teachers who, like Ms. Smith, face students from diverse racial, linguistic, and religious backgrounds adapt and change their beliefs and practices about science instruction and project work. Two bodies of research address this question. In the first, researchers are interested in how to move teachers from the highly teacher-directed forms of science instruction to a more student-centered and constructivist approach (e.g., Beck, Czerniak, & Lumpe, 2000; Kinnucan-Welsch & Jenlink, 2001; Luft, 2001; Maor, 2000). The second, which I refer to as the multicultural education and science literature (e.g., Lee, 2004; Pate, Nichols, & Tippins, 2001; Shymansky, Solano-Flores, & Nelson-Barber, 2001), is also concerned with constructivist science instruction but adds to the question of how teachers can adapt instruction and curriculum to meet the needs of diverse school populations. Both advocate a hands-on and constructivist approach to teaching science, which is embodied in specific discussions of science teaching methods (e.g., Amaral, Garrison, & Klentschy, 2002; Boyd & Rubin, 2002; Feltham & Downs, 2002; Juliet, 2002; Stoddart, Pinal, Latzke, & Canaday, 2002) and discussions of how the content of science in general can be adapted for ESL students (e.g., Echevarria, Vogt, & Short, 2004; Peregoy & Boyle, 2005). Both attempt to identify how the beliefs and practices of teachers change in response to various experiences.

Missing from this research and the discussions of teaching methods is the question of how teachers of newcomers and ESL teachers in general connect their experiences to issues of race, social class, and religion in science instruction. This gap in the literature is problematic in light of research by Short and Boyson (2005) who document the growing numbers of newcomers in the United States. There are approximately 115 programs throughout the country, and the majority (65%) are organized around a school-within-a-school model. In opposition to the traditional middle school model in which students have a different teacher for each subject, in a school-within-a-school model students take math, science, social studies, and language arts with the same teacher and are released only for physical education, music, or art. Programs are primarily (76%) in urban settings, 17% are suburban, and the remaining 6% are in rural areas. More than 50% of the programs are in one of four states: California, New Jersey, Texas, and New York.

This study adds to the literature on teachers' beliefs by documenting how one teacher of newcomers, Ms. Smith, moved from a teacher-centered model of science instruction to a constructivist framework. Project work, an approach that is consistent with a constructivist framework, is used as a centerpiece for discussion. Data are drawn from a larger 2-year study on the practices of middle school teachers of newcomers conducted between 1999 and 2001 and a second set of follow-up interviews conducted in the fall of 2004.

LITERATURE REVIEW

Doherty and Eyring (see Chapter 6) find that only a limited amount of empirical research has been conducted on project work. In the available research, Eyring (1989, 1997) and Doherty and Eyring (see Chapter 6) explore the ways that conducting project work impacts planning time and organization. Although these studies are valuable because they open a much-needed discussion on the workings of project work in the ESL class-room, Doherty and Eyring do not place their findings on how instruction and assessment are transformed within a larger theoretical framework. The bodies of research into constructivism and science instruction (e.g., Beck et al., 2000; Kinnucan-Welsch & Jenlink, 2001; Luft, 2001; Maor, 2000) and multicultural education and science (e.g., Lee, 2004; Pate et al., 2001; Shy-mansky et al., 2001) are valuable complements to research into project work, because they provide the needed theoretical foundation to discuss why beliefs and practices change. Following a brief introduction to the con-structivist philosophy as it relates to instruction, I detail these bodies of research and argue that they provide a needed framework to understand the changes in teachers' beliefs that must accompany conducting project work for the first time.

Learning the practices of constructivist instruction obligates teachers to a philosophical set of beliefs about how students learn, the nature of knowledge, and an associated body of teaching techniques. According to Oxford (1997), "constructivism refers to the philosophical belief that peo-ple construct their own understanding of reality" (p. 36). Sewell (2002) explains that within a constructivist framework "learning is not the result of teaching; rather, it is the result of what students do with the new informa-tion they are presented with" (p. 24). The practicing constructivist teacher then provides multiple opportunities for the students to confront their previous beliefs about a topic with new information.

Project work and its various principles provide a strong example of an approach rooted in the constructivist philosophy. In it, students identify their initial beliefs about the selected topic and formulate their own research questions and methods for investigating the topic. As the students begin work on their study, the teacher searches for activities, assignments, and readings that will challenge their initial misconceptions about the topic. Consistent with the tenant of constructivism described previously, the teacher acts as a facilitator or guide who finds ways for students to grow intellectually as a function of confronting and exploring misconceptions.

As mentioned previously, the research into constructivism as it relates to science instruction spans at least two teaching populations and foci. The majority centers on documenting how to initiate change from practices and beliefs that are teacher directed and transmission based to ones that are organized around constructivism among pre- and in-service mainstream science teachers (e.g., Beck et al., 2000; Kinnucan-Welsch & Jenlink, 2001; Lee, 2004; Maor, 2000). Most often, the researchers prepare a sequence of courses or workshops aimed at challenging and changing the beliefs and practices of the participants. A pre- and posttest design is used to track changing beliefs, and classroom observations provide data on the extent to which the participants are employing constructivist teaching techniques.

A smaller number of researchers are beginning to explore the field of multicultural science, or how teachers can adjust the curriculum of science to meet the needs of the growing population of ethnically diverse learners (e.g., Lee, 2004; Pate et al., 2001; Shymansky et al., 2001). These researchers also find that learning for teachers and students emerges from the constructivist cycle and that the content of science need not be presented as a fixed set of facts and theories. To this end, they present a variety of constructivist-based teaching and assessment practices aimed at inspiring teachers to depart from transmission-based techniques. The difference, however, is that these researchers search for constructivist-based practices that are consistent with the forms of classroom talk, norms around classroom teacher-student relations, and expectations found among ethnically diverse groups.

From both bodies of research, findings suggest that at least two elements are necessary for teachers to change their beliefs and practices. First, teachers need to learn a set of teaching and assessment techniques organized within a constructivist framework. Researchers present teaching techniques, ways of organizing curriculum and assessment, and procedures for planning lessons that are organized around constructivist principles and in direct contradiction to the teacher-centered practices they are currently engaged in.

Second, the research provides a useful heuristic as to how teachers change. Consistent with the constructivist philosophy, participants move through three stages during the course of the study. The first stage involves the participants taking into account their own beliefs. For instance, Luft (2001) used standardized interviews to gather baseline data on teachers before coursework and then after. Group and class discussions were also employed to allow the participants to describe their beliefs at an informal level as well. In the next stage, new information about various constructivist-based teaching and assessment techniques is introduced by the researchers and then tried out by the participants in their classrooms. These are intended to act as a conduit for change by causing dissonance between the participants' current practices and beliefs and what they are learning. The conversations change from describing their beliefs in the first stage to grappling with the conflict between what they are learning and what they currently believe. The final stage is for the participants to resolve the conflict between what they once believed and practiced regarding instruction and assessment and what they have learned. Their beliefs have changed when they implement their newly learned constructivist-based practices.

In summary, these broad findings on constructivism and science education in connection with teacher beliefs provide background that can be used to contextualize specific findings on project work not seen in the current research by Eyring (1989, 1997) and Doherty and Eyring (see Chapter 6) in at least three ways. First, research into the broader area of science and constructivism documents the stages—a heuristic—teachers pass through as their beliefs and practices change from a teacher- to a student-centered and constructivist orientation. Second, research into multicultural science shows the role that diversity plays in implementing a constructivist approach and mirrors the struggles faced by ESL teachers who work exclusively with diverse populations. Finally, both speak to the importance of providing teachers with a number of constructivist-based techniques to add to their current practices. What follows is an explanation of the specific concepts within the constructivist philosophy that can be used to document changes in beliefs and practices among teachers.

THEORETICAL FRAMEWORK

Underpinning the research on constructivism, science education, and beliefs (e.g., Beck et al., 2000; Kinnucan-Welsch & Jenlink, 2001; Luft, 2001; Maor, 2000) are Piaget's (1977) concepts of accommodation, dissonance, and assimilation. Collectively, these three terms operationalize the process of change learners pass through when confronted with new information. Using examples from the constructivism and beliefs literature, I show how these terms are used to track the development of change in teachers' beliefs and practices.

Intellectual and cognitive growth is a process that Piaget (1977) called accommodation. When individuals encounter new information or concepts that are foreign to them, an imbalance occurs which requires a rebalancing of the learning structure. Learning structures are cognitive schemes or ways in which learners organize information around a particular concept. The concept itself is organized and connected to a network of information that forms a schema in the minds of learners.

According to Piaget (1977), when individuals' learning structures change, they move through a three-stage process. The first stage is called *accommodation* and occurs when new information becomes a part of the existing framework, but there is no change to the learning structure. An example is a teacher who is taking a class on constructivist learning and teaching. The teacher is aware of the importance of using hands-on activities during instruction for ESL students but has just begun studying project work and has not fit it into an understanding of the more general learning structure of constructivism.

The second stage is referred to as *dissonance*. This stage occurs after learners recognize the conflict between their current understanding of a phenomenon and the new information they have gathered. Kinnucan-Welsch and Jenlink (2001) provide an excellent example of a teacher in dissonance. The data are drawn from teachers who are grappling with the concept of constructivist pedagogy in their classrooms for the first time. As one teacher in their study explained,

> As an old, experienced teacher who has seen fads (trends) come and go, do I have the flexibility and open-mindedness to change in my thinking and implement changes in my classroom. . . . Can I let some old ways go and take a risk? (p. 300)

The new information given in the class has clearly placed the teacher in a state of dissonance as she must now compare the information to her existing structure of teaching.

A change in her teaching structure, or *assimilation* of the new constructivist practices being advocated, is the third stage. It occurs when the teacher is able to "let some old ways go and take a risk." Kinnucan-Welsch and Jenlink (2001) place the students in cohorts or cadres to facilitate the process and draw on comments and quotes from the participants to illustrate the process. The following quote is taken from a participant who recently completed the program and illustrates the resolution or assimilation of constructivist practices into the teaching structure.

> Really, I think that I have many of the pieces of a constructivist classroom in my classroom. Now . . . and all of us did, but none of us felt that we were constructivist teachers. You can have all of the pieces and not be a constructivist. It's, I think, what you do with it.

The last two sentences of the quote are particularly informative. The participant first explains that learning begins with recognizing new knowledge but understanding that it does not necessarily lead to a change in the particular learning structure. This, of course, is the process of accommodation. Next, the participant explains that cognitive growth is in its final state when the learner is able to do something with the new information—a resolution of the conflict. The act of doing something with what one has learned implies that a change has taken place and is the essence of assimilation.

As mentioned, Piaget's (1977) concepts of accommodation, dissonance, and assimilation can be mapped to the teacher education literature on constructivism, science education, and beliefs. Table 7.1 lists the stages of change reviewed previously and shows how accommodation, dissonance, and assimilation provide a consistent theoretical framework.

Table 7.1.   Integration of Beliefs Literature and Piaget

Stages of Change From the Literature	Piaget's Stages of Change
Accounting for previous beliefs	Stable beliefs and learning structure
Introducing new information in the form of constructivist practices	Accommodation
Reflecting on differences between past beliefs and practices and new information	Dissonance
Changing beliefs and practice	Assimilation

Within this study, I draw on the concepts of assimilation, accommodation, and dissonance to frame the findings. They bring richness and specificity to the discussion of beliefs and change and are consonant with the literature reviewed in the previous discussion. In the following section, I explore the methods I use to collect data concerning Ms. Smith's change in beliefs and practices and locate my questions within the concepts of accommodation, dissonance, and assimilation.

METHODOLOGY

The project and subsequent data described in this study emerged from a larger 2-year case study of newcomers programs in Midtown, Missouri. Ms. Smith, the teacher in the newcomers program, agreed to participate. Because this represented a significant commitment of time and energy for Ms. Smith, I agreed to teach her how to plan, organize, and implement a project-based unit that combined literacy and science instruction. It was the first time that she had ever used project work in her classroom. My part involved instructing her on the instructional practices and background of project work after school. Each day, we planned and collaboratively taught the lessons. The project lasted 12 weeks and engaged the students in an investigation of plant life and an introduction to basic literacy skills.

Ms. Smith had only taught newcomers for 2 years when we began using project work. She had previously taught elementary school students who were native English speakers, but she began her ESL teaching experience in the newcomers classroom. The social, economic, and academic challenges that newcomers face were new to her, and how she would change her science instruction to meet the needs of her students and the circumstances surrounding that change were the foci of data collection.

Data were collected during two time periods. The first was between 1999 and 2001. A qualitative case study method (Stake, 1994) guided data collection and spanned from 1998 to 2001. Data collection focused on building an understanding of how the social and academic lives of the students can be understood within Peirce's (1995) poststructuralist framework. Approximately 300 hours of fieldwork was conducted (much of it on videotape), 15 audiotaped interviews were conducted, and over 100 pages of student work were collected. Thirty hours of field notes provided data of how Ms. Smith and I designed the project-based unit as well as the instructional routines and practices. Careful descriptions of the classroom, the school, and the district were written as well. Interviews were conducted on a regular basis and provided insights into Ms. Smith's early reactions to beginning project work within the newcomers setting. Student work was collected after each lesson and discussed during interviews.

The second time period of data collection was in the fall of 2004. Six interviews were conducted over the telephone. By this time, Ms. Smith had been using project work to organize science instruction for 3 years. These interviews provided data on the process of change she had passed through over the last 3 years and what beginning project work in a newcomers program meant for that change. Data collection was organized around the following questions:

1. What are the forces in the newcomers class that spur discontinuity and eventual assimilation of project work and other constructivist practices?
2. What role does project work play in facilitating that change?

In the first question, I examine the racial, social, and religious forces inherent in teaching within a newcomers program that caused Ms. Smith to change her beliefs from a highly teacher-directed focus to one that is constructivist based and employs a project work approach to teaching science. In the second question, I examine the role that project work plays in facilitating that change.

Throughout data collection, Stake's (1994) procedures for establishing validity were employed. The thrust of Stake's approach is to erase the researcher's voice from the findings and present an accurate account of the participant's voice. Researcher and participant work cooperatively, checking findings with each other and searching for new relationships during all stages of the study. To establish the validity of the data collected in the fall of 2004, all notes along with a final draft of this study prior to its publication were sent to Ms. Smith. Additionally, contemporary ethics were employed throughout the data collection. The participant had the right to withdraw at any time during the study. Pseudonyms were used in place of the participant's name and place of work.

As is common practice in case study research, data analysis was recursive, ongoing, and informed data collection (Bogdan & Biklen, 1998). The constant comparative method was selected to analyze the data. In it, the data are organized into broad themes. Coding is conducted and followed by a series of theoretical memos. The purpose is to find elements in the data that are theoretically salient, fracture those elements, and then use them to generate more avenues for investigation. When the data reach what Strauss (1987) called "theoretical saturation," the analysis is done. In this study, the concepts of accommodation, dissonance, and assimilation within the constructivist philosophy provided the codes.

FINDINGS

The findings are organized into three different sections and reflect the literature on constructivism and science education and multicultural science: (1) Stable Beliefs: The Elementary Years, (2) The Introduction of New Information: Surviving the First Year, and (3) Toward Assimilation of New Practices: Project Work as a Conduit for Change. Data from the first section are descriptive and provide a baseline account of the beliefs about teaching that Ms. Smith brought to the newcomers classroom. The second section provides data on the forces that brought about change in Ms. Smith. These data highlight the elements that are specific to teaching newcomers. In the third section, data reveal how project work acts as a conduit for change in Ms. Smith's classroom. She confronts the racial and religious issues from her first years with the newcomers and then moves from dissonance to assimilation of project work in the classroom. Finally, she changes her beliefs. What she has learned about the constructivist-based practices of project work and the social and academic needs of her students has been assimilated.

Stable Beliefs: The Elementary Years

After finishing a degree in elementary education, Ms. Smith began her teaching career at a small elementary school in rural Missouri. She spent 3 years there, coming in contact with ESL students on only rare occasions. Ms. Smith had gained some familiarity with the practices and philosophy surrounding constructivist education through her coursework in college. Many of the courses stressed a student-centered type of teaching in which teachers developed hands-on types of activities that allowed students to experiment and discover for themselves the relevant concepts. In reference to her students, Ms. Smith said, "I knew just what they liked, so it was easy to teach them. . . . I knew, for instance, that my third-graders would be interested in the wagon trains that moved across the Midwest and the different explorers that passed through."

The Introduction of New Information: Surviving the First Year

The move from a rural Missouri elementary school to the middle school newcomers program in the inner city of Midtown, Missouri, would spur a change in the teaching structures that Ms. Smith had built up during her 3 years as a third- and fourth-grade teacher. Consistent with the process of change described by Piaget (1977), the data reveal how individuals move through a predictable process of change. When they are placed in a new situation and confronted with new information, they must find ways to reorganize their present beliefs in light of what they have learned. Accommodation is the first stage of change and is present when individuals hold two sets of conflicting beliefs about the same concept. In the following discussion, I show how, in Ms. Smith's case, this is spurred by a change in school and the introduction of project work. I begin with the change in schools.

The contrast of Midtown Middle School with rural Missouri is striking. Midtown Middle School is an inner-city middle school that serves a predominantly minority and poor population. It represents one of two newcomers programs in Midtown. In both programs, students attend classes with one instructor for the majority of the day. Students typically take just two electives outside of the newcomers classroom. These may be art, physical education, or keyboarding. In 2000, 1,386 ESL students representing 20 different countries populated the five schools in Midtown providing ESL services. The ESL student population in the district had risen from an average daily attendance of 350 to 1,074 over the last 12 years. At Midtown Middle School, there were 1,000 students at the time of this study, 175 of whom spoke English as a second language. Spanish is the largest language group at 70%, followed by Somali at 9% and Vietnamese and Bosnian at 8%. The remaining students represent 14 different language groups.

As Ms. Smith learned about the religious, economic, and home lives of her newcomers, the discontinuity between her teaching experiences in rural Missouri and at Midtown Middle School emerged. She recalls that approximately half of her students in her first-year class were Muslims. These students brought their religious traditions with them into the classroom and the school. Dietary restrictions, fasting, Ramadan, praying to Mecca, and a strict separation of the sexes all represented new variables to consider when planning instruction. Three months passed before she could coax them into coed groups, and then boys and girls would often refuse to speak with each other. Arguments were common and often resulted in students spitting on each other. Muslim students refused to shake hands with other students who did not practice Islam.

Health became an issue of concern as well, but not just among the Muslim students. Ms. Smith was concerned about all of the students, to some degree. Visits from the school nurse were frequent, as many of the students had not received the required inoculations. She learned from the nurse that many of the students were struggling with malnutrition. Often, it was not so much that they did not have enough calories but that their selection of foods was poor. She also kept a constant watch on whether or not the students were actually eating healthful food when they went to lunch or if they were snacking on chips and soda. When Ramadan arrived, she found that the students were often exhausted and experienced difficulty paying attention in class as a result of the fasting that they had endured.

When Ms. Smith began teaching at Midtown Middle School, the newcomers program had not adopted or developed a formal curriculum or even purchased textbooks for the students. She was expected to base the curriculum and her instruction on the students' immediate needs. After talking with the teachers in various content areas, she realized that the gap between what was expected in the content courses and the newcomers' level of academic achievement was too great to fill in just 1 year. None of the students had had more than 3 years of schooling in their native countries, and few had advanced beyond a rudimentary command of reading and writing in their native language.

Ms. Smith describes this first year as a survival period, one in which she would be forced to confront and reconcile her past beliefs about teaching with what she was learning from her time in the newcomers program. As she stated in an interview,

> *Smith:* When you first start teaching, everything is so hectic and
> so much is coming at you. So, the first year was more sur-

vival skill.... When you are a new Americans teacher, you are willing to try whatever will help the majority of the students...You are very willing to try anything.

Interviewer: Where did your experience as an elementary teacher fit in?

Smith: It was helping me to understand the importance of hands-on work.... I started doing more hands-on work with the newcomers. This was to develop fine motor skills: cutting, playing with a ball, coloring.... But, I didn't realize the importance of oral language...nor did I really see how important the things (malnutrition, religious practices and low literacy) that we just discussed were...I didn't realize how much I had relied on the fact that the elementary students could read and write.... This came along also because they were so shy, they would get lost and freeze up. So, then we started developing oral language as a survival skill.

Here, it is possible to see the workings of dissonance. As Ms. Smith learns about the religious, social, and economic issues that her students face, she is forced to re-examine the beliefs that she brought in about her teaching from teaching elementary school. Her previous understanding of constructivism included hands-on instruction, group work, and the importance of student-directed instruction, but it was formed in an environment that was very different from the newcomers classroom. Until she entered the newcomers classroom, religious, social class, and literacy issues did not complicate her beliefs about constructivism. She now had to think about students who had very different experiences from her own experiences. Religious, social class, and literacy practices all represented new information that conflicted but coexisted with her past beliefs about constructivism.

Toward Assimilation of New Practices: Project Work as a Conduit for Change

Developing a curriculum and teaching science represented an interesting challenge for Ms. Smith. As she learned more about the students, she came to realize that many of the science texts used by mainstream science teachers were of little value. The language was far too advanced; the subjects, while interesting, were not consistent with the students' immediate needs and interests. Ms. Smith turned to an emphasis on health, diet, and the body. Students learned about the senses, the organs of the body, the muscles, illness, and nutrition. There was also a significant portion of time devoted to the language and routines associated with visiting a doctor in the United States. While Ms. Smith felt that this held the students' interest and met their needs, she still struggled to accommodate what she had learned about her students with her current beliefs about teaching. This struggle could be seen in how she describes her science teaching.

> Sometimes, I really didn't know what to expect from the students ... or what exactly they would know about a subject, so I turned to worksheets. ... The students were led in the direction that I wanted them to go. ... I had lots of posters, displays were bought in from the stores. It wasn't really constructivism. I would direct them in the way that I planned to go.

While her decision to rely on worksheets and a teacher-directed approach contradicts both the beliefs that she brought in as an elementary teacher and what she had learned in her newcomers class, Ms. Smith explained that this was a survival mechanism. In her own words, "I didn't feel that I knew enough about the students to turn them loose on an experiment in groups." By not knowing "enough about the students," Ms. Smith is speaking of their religious, social, and economic circumstances. She describes entering the classroom each day as a roller coaster of experiences and recounts how she would have to debrief at the end of each day with close friends or family members about all of the things she had seen during the day.

By the beginning of her third year in the newcomers class, Ms. Smith felt that she had passed the survival period. She had begun to learn about the students through home visits, her daily observations, reading, and talking with other teachers. She also felt she was at a point in her instruction where she could make it through the day without, in her own words, "being totally shocked" at what she was seeing. While not completely unhappy with her instruction in science or the general curriculum, she explained that she was ready for a change. In her own words, "I felt like I could keep my head above water now. ... I mean I didn't have to struggle just to teach the class now, so I was really ready to change when you came in."

It was at this time that I suggested that we begin developing a science and literacy curriculum around a project work model. Working after school, we identified areas of interest that the students might have, located community and library resources, and then began planning the first days of instruction. Because Ms. Smith wanted to explore ways to use student-centered instruction, we selected science as the content area. The broad topic for investigation was plant life in and around Midtown. Because literacy instruction was an emphasis in the newcomers class, she decided that there should also be a significant focus on the processes of research writing. The students would learn the skills of summarizing, documentation, and identifying relevant sources as they investigated the topic of plant life. An outline of the project is shown in Table 7.2.

Table 7.2.   Stages of Project Work

Stage	Research Skill Addressed	Selected Activities
1	Writing research questions	Experiment with seeds
		Field trip to a nursery
		Creating a play
		Dance lesson
2	Summarizing and paraphrasing	Instructional conversation
		Paragraph writing
		KWL charts
		Adapting texts
3	Developing final research project	

Despite Ms. Smith's interest in project work and her willingness to learn new approaches, our agreement to begin project work was of some concern to her. As the researcher, I had occupied the role of what Bogdan and Biklen (1998) refer to as participant observer. I spent my time in her classroom observing the students and documenting their academic progress, not assisting her in teaching the class. Despite the fact that I was a professor at the local university, for that year Ms. Smith had been the expert on the lives of the students and the workings of the newcomer program. The decision we made would reverse this relationship. While I had never taught her class and Ms. Smith had not taken a class from me, I would be the one with the answers and the one who would guide decisions about how instruction should proceed. This required Ms. Smith to trust me, and, as such, she began project work with some reservations. As she explained,

> I thought that it was a good thing to try, but I was cautious. The fact that there wasn't a direction seemed like it would be a problem.... It was hard to prepare because you give the students some material and let them go.... Even though the students were doing it, I was concerned about consistency.

As work progressed, Ms. Smith began to grow more confident that project work was something that could be used successfully with her students. Success came as we moved through each stage of instruction. As Ms. Smith commented, "By the third week, I could see that this is working.... I could see that we had a pattern for the instruction, a routine and some structure."

In stage 1, for instance, I led a very active class discussion in which the class talked about seeds that I planted in small cups under different conditions. Some were planted with soil but no light, others were planted with soil and light, and another group of seeds was given soil and light. The students were asked to predict what would happen under the different circumstances. Stage 2 again brought out a tremendous amount of oral language, as I demonstrated how to use the instructional conversation described by Tharp and Gallimore (1991). In the small group discussion, students initiated over 60 potential questions that they would like to investigate. In stage 3, the students demonstrated what they had learned by making murals.

Equally important, project work provided a conduit for change. In the course of the project, Ms. Smith moved from the imbalance she was struggling with trying to accommodate the new information about newcomers to an assimilation of the constructivist practices that are rooted in an understanding of the students' lives that project work offers. As Ms. Smith explained,

> Project works wonderfully because it is based on what students' needs and interests are.... I recall that it was really difficult to find out what they wanted to know, but now I feel that I have a sense of what that is and what it means for my teaching.

This new belief about teaching, while rooted in her past constructivist-based beliefs she brought from teaching elementary school, has been reshaped and become assimilated into her instruction. As Ms. Smith stated, "Now I can see how important their home lives are, their religions and cultures... and how that should play out in the classroom."

Three years have passed since Ms. Smith first began to use project work. To date, it remains the dominant model of how she organizes science instruction. Home visits to the parents are common; discussions with content teachers are conducted regularly; and a sense of curiosity about the nature of students' personal, religious, and cultural lives is a regular thread throughout conversations with her. From barely making it her first year, through confusion, and then on to a set of practices rooted in deeper understanding of her students' lives, she has come a long way.

DISCUSSION

While the examination of the circumstances, reasons, and events that cause in-service and pre-service teachers to change their beliefs about science instruction has been well documented in general education classrooms (e.g., Beck et al., 2000; Kinnucan-Welsch & Jenlink, 2001; Luft, 2001; Maor, 2000) and classrooms with diverse learners (e.g., Lee, 2004; Pate et al., 2001; Shymansky et al., 2001), these researchers have ignored the question of how and why ESL teachers in general and teachers of newcomers in particular develop those beliefs. This study followed a case study approach to examine how and why one teacher, after taking an assignment as a newcomers instructor, changed her beliefs and practices. Project work served as a conduit for those changes in beliefs and practices. Piaget's (1977) concepts of assimilation, dissonance, and accommodation provided the theoretical framework, and the findings contribute to two bodies of literature.

The first finding addresses the question of what forces in the newcomers class spur dissonance and eventual assimilation of project work and other constructivist practices. Data suggest that confronting issues such as health, poverty, religion, and social class spurred a dissonance in Ms. Smith's belief system about diversity and instruction, which prepared her to move toward a more constructivist-based instructional approach. Research from the multicultural science literature (e.g., Lee, 2004; Pate et al., 2001; Shymansky et al., 2001) indicates that these are valuable experiences that impact instruction. In a study of six ESL teachers learning to adapt their science instruction for ESL students, Lee (2004) found that reflecting on issues of diversity readied the teachers to change their instructional practices so that they are consistent with the learning styles and cultural expectations of the students.

A second finding is that project work acts as a conduit for change from which to plan instruction. Following the research into both the science and constructivism literature (e.g., Beck et al., 2000; Kinnucan-Welsch & Jenlink, 2001; Luft, 2001; Maor, 2000) and the multicultural science literature (e.g., Lee, 2004; Pate et al., 2001; Shymansky et al., 2001), there are at least two reasons for this success. First, data from this study suggest that the well-defined stages of instruction and assessment of project work allow students a voice in their learning without requiring teachers to relinquish control of the classroom to their students. The importance of this finding is echoed in Kinnucan-Welsch and Jenlink's (2001) study of in-service teachers learning to implement constructivist practices for the first time in their classrooms. While they saw the value of student-directed instruction, they also struggled with how much control they should give over to their students during lessons.

The second reason that project work functioned successfully as a conduit for instruction is the attention it places on planning curriculum based on student interests and needs. According to the research in multicultural science (e.g., Lee, 2004; Pate et al., 2001; Shymansky et al.,, 2001), this is particularly important in diverse settings where teachers must find ways to integrate the students' cultural backgrounds, learning styles, and academic interests into their instruction and assessment. While project work was not designed to be used either for ESL or for science, the findings from this study suggest that it provides an effective instructional framework for both. As such, it adds another instructional bridge from teacher-directed instruc-

tion to student-centered and constructivist-based instruction to the literature on multicultural science.

While the two bodies of research addressed in this study—science and
constructivism and multicultural science—provide a foundation for documenting how beliefs and practices change in the newcomers classroom
when project work is introduced, more research is needed. The special circumstances surrounding ESL classrooms in general and newcomers in particular warrant special attention when questions arise as to how beliefs and
practices change. Next, this study demonstrated that project work was
uniquely suited to understanding the role that project work can play in
teacher change as well, but few have explored its relevance. Finally, a more
inclusive model of constructivism and teacher change would benefit future
research. As an example, this study drew on Piaget's (1977) concepts of
accommodation, dissonance, and assimilation to trace the progress in Ms.
Smith's change.

CONCLUSION

The purpose of this study was to examine the unique circumstances surrounding ESL teacher change. While the findings of this study are limited
by the small amount of research into ESL teacher beliefs and the case study
design, the following conclusions can be drawn: (1) Issues concerning
race, social class, literacy, and religion faced by teachers of newcomers
press teachers into a state of imbalance or questioning about how to enact
constructivist-based instruction and project work. (2) Project work,
because of its focus on developing curriculum out of student interest, provides a unique conduit for that change.

REFERENCES

Amaral, O. M., Garrison, L., & Klentschy, M. (2002). Helping English learners
    increase achievement through inquiry-based science instruction. *Bilingual
    Research Journal, 26,* 213–239.
Beck, J., Czerniak, C. M., & Lumpe, A. T. (2000). An exploratory study of teachers'
    beliefs regarding the implementation of constructivism in their classroom.
    Journal of Science Teacher Education, 11, 323–343.
Bogdan, R. C., & Biklen, S. K. (1998). *Qualitative research in education* (3rd ed.).
    Needham Heights, MA: Allyn & Bacon.
Boyd, M. P., & Rubin, D. L. (2002). Elaborated student talk in the elementary
    ESOL classroom. *Research in the Teaching of English, 36,* 495–530.
Case, R. (2000). Project work as an introduction to research writing. *The CATESOL
    Journal, 12*(1), 7–21.

Cuthbert, K. (1995). Project planning and the promotion of self-regulated learning: From theory to practice. *Studies in Higher Education, 20*(3), 267–277.

Echevarria, J., Vogt, M., & Short, D. (2004). *Making content comprehensible for English learners: The SIOP model.* Boston: Allyn & Bacon.

Eyring, J. (1989). *Teacher experiences and student responses in ESL project work instruction: A case study.* Unpublished doctoral dissertation, University of California, Los Angeles.

Eyring, J. (1997). *Is project work worth it?* (ERIC Document Reproduction Service No. ED 407 838)

Feltham, N. F., & Downs, C. T. (2002). Three forms of assessment of prior knowledge, and improved following and enrichment programme, of the English second language biology students within the context of a marine theme. *International Journal of Science Education, 24,* 157–184.

Juliet, E. (2002). Inclusive science: Supporting the EAL child. *Primary Science Review, 74,* 4–6.

Kinnucan-Welsch, K., & Jenlink, P. M. (2001). Stories of supporting constructivist pedagogy through community. *The Alberta Journal of Educational Research, 157,* 294–308.

Lee, O. (2004). Teacher change in beliefs and practices in science and literacy instruction with English language learners. *Journal of Research in Science Teaching, 41*(1), 65–93.

Luft, J. A. (2001). Changing inquiry practices and beliefs: The impact of an inquiry-based professional development programme on beginning and experienced secondary science teachers. *International Journal of Science Education, 23,* 517–534.

Maor, D. (2000). A teacher professional development program on using a constructivist multimedia learning environment. *Learning Environments Research, 2,* 307–330.

Oxford, R. L. (1997). Constructivism: Shape-shifting, substance, and teacher education applications. *Peabody Journal of Education, 72*(1), 35–66.

Pate, P. P., Nichols, S. E., & Tippins, D. J. (2001). Preparing science teachers for diversity through service learning. *Science Educator, 10,* 10–18.

Peirce, B. N. (1995). Social identity, investment, and language learning. *TESOL Quarterly, 29,* 9–31.

Peregoy, S. F., & Boyle, O. F. (2005). *Reading, writing and learning in ESL: A resource book for K–12 teachers* (4th ed.). Boston: Pearson Education.

Piaget, J. (1977). *The development of thought: Equilibration of cognitive structures.* New York: Viking Press.

Polman, J. L. (2000). *Designing project-based science: Creating learning through guided inquiry.* New York: Teachers College Press.

Sewell, A. (2002). Constructivism and student misconceptions: Why every teacher needs to know about them. *Australian Science Teachers' Journal, 48*(4), 24–28.

Short, D., & Boyson, B. (2005). *Secondary newcomer programs in the United States: Directory.* Washington, DC: Center for Applied Linguistics.

Shymansky, J. A., Solano-Flores, G., & Nelson-Barber, S. (2001). On the cultural validity of science assessment. *Research in Science Teaching, 38,* 553–573.

Stake, R. E. (1994). Case studies. In N. K. Denzin & Y. S. Lincoln (Eds.), *Handbook of qualitative research* (pp. 236–246). Thousand Oaks, CA: Sage.

Stoddart, T., Pinal, A., Latzke, M., & Canaday, D. (2002). Integrating inquiry science and language development for English language learners. *Journal of Science Teaching, 39,* 664–687.

Strauss, A. L. (1987). *Qualitative analysis for social scientists.* Cambridge, UK: Cambridge University Press.

Tharp, R., & Gallimore, R. (1991). *The instructional conversation: Teaching and learning social activity* (Research Rep. No. 2). Washington, DC: National Center for Research on Cultural Diversity and Second Language Learning.

CHAPTER 8

PROJECT-BASED ENGLISH AS A FOREIGN LANGUAGE EDUCATION IN CHINA

Perspectives and Issues

Yan Guo
University of Calgary

As Nunan (2003) reports, in September 2001, the Ministry of Education of China instructed all colleges and universities to use English as the main teaching language in the following areas: information technology, biotechnology, new-material technology, finance, foreign trade, economics, and law, an enormous undertaking that calls for an integrated approach to language and content teaching. However, English language has traditionally been taught separately from subject matter content in China. As a result, China has produced many language experts who are not knowledgeable in content or, vice versa, content experts who cannot communicate in English. Another problem resulting from this approach, teaching language as separate subject matter, is that Chinese university professors have not

Project-Based Second and Foreign Language Education, pages 143–155
Copyright © 2006 by Information Age Publishing
All rights of reproduction in any form reserved.

been prepared to teach language and content integratively. Many Chinese colleges and universities have been exploring ways to incorporate English language and subject content.

Project-based learning is one possible means for promoting language and content learning in English as a foreign language (EFL) classrooms. It originated more than a century ago with John Dewey and his followers (Dewey, 1916, 1938; Kilpatrick, 1918). Project-based learning requires a fundamental shift in the roles of teachers and students from traditional education. In traditional education, teachers serve as mere agents to transfer knowledge from books, especially textbooks, which are considered the chief representatives of the wisdom of the past (Dewey, 1938). Project-based learning aims for the reconstruction of experiences through interactive processes with one's environment. Learning is viewed as the outcome of the learner's personal experiences. The teacher's task is to guide, direct, and evaluate these experiences (Dewey, 1938). Project-based learning aims to engage students in the investigation of real-life problems and develop students' creativity, problem-solving skills, and lifelong learning (Barron, 1998; Blumenfeld et al., 1991; Breault & Breault, 2005). In this chapter, a project, to borrow from Beckett (2002), "is defined as a long-term (several weeks) activity that involves a variety of individual or cooperative tasks such as developing a research plan and questions, and implementing the plan through empirical or document research that includes collecting, analyzing, and reporting data orally and/or in writing" (p. 54). Is it possible to implement project-based learning in an EFL setting such as China where teaching and learning are teacher centered? How do Chinese professors, who may be asked to apply a project-based learning approach in their teaching, respond to it? The purpose of this chapter is to explore Chinese professors' perspectives on project-based EFL instruction. To accomplish this, I begin with an overview of project-based EFL learning and a summary of the benefits and constraints reported by scholars and practitioners. These sections are followed by a discussion of the benefits and concerns of project-based EFL learning from the perspectives of the Chinese professors. The chapter concludes with the implications for Chinese educators of implementing project-based EFL learning.

BENEFITS OF PROJECT-BASED LEARNING IN EFL CONTEXTS

Project-based learning has been advocated as an effective means for promoting language and content learning in English as a second language (ESL) classrooms (Beckett & Slater, 2005; Fried-Booth, 1986, 2002; Ho, 2003; Mohan & Beckett, 2003; Sheppard & Stoller, 1995; Stoller, 1997).

There are few research articles that examine project-based learning in EFL contexts. Most of the available literature consists of anecdotal reports of how language teachers organized project work for the purpose of English learning. In an anecdotal report, Alan and Stoller (2005) discuss a real-world project designed for intermediate and high-intermediate EFL students in the English preparatory program at a university in Turkey. Students evaluated the effectiveness of the local tramcar system. The project followed the 10 steps suggested by Stoller (1997) and Sheppard and Stoller (1995):

1. The students and instructor agree on a theme for the project.
2. The students and instructor determine the final outcome of the project.
3. The students and instructor structure the project.
4. The instructor prepares students for the demands of information gathering.
5. The students gather information.
6. The instructor prepares the students for the demands of compiling and analyzing data.
7. The students compile and analyze information.
8. The instructor prepares the students for the language demands of the culminating activity.
9. The students present the final product.
10. The students evaluate the project.

By the end of the project, students had improved their language and content knowledge and enhanced their critical thinking and decision-making abilities.

Gu (2002) reports on a successful 12-week project that teachers organized at Suzhou University in China. Twenty Chinese students were paired with 28 American students at the Southern Polytechnic State University of Georgia. The Chinese students were doing projects about a Chinese silk pajamas exhibition and marketing strategies of Suzhou freshwater pearls in Georgia. Gu (2002) finds that project-based learning enhanced Chinese EFL learners' motivation, improved their performance in writing and communication, and initiated their active roles in learning. In a related report, Gu (2001) cites a Chinese student's comment to show that project-based learning offered an opportunity for EFL learners to communicate meaningfully. The following student was paired with a student in the United States and she was responsible for introducing tourism in Suzhou to her American pen pal:

> Although I am an English major, I did not have many chances to really use
> my English. Instead, I just have to attend various activities organized by

classes at schools. More often than not, they are not true communication.... But when doing this project, I usually write something purposefully, for example asking for some information and giving some explanations. Thus, I can see the usage (use) of English as a tool for communication, which really arouses my interest. (p. 17)

This student's comment suggests that project-based learning increased authentic interaction and purposeful language learning.

Fang and Warschauer (2004) report on a 5-year study conducted at the same university as that in Gu's study. They find that Chinese EFL students interacted far more often in project-based learning than they would have in other EFL courses, they had more autonomy in their learning, and they perceived that the learning process was more relevant to their lives. The following comment by a student illustrates the learners' autonomy:

To be frank, the project is the best teaching pattern that I've ever experienced. It broke the traditional monotonous teaching method and established a brand-new uninhibited setting for us. In these activities, we play a more active role which made us feel happy and had a desire to learn more. (p. 311)

Tomei, Glick, and Holst (1999) discuss their successful experience in organizing small survey projects in an English course in a Japanese university. They were pleased that their Japanese students improved their motivation, learned authentic language, and became familiar with communicative presentations. Papandreou (1994) introduces project-based learning in English teaching in Cyprus. He emphasizes the teacher's role in project-based learning. For example, the teacher needs to help students find the resources that may help them in the project, be a source of information, coordinate the entire process, and provide feedback to help students get through the process.

M. M. T. Lee, Li, and Lee (1999) assert that choosing a suitable topic for the project is significant. They suggest that teachers should (1) consider the background of students, (2) make sure the topic is interesting and relevant, (3) ensure that the topic is challenging but not too difficult, (4) allow for imaginative and creative thinking, (5) choose a topic that will sustain student interest for the whole duration of the project, and (6) connect this topic with recently covered topics in their teaching or in other content areas. Following M. M. T. Lee et al., I. Lee (2002) discusses an environmental project she designed for secondary EFL students in Hong Kong. She notes that it is important for teachers to provide language support and that project-based learning does not exclude direct teaching.

As discussed previously, project-based learning has been reported to assist students in learning language, content, and skills simultaneously, increasing student motivation and learner autonomy. However, the same researchers and others have also pointed out some of the constraints of project-based learning. For example, Gu (2002) finds that project-based learning seems to be a great challenge to Chinese teachers and students, who are used to teacher-centered classrooms. Both teachers and students need to make adjustments in transitioning from a teacher-centered structure to one that encourages student autonomy (see Levy, 1997, for a similar discussion). Fang and Warschauer (2004) report that a number of Chinese students expressed discomfort with the emphasis on learner control and responsibility. For example, as one student commented, "if all the students were asked to teach themselves, what do we need teachers for?" (p. 312). Fang and Warschauer (2004) report that faculty members were also reluctant to teach project-based courses "because they require more time and effort and because project-based courses do not accord with norms of Chinese higher education" (p. 308). Faculty members were more comfortable with the traditional teacher-centered approaches that are based on the notion of transmitting a predetermined body of knowledge to the learner. They felt uncomfortable to lose teacher control in student-centered project-based learning. Many faculty members felt unprepared to engage in project-based learning.

CHINESE PROFESSORS' PERSPECTIVES ON PROJECT-BASED EFL LEARNING

Due to the demands for professional development in content-based instruction (Zhang, 2003) in Chinese universities, in 2004 I was invited to show some Chinese professors how to teach language and content simultaneously. Nineteen English professors participated in the seminar. The professors, 2 of whom were teaching English majors and 17 of whom were teaching non-English majors, came from 15 universities in the Shandong Province of China. They were all Chinese native speakers and had been teaching English for more than 10 years. Out of the 19, 3 professors used project-based learning in their English courses.

Project-based learning has been advocated as an effective means for promoting language and content learning in EFL classrooms and is an approach that has been explored by language researchers in China. Thus, I introduced the principles and procedures of project-based instruction in my seminar. Specifically, I explained the Project Framework proposed by Beckett and Slater (2005). The Project Framework is a tool that helps students learn language, content, and skills simultaneously. It consists of two components: the planning graphic and the project diary. The former provides for the categorization of the target language, content, and skills, and the latter provides students with a weekly summarization task (see Beckett &

Slater, 2005, for details). I showed them how students can use the planning graphic and project diaries to keep a weekly summary and for reflection. I also introduced the 10 steps of project-based learning suggested by Stoller (1997) and Sheppard and Stoller (1995), introduced earlier in this chapter.

During the seminar, I distributed a questionnaire to the professors in order to understand their perspectives about project-based learning. All 19 professors responded to the questionnaire. Project-based learning generated a heated discussion among the Chinese professors during and after the seminar. The professors were enthusiastic about employing project-based learning because they recognized its value. At the same time, they also discussed a variety of constraints that might inhibit the adaptation of project-based learning in China. I will discuss the benefits of project-based learning from the Chinese professors' perspective first, followed by the constraints reported by the professors.

Benefits of Project-Based EFL Learning

After studying the principles and procedures of project-based instruction in the seminar, the professors agreed that project-based learning can be an effective tool for the integration of language, content, and skills (Beckett & Slater, 2005; Mohan, 1986; see also Chapters 2 and 4). For example, one of the three professors who used project-based learning in their teaching reported that she asked her students to interview 10 Chinese university students and 10 international students on campus to elicit their opinions about online dating. Her students presented their results orally to the class. At the end of the project, her students reported that they had learned interview skills, acquired new vocabulary about online dating, used English for a real purpose when they communicated with the international students, and developed their critical understanding about the issue of online dating.

Most of the professors noted that project-based learning is urgently needed because it might address the weakness of Chinese students. They noticed that many of their students had successfully passed various tests in English, but not many had developed necessary communicative competence (Canale & Swain, 1980). Communicative competence, as Canale and Swain (1980) propose, consists of grammatical competence (a knowledge of the linguistic system of the target language), sociocultural competence (an understanding of the social rules of language use in social contexts), discourse competence (the ability to interpret the connection of a series of sentences or utterances to form a meaningful whole), and strategic competence (the ability to use strategies to compensate for imperfect knowledge or limiting factors such as fatigue or distraction). The professors stated that many Chinese students develop a strong metalinguistic knowledge about English, namely, the students are able to state grammatical rules, memorize vocabulary, and analyze English texts, but they are weak in the other three competences. The students have been studying English for many years, but are unable to use English for communication. The professors mentioned that, in reality, students study English for examinations. As a result, students have developed "mute English"—poor listening comprehension and speaking ability (Q. D. Wu, 2004). The Chinese professors realized that project-based learning is an educational activity that provides students with opportunities for authentic and purposeful communication and developing their listening comprehension and speaking ability (Beckett, 2002; Gardner, 1995; Stoller, 1997).

Out of the 16 people who had not previously used project-based learning, all planned to experiment with it in their teaching after the seminar. In their responses to the questionnaire, they expressed their belief that project-based learning may "enhance students' motivation" and "develop students' ability to learn more independently and autonomously." This is consistent with findings by other researchers (Debski, 2000; Gu, 2002; Levy, 1997; Moss, 1998; Sarwar, 2000; Warschauer, 1996). Gu (2002) studies the effects of a project-based computer-assisted language learning (CALL) program. Gu (2004) finds that CALL projects had potential in motivating Chinese EFL students. For instance, those undergraduates who had never previously written a single e-mail message in English, each composed about 51 e-mail messages for teachers and peers by the end of the project.

Professors' Concerns About Project-Based EFL Learning

While the professors could see the benefits or possibilities that project-based instruction has to offer to the EFL field, they also raised some concerns. Many of the professors expressed concerns with regard to implementing project-based learning in China. The professors reported that their students might resist such a mode of learning for a number of reasons. First, the professors were concerned that project-based learning challenged the traditional view of learning and their students might not value it. Project-based learning encourages learning by doing and requires critical thinking and active and independent learning (Breault & Breault, 2005). The professors were concerned that their students might not consider it as serious teaching if they asked their students to do projects, because their students regard the teachers as the knowledge provider and the textbook as the knowledge source. One professor explained that he spent a lot of time in class on a detailed study of the text, including the introduction of some background information and the explanation of some key words and the meaning of the text. His students would listen to his lectures and take notes. This approach of focusing on a detailed analysis of texts is still popular in teaching English in China (Hu, 2002). As Cuban (1993) suggests, deeply held cultural beliefs about the nature of knowledge, and about how teaching should occur and students should learn militate against project-based learning.

Second, as mentioned earlier, many students study English for examinations. In China, all non-English majors need to pass College English Test Band 4 (CET4) in order to obtain their bachelor's degree. This means that those who fail CET4 can graduate, but without a degree certificate. Chang (2004) explains that college English consists of six bands, Bands 1–4 are required for all university students, and Bands 5–6 are optional. CET4 is also a prerequisite for admission into a master's program. In addition, the test results provide documentation of English proficiency while the graduates seek employment. Projects take time to plan, search for interesting topics, conduct research, and write and present a report. The professors argued that under the pressure of this nationwide mandatory examination system, students believe it is more important to get a right answer from the teacher or the textbook than doing a project. This view is consistent with the findings in the study by Fang and Warschauer (2004). They report that some Chinese university students rejected project-based learning, illustrated by the following student comment:

> We managed to interview some hotels as well as tourism bureau. We learned from them something new, but by and large, the result was not satisfactory. Because in communicating with them we realize that we knew very little about this specific field and readings books by ourselves could complement little about that. Anyway, if all the students were asked to teach themselves, what do we need teachers for? (p. 312)

This comment clearly shows that the student had difficulty in accepting the idea that students are the active agents of their own learning as part of project-based learning (Breault & Breault, 2005).

Some professors reported that they needed further professional development. When I went through the 10 steps of project-based learning (discussed earlier; Stoller, 1997), I emphasized the importance of the teacher's guidance (Beckett & Slater, 2005; M. M. T. Lee et al., 1999; Papandreou 1994) in each step. Several professors mentioned that they needed to learn how to manage these steps first before they would be able to help their students. Several professors explained that their training was focused on English proficiency levels and perhaps a little on knowledge about English, but they never received any training in language-learning and language-teaching philosophies and methodology. Some of them explained that they had never heard about project-based learning. As a result, the professors were concerned that they would be unable to provide appropriate guidance for students. Thirteen of the 19 professors received their degrees from foreign language colleges or universities, and 6 of them received degrees in economics, engineering, or other disciplines. Among the 13 professors, only 2 were teaching English majors; the rest were teaching English nonmajors. Those who received their degrees in English but taught English nonmajors felt they were incapable of providing content guidance to students because they had little knowledge of their students' disciplines such as engineering, agriculture, and economics. They felt it would be easier to deliver a traditional lecture in English rather than to implement project-based learning in various disciplines. The concerns and desires of these professors seem to be consistent with Y. Wu's (2001) statement that teacher professional development is often threefold: "in (a) English proficiency levels; (b) knowledge about language in general, English in particular, and language learning; and (c) language teaching philosophies and methodology" (p. 193).

However, the professors did not seem to understand that they do not have to be content experts in order to act as guides and facilitators and that students can do the rest, using their work to satisfy their needs and interests. For example, as Papandreou (1994) suggests, the teacher needs to help students find the resources that may help them in the project, be a source of information, coordinate the entire process, and provide feedback to help students get through the process.

The professors also pointed out the limited resources available to students of English in China. It was difficult for Chinese EFL students to get access to authentic materials in English to conduct documentary research for their projects. Even though the Internet is widely accessible in most cities in China, the professors questioned the use of language on the Internet. There are many, to use their words, "inaccurate English" texts on the Internet, which may provide a bad model for their students. In terms of print resources, many professors commented that the English books in their university libraries are usually outdated and their universities do not have funding for new books and journals. It is worth noting that projects can be done without all of these resources. However, professors and students should be educated in how to be creative with the available resources and conduct project work to create resources for teaching and learning.

Another concern is the class size. Two of the professors normally had 30 students enrolled in their classes, and 17 professors had a range of 40 to 120 students in their classes. Those who had over 100 students in a class said they liked project-based learning because it allows students to develop their listening, speaking, reading and writing skills in a real context. However, they also said it would be difficult to manage group work. The professors liked the project diary idea (Beckett & Slater, 2005) because it provides a tool for students to reinforce the language, content, and skills that they learned in the classroom every week. But several professors said it would be impossible to provide weekly constructive feedback to a group of 100 students (see Locastro, 2001, for a similar discussion).

IMPLICATIONS

This study does not follow the procedure of formal research. However, it has implications for project-based EFL education in China on both conceptual and practical levels. On a conceptual level, first of all, it provides guidelines for future research on investigating how Chinese professors implement project-based EFL learning and how their students react to such an approach. Second, Chinese professors need to shift their educational philosophy from providing knowledge to students to helping students to construct their knowledge (Dewey, 1938; Vygotsky, 1978). Project-based learning moves a teacher from a source of knowledge to the status of a facilitator or manager of learning situations. Teachers do not have to be the expert on every topic that students choose, but can be a resource to help direct them. This philosophical shift takes time. However, as the macrosocietal culture in China seems to have shifted in thinking and now demands a different kind of education, teachers and students may need to rethink and adjust their notion of teaching and learning, I make the following suggestions that professors and students may consider adopting during this transition.

On a practical level, first of all, in response to potential skepticism about project-based learning from their students, the professors might use the Project Framework to raise students' awareness of learning language, content, and skills simultaneously (Beckett & Slater, 2005). Professors should understand that they do not need to abandon their traditional English language teaching as it is possible to draw from their traditional English language teaching and from project-based learning. Instead, teachers can learn to include traditional grammar instruction when they identify a common error in students' projects as the teachers in Mohan and Beckett (2003) and Beckett and Slater (2005) did. Second, the current examination system in China needs to change if project-based learning is to be successfully implemented. CET4, as mentioned previously, is the nationwide mandatory examination for all university students in China. The current universal standardized tests pressure students to study for examinations and teachers to "teach to the test." This has become a major obstacle for implementing project-based learning. Project-based learning enhances student performance in authentic communication and decision making, which cannot be evaluated through the current standardized tests. A holistic alternative assessment such as the ones suggested by Slater, Beckett, and Aufderhaar (see Chapter 15) should be considered. Such assessments evaluate students' research abilities, oral presentation skills, and reporting writing abilities through their projects. Third, as discussed earlier, the Chinese professors were concerned that ongoing constructive feedback and assessment for students cannot be done during the course of project-based learning because of the large size of classes. One of the ways to tackle this issue is to train a small group of graduate students and then ask them to be tutors for undergraduate students (Gu, 2004). Chinese professors can also train undergraduate students to provide peer feedback to each other so as to allow students to become active agents of their own learning. Further research is needed to examine how Chinese professors creatively manage group work in project-based EFL learning within the unique context of China.

REFERENCES

Alan, B., & Stoller, F. L. (2005). Maximizing the benefits of project work in foreign language classrooms. *English Teaching Forum, 43*(4), 10–21.

Barron, B. J. S. (1998). Doing with understanding: Lessons from research on problem- and project-based learning. *Journal of the Learning Sciences, 7,* 271–311.

Beckett, G. H. (2002). Teacher and student evaluations of project-based instruction. *TESL Canada Journal, 19,* 52–66.

Beckett, G. H., & Slater, T. (2005). The project framework: A tool for language and content integration. *English Language Teaching Journal, 59,* 108–116.

Blumenfeld, P. C., Soloway, E., Max, R. W., Krajcik, J., Guzdial, M., & Palincsar, A. (1991). Motivating project-based learning: Sustaining the doing, supporting the learning. *Educational Psychologist, 26,* 369–398.

Breault, D., & Breault, R. (Eds.). (2005). *Experiencing Dewey: Insights for today's classroom.* Indianapolis: Kappa Delta Pi.

Canale, M., & Swain, M. (1980). Theoretical bases of communicative approaches to second language teaching and testing. *Applied Linguistics, 1*(1), 1–47.

Chang, J. (2004). *Communicative language teaching and college English reform in China.* Unpublished master's thesis, University of Alberta, Edmonton.

Cuban, L. (1993). *How teachers taught: Constancy and change in American classrooms 1890–1980* (2nd ed.). New York: Longman.

Debski, R. (2000). Exploring the re-creation of a CALL innovation. *Computer Assisted Language Learning, 13,* 307–332.

Dewey, J. (1916). *Democracy and education.* New York: Macmillan.

Dewey, J. (1938). *Experience and education.* New York: Collier Books.

Fang, X., & Warschauer, M. (2004). Technology and curriculum reform in China: A case study. *TESOL Quarterly, 38,* 301–323.

Fried-Booth, D. L. (1986). *Project work.* New York: Oxford University Press.

Fried-Booth, D. L. (2002). *Project work* (2nd ed.). New York: Oxford University Press.

Gardner, D. (1995). Student produced video documentary provides a real lesson for using the target language. *Language Learning Journal, 12,* 54–56.

Gu, P. (2001). *Multimedia English teaching in China: Theory and practice.* Research report prepared for Advisory Committee of Tertiary Foreign Language Teaching. Retrieved February 14, 2005, from http://www.tc.columbia.edu/centers/coce/pdf-files/cb.pdf

Gu, P. (2002). Effects of project-based CALL on Chinese EFL learners. *Asian Journal of English Language Teaching, 12,* 195–210.

Gu, P. (2004). Tech view: Leaving the bathtub to make waves. *Essential Teacher, 1,* 32–35.

Ho, R. (2003). *Project approach: Teaching* (2nd ed.). (ERIC Document Reproduction Service No. ED 478 224)

Hu, G. (2002). Potential cultural resistance to pedagogical imports: The case of communicative language teaching in China. *Language, Culture and Curriculum, 15,* 93–105.

Kilpatrick, W. H. (1918). The project method. *Teachers College Record, 19,* 319–335.

Lee, I. (2002). A touch of... class. *Canadian Modern Language Review, 59,* 282–290.

Lee, M. M. T., Li, B. K. W., & Lee, I. K. B. (1999). *Project work: Practical guidelines.* Hong Kong: Hong Kong Institute of Education.

Levy, M. (1997). Project-based learning for language teachers: Reflecting on the process. In R. Debski, J. Gassin, & M. Smith (Eds.), *Language learning through social computing* (pp. 181–191). Melbourne: Applied Linguistics Association of Australia and Horwood Language Center.

Locastro, V. (2001). Large classes and student learning. *TESOL Quarterly, 35,* 493–496.

Mohan, B. (1986). *Language and content.* Reading, MA: Addison-Wesley.

Mohan, B., & Beckett, G. H. (2003). Functional approach to content-based language learning: Recasts in causal explanations. *The Modern Language Journal, 87,* 421–432.

Moss, D. (1998). *Project-based learning and assessment: A resource manual for teachers.* Arlington, VA: Arlington Education and Employment Program.

Nunan, D. (2003). The impact of English as a global language on educational policies and practices in the Asia-Pacific region. *TESOL Quarterly, 37,* 589–613.

Papandreou, A. P. (1994). An application of the projects approach to EFL. *English Teaching Forum, 32,* 41–42.

Sarwar, Z. (2000). The golden gates of English in the golden context. In W. K. Ho & C. Ward (Eds.), *Language in the global context: Implications for the language classroom* (RELC Anthology Series 41, pp. 32–56). Singapore: SEAMEO Regional Language Centre.

Sheppard, K., & Stoller, F. L. (1995). Guidelines for the integration of students projects in ESP classrooms. *English Teaching Forum, 33,* 10–15.

Stoller, F. L. (1997). Project work: A means to promote language and content. *English TeachingForum, 35,* 2–9, 37.

Tomei, J., Glick, C., & Holst, M. (1999). Project work in the Japanese university classroom. *The Language Teacher, 23,* 5–8.

Vygotsky, L. S. (1978). *Mind in society*. Cambridge, MA: Harvard University Press.

Warschauer, M. (1996). Comparing face-to-face and electronic discussion in the second language classroom. *CALICO Journal, 13,* 7–26.

Wu, Q. D. (2004). *Jiao yu bu: Wu Qidi zai da xue ying yu jiao xue gai ge shi dian gong zuo shi pin hui yi shang de jiang hua* [Ministry of education: Qi Di Wu's speech at the college English teaching pilot reform teleconference]. Retrieved October 26, 2005, from http://www.openedu.com.cn/suxin2/read.php?id=1902

Wu, Y. (2001). English language teaching in China: Trends and challenges. *TESOL Quarterly, 35,* 191–194.

Zhang, H. (2003, May). *English in China: Which direction?* Paper presented at the Annual Conference of the American Association for Applied Linguistics, Portland, Oregon.

PART II

APPLICATION: FRAMEWORKS AND MODELS

CHAPTER 9

"LEARNERS' LIVES AS CURRICULUM"

An Integrative Project-Based Model for Language Learning

Gail Weinstein
San Francisco State University

INTRODUCTION

This chapter explores a model for integrative project-based language learning, "Learners' Lives as Curriculum." It builds on the premise that teachers must listen for learner stories to discover the most pressing issues that will bring language learning to life. In the first part of the chapter, I contrast "mastery" versus "constructivist" orientations to curriculum and argue for a model for learner-centered teaching that integrates these two orientations. Then, I discuss some possible challenges in implementing the proposed model as both English language learners and teachers struggle to shift from pure mastery-only orientations to a constructivist approach in which mastery of certain skills, structures, and competencies are still integral to the process, but are part of a larger meaning-making endeavor. The chapter concludes by arguing that teachers are also learners who benefit

Project-Based Second and Foreign Language Education, pages 159–165

from communities of peers who engage in project-based learning for their own professional development.

THE MODEL: "LEARNERS' LIVES AS CURRICULUM"

Orientations to Adult ESL

There are a variety of approaches to English as a second language (ESL) instruction, each with underlying assumptions about teaching and learning as well as associated techniques and procedures. While it is problematic when a program pursues one approach with a rigidity that precludes responding to learner styles or changing learner needs, Wrigley and Guth (2000) caution that there is cause for equal concern when programs become so "eclectic" that they have no philosophical coherence or unifying vision. For example, an orientation toward *mastery or transmission of knowledge* aims to help students learn facts, concepts, and skills (procedural knowledge) through guided and sequenced practice. One role of the teacher is to provide learners with information and practice to master the components of language. These may include a focus on linguistic structure (i.e., grammar), the four "language skills" (i.e., listening, speaking, reading, and writing) along with the addition of vocabulary, pronunciation, and language functions. Such curricular components illustrate an orientation toward mastery in which the teacher provides information and opportunities to develop knowledge and skills, where learners practice the skills and forms to be taught and then are assessed by the teacher. One criticism of mastery-focused approaches is that they do not provide enough opportunity for learners to use language to express their own intentions; another is that the teacher is seen as the "knower," when, in fact, while language teachers hold linguistic knowledge, adult learners bring other kinds of knowledge to the learning enterprise which are valuable if they are tapped.

A *constructivist orientation* to teaching and learning is one in which it is assumed that knowledge is not only transmitted to learners from teachers or books, but rather, that both meaning and knowledge can be created collectively by learners or by learners and teachers. A variety of approaches, methods, and techniques may be associated with this orientation as well. The *whole language approach* created the context for viewing language as social and as learned in interaction with other speakers, readers, and writers. One technique adapted from this approach for adult education is the language experience approach (LEA), which enables adult ESL literacy learners to engage with print from the outset by drawing on stories that they dictate to a teacher or more literate classmate, either in their native language or in English. These stories become the basis for a language or literacy lesson. A *participatory*, or *Freirean*, approach to adult literacy education revolves around the tenet that education and knowledge have value only insofar as they help people liberate themselves from the social conditions that oppress them (Freire, 1972) as it has been applied to the teaching of ESL (see Spener, 1992). A common criticism of participatory approaches is that not all learners share the teachers' goals of changing their situations; another criticism is the loss of systematic focus on language acquisition as advocacy takes center stage.

The Case for an Integrated Approach and the Promise of Project-Based Learning

ESL programs for adults, as well as the teachers who work with them, tend to prefer either a mastery orientation or a constructivist orientation, neglecting the fact that adults who come to family literacy or any other adult ESL program need both. These students benefit most when they have the opportunity to discuss and resolve their most pressing concerns related to family life, to gain information about how the English language works, and to learn how the "nuts and bolts" of literacy can be used in service of addressing those concerns. *Project-based learning* is an approach in which learners investigate a question, solve a problem, plan an event, or develop a product. As the chapters in this volume illustrate richly, learners do not receive knowledge only from a teacher or book. Rather, they collectively share and create knowledge for real readers or listeners outside the classroom (see Chapters 2 and 4). In adult nonacademic education, several examples illustrate this approach. As discussed in Agard (1999), Mien hill tribe women worked in groups to describe photos of village life in Laos. With help from a bilingual aide, they created a book that was to be given to their children born in the United States A mixed group of ESL learners created "family Web pages" with their art and writings for their school's Web site (Hovanesian, 1999). Students at El Barrio Popular investigated neighborhood problems that they identified and compiled their research for collective advocacy (Rivera, 1999). Learners carried out these activities using language to create projects for real audiences. In many adult ESL classrooms and programs that employ project-based learning, participants engaged in their projects while systematically documenting language that is acquired in the process, achieving and documenting both linguistic and nonlinguistic outcomes. While Wrigley and Guth's (2000) warning about chaotic eclecticism without grounding in a coherent vision is well taken, there is a case to be made for an integrated project-based approach to curriculum that provides systematic information about the building blocks of language and uses those building blocks to talk about as well as to take action about things that matter.

Integrated Approach: "Learners' Lives as Curriculum" Projects

One way to implement the integrated approach is through the "Learners' Lives as Curriculum" projects. "Learners' Lives as Curriculum" (LLC) is a model for curriculum development in which learner texts (e.g., language experience dictation, poem, story, folktale, or interview) are used as catalysts for discussing themes of interest or concern to learners (Weinstein, 1999). A *thematic unit,* according to this model, provides learners with personal stories of others like themselves, along with an opportunity to respond to those stories, generate their own narratives, and prepare for a collective project while learning specific language skills and structures. As such, it can be considered or easily adapted to fit into the project-based learning approach. There are three components to LLC projects: (1) narratives or stories from learners and teachers with a contextualized focus on themes and hot topics of interest to learners; (2) language skills, structures, and competencies; and (3) creating a sense of classroom community. While researchers and curriculum designers agree that these are all wonderful learner goals, some teachers resist using such an approach, because they find it difficult to show how these goals can be achieved, particularly to stakeholders such as administrators and sponsors.

Challenges

Shifting paradigms is neither easy nor comfortable for anyone involved. Immigrant learners may not think that they have anything valuable to say. They may come from a culture or situation where discussing personal stories is not safe or is not culturally appropriate. In addition, learners may be suspicious when teachers ask them what they want to learn or when lessons are not organized around grammar points. For many learners (and teachers) from a traditional educational system, learning of grammar is the only kind of learning that "counts." It becomes especially important to help learners document not only what they are learning *about* language, but also to document the increasing range of functions they can do *with* language.

A challenge for both teachers and learners is that when adults begin to discuss issues that matter most to them in their lives, difficult stories and events may arise. In the refugee community in particular, there are few families who have not experienced some sort of trauma in the process of being uprooted. In a classroom that is authentic and where participants share their lives, difficult stories are certain to emerge. Teachers will be challenged to share tools and skills for creating a safe environment where difficult stories can be shared and witnessed, and where learners can be referred to other resources when their challenges are greater than the ability of the class or the teacher to address them.

Project-based learning for teachers also involves a paradigm shift that is difficult for them as well. The shifting of roles may be extremely uncomfortable for some participants. The shift to a constructivist orientation, where participants create rather than receive meaning, is also uncomfortable in other ways. Planning a thematic unit is messy and entails problems for which the teacher/facilitator may not have easy answers. In a sound-bite society with multiple-choice tests and quick answers, learners understandably want easy solutions and a person who knows all the answers. Authentic projects and learner-centered curricula do not lead to quick answers and "correct" solutions from an answer key.

A third challenge presented by an approach such as "Learners' Lives as Curriculum" for both teachers and learners is that it requires time, experimentation, and opportunity for reflection. Teachers who are juggling several part-time jobs rarely have support for listening to learners, investigating resources, and sharing ideas with colleagues. In the next section, I discuss how these concerns may be addressed.

Preparing Teachers to Become Listeners: Initial Training

There are many ways to train teachers how to demonstrate learner achievements. In my initial training, teachers are introduced to the writing process by writing some narratives of their own and writing a collective piece with colleagues. After experiencing the process as writers, we begin to explore how to create the same conditions for ESL learners by looking at learner stories and following specific steps for creating language lessons. By the end of the initial training, teachers have received from me and from one another many ideas about how to tune in to learners' lives by collecting snippets of experience through conversations, learner writings, language experience, and dialogue journals. Learner stories remind us of our own stories; our own stories raise questions we want to ask our students. Soon, we are ready to return to the classroom with eyes and ears open for material that can bring language lessons to life.

Preparing Teachers to Become Writers: Tools and Training

Listening to learners, hearing their stories, and identifying "hot issues" are the first step. But language learners need something more—they also need a systematic tour of how the language works. The next step is to show teachers how to create thematic projects that include the skills, vocabulary, functions, and competencies that learners need to use language effectively in talking about their most heartfelt concerns, and where appropriate, creating "tools" to help teachers plan projects that contain all of these components. For example, a tool, called the *Thematic Unit Project Worksheet*, would list all of the components that go into a fully integrated thematic unit. It would contain spaces to jot down ideas for themes and projects, language development, community building, and monitoring progress. Teacher-authors could use this as a planning tool for addressing both language and content needs. For one such tool, see Beckett and Slater (2005), who present the Project Framework and a project diaries and illustrate how they are used by teachers to help students assess their learning process as well as their learning outcomes through their own testimonies. Further along in the project, teachers can use a *storyboard* to lay out the progression of activities. This helps the teacher and authors visualize and create scaffolding for each task to be included in the project.

"Learners' Lives as Curriculum" and Project-Based Learning: The Project as Organizing Principle

Experience from scores of workshops indicated that teachers are accustomed to starting with a grammar point or vocabulary list and planning a lesson from there. Working teams often start with some language structure, and then think up some scenario to practice the structure. With "Learners' Lives as Curriculum" projects, language structures and functions grow out of the themes and projects. To do this, one can develop a *Thematic Unit Summary Planning Sheet*, which guides the teacher to select an opening story first, identify the themes that will be addressed, select a project, and *then* analyze what language structures and functions should be taught. This way, systematic language *is* taught, but it grows from the activities and communicative purposes rather than the other way around. This way of working turns on its head the paradigm familiar to most English language teachers who have often used linguistic structures as the organizing principle for their curriculum.

When learner narratives are the catalyst, teachers have the raw material they need to examine the pressing issues in learners' lives. The next question they have to ask is, What can learners discuss, learn, or do about this issue? The linguistic resources needed to complete it will be useful, motivating, and meaning based in the most fundamental sense. As one learner in Chicago commented on why the students loved their teacher so much, "This class isn't about English. It's about us" (Weinstein-Shr, Huizenga, & Bernard-Johnston, 1996).

CONCLUSION

In this chapter, I have described a process for language learners and for language teachers in which learners' lives become central to the teaching and learning process. I have tried to show that project-based learning is philosophically consistent with this approach, and, in fact, that such project orientation strengthens and provides an organizing structure for the model. I have argued that adult English language education has tended to focus on either mastery or constructivist orientations and that learner-centered teaching with project-based learning at its heart can integrate both of these orientations to provide skills and structures as well as opportunities to make meaning and create knowledge

While the promise for a "Learners' Lives as Curriculum" project is great, there is much to be done. Developing and streamlining tools, developing ways to capture and document progress, creating opportunities for other teachers and learners to come aboard, and supporting communities of learners and communities of teachers all require resources. The only way to usher in a shift of paradigm is to invite teachers and learners to participate in the shaping and direction of the shift.

REFERENCES

Agard, A. (1999). For the children: Remembering Mien life in Laos. In G. Weinstein (Ed.), *Learners' lives as curriculum: Six journeys to immigrant literacy* (pp. 23–30). McHenry, IL: Delta Systems.

Beckett, G. H., & Slater, T. (2005). The project framework: A tool for language, content, and skills integration. *ELT Journal, 59*(2), 108–116.

Freire, P. (1972). *Pedagogy of the oppressed.* New York: Herder & Herder.

Hovanesian, S. (1999). Building community through family: Family web page and quilt project. In G. Weinstein (Ed.), *Learners' lives as curriculum: Six journeys to immigrant literacy* (pp. 59–68). McHenry, IL: Delta Systems.

Rivera, K. (1999). Popular research and social transformation: A community-based approach to critical pedagogy. *TESOL Quarterly, 33,* 485–500.

Spener, D. (1992). *The Freirean approach to adult literacy education* (Rev. ed.). Washington, DC: National Clearinghouse on ESL Literacy Education. Retrieved September 1, 2005, from http://www.escort.org/products/freireQA.html

Weinstein, G. (Ed.). (1999). *Learners' lives as curriculum: Six journeys to immigrant literacy.* McHenry, IL: Delta Systems.

Weinstein-Shr, G., Huizenga, J., & Bernard-Johnston, J. (1996). *Collaborations 1: English in our lives.* Boston: Heinle.

Wrigley, H., & Guth, G. (2000). *Bringing literacy to life: Issues and options in adult ESL.* San Mateo, CA: Aguirre International.

CHAPTER 10

GLOBAL ISSUE PROJECTS IN THE ENGLISH LANGUAGE CLASSROOM

Kip A. Cates
Tottori University

George Jacobs
JF New Paradigm Education

INTRODUCTION

What is your opinion? When you manage to get away from the everyday emergencies of dealing with classes, family, and the other aspects of a teacher's life and look at what is going on in the world, are you optimistic or pessimistic about the future of the human race and of our fellow residents on the planet Earth? Do you believe that we in our role as second language teachers can have any impact on what is going on in the world, or should our teaching concentrate solely on improving our students' language proficiency?

In this chapter, we propose an optimistic view of the future of this planet. We propose that as our tiny globe spins round the sun, we second language teachers can play a role in making this world a better place at the

Project-Based Second and Foreign Language Education, pages 167–180
Copyright © 2006 by Information Age Publishing
All rights of reproduction in any form reserved.

same time that we improve our students' language proficiency. The means by which we and many of our colleagues have been attempting to do our part for the planet lies in the use of global education projects as a component of the second language curriculum.

This chapter has three main parts. First, we describe what global education entails and provide a list of organizations of second language teachers who include global education in their teaching. Second, we describe how global education links with trends in second language instruction and, in particular, with the use of projects in second language instruction. Third, we provide specific examples of global education projects completed by students as part of their second language development and highlight key elements of these projects and pedagogical issues arising from the projects.

WHAT IS GLOBAL EDUCATION?

Definitions

Global education came into prominence in the last third of the 20th century. Two definitions of this field are:

> Global education is the lifelong growth in understanding, through study and participation, of the world community and the interdependency of its peoples and systems—ecological, social, economic, and technological. (Sny, 1980, p. 3)

> Global education involves learning about those problems and issues that cut across national boundaries and about the interconnectedness of systems—cultural, ecological, economic, political, and technological. Global education also involves learning to understand and appreciate our neighbors who have different cultural backgrounds from ours; to see the world through the eyes and minds of others; and to realize that other people of the world need and want much of the same things. (Tye, 1991, p. 5)

Several points in the preceding definitions merit highlighting. Sny (1980) emphasizes that global education needs to be part of a lifelong process, not just something studied for a test, and that the world is an interdependent community, not just separate nations. Tye's (1991) definition also underlines our global interdependence. Plus, he directs our attention to the importance of the affective, such as cultural understanding and empathy. We believe, however, one area is missing from the two definitions. With the growth of the concept of animal rights/welfare and efforts to address speciesism (Dunayer, 2001), definitions of global education should be expanded to include not just humans but also other sentient beings.

Topics in Global Education

Topics within the realm of global education include sexual preference, peace, women's issues, environmental protection, development (including eliminating hunger and poverty), human rights, protection of nonhuman animals, AIDS education, and cross-cultural understanding. The use of such global education topics may be seen as bringing bad news into the classroom, causing students to feel depressed and unmotivated. No doubt, there is much in the world about which to be sad, but at the same time, there is much happening to celebrate. Some all-too-familiar examples of the bad news include wars, poverty, racism, disappearing species and rainforests, discrimination against women and those of different sexual orientations, and apathy in the face of all these problems. On the bright side, we can see in the news and in our own lives examples of peace returning to war-ravaged lands; sustainable development helping to lift people out of poverty; people of different races living, working, and learning together harmoniously; protection of endangered species and establishment of protected forests; people working to overcome discrimination and standing up against injustice; and all of this happening because people, including students and their teachers, do care and do believe that they can make a difference.

Teaching Methods for Global Education and Global Education Organizations of L2 Educators

Global education should be seen not just as a set of topics but also as an approach to teaching (Cates, 1990; Greig, Pike, & Selby, 1987). Pedagogical methods and techniques consistent with global education include thinking skills (Benesch, 1993), focus on meaning (Richards & Rodgers, 2001), Freirean methods (Graman, 1988), collaborative skills (Bejarano, Levine, Olshtain, & Steiner, 1997), cooperative learning (Baloche, 1998), service learning (Kinsley & McPherson, 1995), content-based language teaching (Crandall, 1987), and project-based learning (Ribe & Vidal, 1993).

Many second language instructors can be found among the ranks of those educators trying to make a difference by inviting their students to take part in global education. One way that second language educators attempt to have an impact is via global issue subgroups within professional organizations. Examples include the Global Issues Special Interest Group (www.jalt.org/global) of the Japan Association for Language Teaching (JALT), the Language and Gender and the Language and Ecology Scientific Commissions of AILA (International Association for Applied Linguistics; www.aila.info), the Global Issues Special Interest Group (www.countryschool .com/GISIG/about.htm) of IATEFL (International Association of Teachers of English as a Foreign Language), and the TESOLers for Social Responsibility (TSR) Caucus (www2.tesol.org/mbr/caucuses/tsr.html) of TESOL (Teachers of English to Speakers of Other Languages). Additionally, UNESCO founded Linguapax (www.linguapax.org), an organization that works to put language to the service of peace.

GLOBAL EDUCATION, SECOND LANGUAGE INSTRUCTION, AND PROJECT WORK

Global Education and the Paradigm Shift in Education

Global education represents more than just a source of content for second language instruction. Pedagogy is also involved. Indeed, global education fits well with an overall paradigm shift in education (Jacobs & Farrell, 2001). The previously dominant paradigm flows from positivist perspectives, including behaviorist psychology, whereas the alternative paradigm springs from postpositivism, including sociocognitive psychology. Table 10.1 compares the two paradigms and lists some of the ways that this alternative paradigm fits with the integration of global education projects in L2 instruction.

Specific Examples of Links Between Global Education and the New Paradigm

Several prominent features of the alternative paradigm in second language education fit well with global education and project work. First, this paradigm emphasizes a holistic approach to language learning, similar to the whole language approach in L1 learning (Goodman, 1986). Aspects of wholeness in regard to language include using whole texts in a whole-part-whole cycle in which students begin with whole texts and notice particular parts and features of those texts. R. Carter (2003) calls this *language awareness*. Later, students create whole texts of their own, perhaps in collaboration with peers, using the same parts and features. Global education content offers whole texts on a wide range of topics. Students read and listen to these texts as they do research for their projects. Not only do students learn content as they read and listen, they can also be guided to learn about the language used and then to apply that knowledge when they create their own texts. Additionally, the meaningful content provided by global education topics combines with the engaging nature of project tasks. This combination can increase students' motivation to master language so as to successfully use it as a tool for completing projects and for future endeavors.

Table 10.1. Comparing Two Paradigms in Second Language Instruction and Linking the Alternative Paradigm to Global Education and Project Work

Formerly Dominant Paradigm in L2 Instruction	Alternative Paradigm in L2 Instruction	Global Education	Project Work
Emphasizes parts and decontextualization (e.g., individual grammar features).	Emphasizes wholes and contextualization (e.g., whole texts).	Emphasizes that the world is interdependent and that issues must be understood in context.	Offers students opportunities to look at the big picture.
Separates language from other subjects.	Uses content-based language teaching.	Provides content for language learning.	Offers time to delve into content and to learn content language (Beckett & Slater, 2005; Mohan, 1986).
Sees learning as preparation for life.	Sees learning as also being participation in life.	Provides ways to participate in improving the world.	Involves students in tasks through which they can help others (e.g., service learning).
Attempts to standardize the way learning takes place and what is learned.	Encourages diversity as to ways of learning and content of learning.	Encourages understanding of diversity, rather than fear of what is different.	Allows students to learn in different ways and pursue personal interests.
Promotes teacher-centered instruction.	Encourages student-centered learning.	Promotes lifelong learning and involvement.	Allows students choice in the projects they undertake.
Uses mostly whole-class and individual work.	Includes group activities.	Encourages students to work with others and to care about what happens to others.	Is normally done in groups.
Focuses on the product; assessment via discrete point instruments (e.g., questions with right/wrong answers).	Focuses on the process as well as product; assessment via a range of tools (e.g., questions with many possible good answers).	Emphasizes complexity of global issues and differing perspectives.	Involves students in displaying their learning in various ways and thinking about the process they used to build their understanding.
Sees teacher control as key; teacher assessment only.	Encourages teachers to share responsibility with students; peer and self-assessment also used.	Emphasizes that people must understand for themselves and take actions based on their own views.	Gives authority to students to plan their work, carry out their plan, and monitor their performance.

A second aspect of the alternative second language education paradigm that links with global education and projects involves providing choice to students. *Learner autonomy* (van Lier, 1996) is a term often used for this trend in education. Global education encourages learner autonomy by offering a wide range of topics for students to learn about. More important, central to global education is that people participate in the world and make their own choices rather than only following their leaders. Projects invite students to choose, as they work in less teacher-controlled settings and have some freedom on what topics or subtopics they choose as well as what shape their projects take.

A third strand linking the alternative second language instruction paradigm with global education and projects involves integration. Global education urges the integration of culture, ecology, economics, politics, and technology. Indeed, global education is by its very nature cross-curricular. The longer term nature of projects, as opposed to short assignments finished in one class period, makes projects ideal for integrating a range of subject areas with language learning. Another form of integration encouraged by global education involves the linking of classroom activities to students' lives beyond the classroom and to the wider world.

GLOBAL EDUCATION PROJECTS
BY SECOND LANGUAGE STUDENTS

This section presents a variety of global education projects completed by second language students. They are presented with the permission of the teachers who developed the projects and are listed in order from classroom-based projects to community-based projects to international projects. The projects listed, of course, represent only a few examples of many, many possibilities. Of course, any project will need to be adapted to local contexts and to students' language level, learning needs, and interests.

A Student-Produced Global Issue Essay Collection

Type: Classroom-based project
Teachers: Masaharu Nagasaki and Carole Ray (Nagasaki, 2000)
Activity: During a two-semester course, students develop their English skills as they study a variety of world problems. The first semester, Global Studies, focuses on lectures, readings, discussion, and paragraph writing on global issue topics. The second semester, Essay Writing, introduces students to computers and to basic essay writing skills (outlining, writing, editing). The course culminates in a class booklet, titled *Our Windows to*

the Globe, which contains student essays on a variety of global themes. These range from topics such as war, peace, and pollution to overpopulation and development issues.

Comments: (a) Student writing can provide real reading for classmates and future students. (b) Also noteworthy is the way students developed their writing skills and knowledge of global issues before embarking on this project. While students can develop language skills and issue knowledge through doing projects, we must not assume that either will develop on its own. We need to pay attention to how we can help students learn before, during, and afterward. For example, we can facilitate students' understanding of the text type in which they will be writing (Derewianka, 1990), in this case, exposition.

Service Learning Projects with Environmental Organizations

Type: Community-based project

Teacher: Karen Mattison Yabuno (Mattison, 2003)

Activity: After studying about the environment, students spend 20 hours volunteering with an environmental protection organization of their choice. These organizations can include ones that seek to protect endangered species, as well as animals living on highly polluting factory farms (Vegan Outreach, n.d.). Students keep a scrapbook and give a presentation based on their volunteer experience.

Comments: (a) Service learning (Kinsley & McPherson, 1995) links the classroom with the outside world by combining service to others with learning related to students' academic curriculum. Service projects designed within a service learning approach differ from service projects that have no link to the curriculum. Service learning projects offer a rich vein of possibilities for combining language and global education. (b) The students' scrapbooks and presentations provide a language focus. Both the scrapbooks and the presentations can be done in groups, with feedback from group members and from other groups. An example of intragroup feedback is after a group brainstorms the content and organization of their scrapbook, each group member can be responsible for the first draft of one part and then receive feedback on that draft. An example of intergroup feedback is instead of whole-class presentations, in which one person per class talks at a time (what Kagan, 1994, calls *sequential interaction*), groups can present to other groups (i.e., *simultaneous interaction*) and receive feedback from their audience, thereby increasing the amount of student talk. (c) The combination of cooperative learning and writing tasks integrates all four language skills, as students write, read what groupmates have written, talk to groupmates about ideas, and listen to groupmates' responses and feedback. (d) Students should have choices in the topics of their global education projects. For instance, if some students are not interested in environmental issues, they could volunteer with another type of organization. Or, taking the concept of student choice a step further, if some students disagreed with the goals of organizations with which classmates were volunteering, they could volunteer for organizations with opposing views. The goal here is to promote informed, involved, self-motivated citizenship, rather than to foster action on behalf of the teacher's or the majority of classmates' views.

Interviewing Survivors of World War II

Type: Community-based project
Teacher: Jerry Burks (Burks, 1999)
Activity: Students use a set of criteria to interview Japanese senior citizens who lived through the turmoil of World War II in Okinawa. These interviews are written in English, compiled, and distributed as a way to keep alive memories about local people's experiences, the cruelty of war, and the need to work for peace.
Comments: (a) Connecting students with older members of their communities brings together two groups who often have little interaction but who can benefit from shared activities. Students can provide a genuine service to their community by recording and maintaining memories of the past, and students have much to learn from interacting with their elders. (b) The language component flows principally from the written records that students produce. This record offers engrossing material for extensive reading by future students (Robb, 2001) although careful editing is often necessary before student-created texts are ready for use by others. For example, peers can read first drafts and provide feedback on the content. This can help students make their writing more reader-friendly, while students learn ideas for their own writing by reading their peers' drafts. Later, students can check peers' subsequent drafts for such matters as grammar, punctuation, and formatting. Final editing can be done by teachers.

Learning About Visual Impairment and Other Disabilities

Type: Community-based project
Teachers: George Jacobs and Loh Wan Inn (Jacobs & Loh, 2002)

Activity: After reading about visually impaired people and how they cope, students pair up to simulate what it is like to be visually impaired. One person pretends to be visually impaired, while his or her partner ensures that nobody is hurt. Students then reverse roles. After each simulation, students write about how they felt during the simulation, using the past continuous tense. Next, students investigate what forms of support are available on their campus and in their community for the visually impaired or people with other physical challenges. They also investigate what types of support are available in other places and are desired by physically challenged people. Based on their investigation, students formulate what they believe are realistic recommendations and seek to have them implemented.

Comments: (a) Evaluation is a crucial thinking skill. If global education projects are to have an impact, they must be carefully thought out and not done just to get the project over with because it is a graded assignment. Therefore, students' projects must be practical, rather than only sounding wonderfully idealistic. One aspect of being practical is that students have a realistic chance of seeing some impact within the normally brief time span of a project. That said, the hope would be that students will become so excited about their project that they will want to continue pursuing it after the required time span or that other students will wish to take it up. (b) On a language note, having students consider the use of a specific tense in their writing as part of the project is an example of how to maintain a focus on language usage within the overall emphasis on language use that is an essential characteristic of projects.

Investigating the Fishing Industry and Alternatives

Type: Community-based project
Teachers: Syahrir Mappe and Nurnia (Lie, Jacobs, & Amy, 2002)
Activity: Students learn about local fishing practices, including unsustainable ones, such as dynamite fishing. They also learn about nutrition and about plant-based alternatives to eating marine animals. This learning takes them out of the classroom to interact with fishers, food marketers, and nutritionists. Students disseminate their findings in the form of discussions, skits, and articles. Most of these are done in the first language, but second language versions are prepared for feedback from classmates, teachers, and overseas experts, as well as for presentation to other English classes.

Comments: (a) One type of action that students can readily take is educating others. Too often, these education efforts are confined to their teachers. We should look for ways to expand students' reach, so that they present to others beyond the other people in their class. (b) Food was a focus in this lesson. In our increasingly globalized world, what we eat offers many ways for students to have an impact. Examples of global issues related to food include organic food, genetically modified food, vegetarianism, and fair trade. (c) A concern often raised in foreign language situations is that students have little opportunity for communicative use of the target language. Here, this was overcome by students using the target language with classmates and teachers to prepare, critique, and present their out-of-class efforts before translating these into the first language for interaction with the public. In this way, being in a foreign language context does not preclude reaching out to the local community. Indeed, it prepares students for the kind of code switching in which many fluent bilinguals engage. (d) The inclusion in this project of nutrition via plant-based sources suggests that students think about reducing their consumption of other animals and encourage other humans to consider the same step. This fits with the global education topic of protection of nonhuman animals.

Learning from Traditional Culture

Type: Community-based project
Teacher: Leonora Saantje Tamaela (Lie et al., 2002)
Activity: Students investigate traditional practices in regard to the environment and other areas. Teachers begin by relating their own experiences. For example, in some Indonesian villages, farm families have a tradition of donating part of their harvest to the poor. Students evaluate these practices as to whether they offer advantages over current practices. Finally, students and teachers attempt to influence others to maintain or adopt traditional practices that students feel are beneficial.
Comments: (a) Education is seen by some as teaching students to adopt modern ways and to reject tradition. Such wholesale acceptance of the present/future and rejection of the past may not be the best course to take. As seen in this lesson, traditional practices may in some regards be more environmentally friendly than modern ones. Also, with specific relation to the confluence of language education and global education, one aspect of human rights is linguistic rights. Unfortunately, many languages are disappearing, with a small set of languages, led by English, becoming increasingly dominant. Respecting tradition can mean attempting to preserve languages associated with traditional cultures (Skutnabb-Kangas, 2000). (b) Another aspect of the lesson worth noting is the fact that teachers are involved as co-learners. This relates to the paradigm shift discussed earlier, in particular to the move away

from a student-teacher relationship in which teachers reign from in front of the class and issue do-as-I-say edicts. Instead, teachers partici-pate along with students.

A Collaborative Environmental Project to Promote Language Learning and Computer Skills

Type: International project
Teachers: Janpha Thadphoothon, Regina O'Shea, Libby Smith, and Junko Kosaki
Activity: Classes in two countries are paired. Each class collects primary data on an environmental problem in the area near their school. They use the Internet and a range of computer tools to exchange informa-tion with the class in the other country. Students ask questions and make suggestions about the other's problem. Then, in consultation with the other class, students formulate and implement plans for addressing the environmental problem they have investigated.
Comments: (a) The Internet offers a wealth of possibilities for students to engage in real communication about global topics. (b) Knowing about the efforts of peers in another country can inspire students to increase their own efforts. (c) Another example of an Internet project is constructing a Web site to spread information and enlist support for addressing a global issue. (d) When conducting projects using the Internet, we must be sensitive to the digital divide (i.e., the fact that not everyone has the same level of hardware and software and access to a constant flow of electricity). For example, while some students may have high-speed Internet access in their homes, capable of sending and receiving video, other students (and their teachers) may need to rely on sporadic Internet access with very slow connections. (e) Global edu-cation projects must not be condemned to the all-too-common cate-gory of work done only for a grade, only because the teacher assigned it, or only as preparation for an exam. Instead, when students embark on a global education project, they should have a vision of who will ben-efit from their efforts.

An "Asian Youth Forum" EFL Student Exchange Program

Type: International project
Teacher: Kip Cates (Cates, Takayama, Lachman, & Perry, 2001)
Activity: Teachers of English as a foreign language (EFL) and their stu-dents from a number of Asian countries meet together, with one nation

hosting the others, for an "Asian Youth Forum" (AYF) aimed at promoting international understanding. Teachers and students, especially in the host country, need to do a great deal of preparation to facilitate this event. During the forum, students learn together about leadership skills, cultural differences, stereotypes, and global issues such as peace, human rights, and the environment. While in the host country, visiting students stay with the families of host-country students who act as guides to the local culture. Visiting students teach local hosts about their own society. Students—both visitors and hosts—can maintain journals of their experiences. Furthermore, communication continues after the visits have ended, and plans are made for future trips in which the roles of visitor and host are switched.

Comments: (a) This project fits with the peace and cross-cultural areas of global education. (b) Negative stereotypes and generations-old ill-will often plague relations between people from different countries. Much can be done in the classroom to address these noxious beliefs. However, face-to-face interaction and visits to each other's countries may well be the most effective means of overcoming misunderstandings and moving toward mutual understanding and harmonious relations. For instance, these exchange programs have been used with success to bring together students from Korea and Japan, two countries with a history of animosity. (c) From a language acquisition perspective, when the target language acts as the *lingua franca* for student-student interactions, an immersion situation is created rife with opportunities for communicative language use. Furthermore, students see the utility of second language acquisition, potentially increasing their motivation. (d) Another way to promote cross-cultural interaction is for second language students to teach about their culture to younger students from the host country (e.g., university students of English as a second language [ESL] in the United States teach about their home cultures to local elementary school students) (G. Carter & Thomas, 1986).

CONCLUSION

We began this chapter by stating our optimism about the ability of second language students and teachers to have a positive impact on the future of the human race and on our fellow residents on planet Earth. Global education projects offer an outstanding way to have such an impact. This chapter has outlined what global education involves, described ways in which global education projects can contribute to second language acquisition as they positively impact the planet, sketched examples of global education projects completed by second language students, and highlighted lessons that can be learned from these examples.

The chapter also provided a list of organizations that promote global education. It is by recommending these organizations for readers' consideration that we would like to conclude this chapter. Both of us have been involved with establishing and managing such groups. We know the frustrations that are inescapable in any conglomeration of volunteers who have full-time jobs and are spread across the globe. Despite the convenience and speed that modern communication technology offers, and despite the genuine desire of many education professionals to do their part to promote global education, much of the work in such organizations too often falls on the shoulders of too few members.

Nonetheless, we believe in the role of organizations of second language educators dedicated to global education. These organizations inspire us when we hear about what other educators and their students are doing; make us proud when we share the excitement of what we and our students have done; inform us when we learn about global education resources that are available and appropriate to our students' language level; connect us when we meet global education colleagues face to face at conferences or online and when we establish ties for our students with others around the world. All these benefits enrich our use of global education projects in our second language teaching and make the organizational frustrations worth bearing.

REFERENCES

Baloche, L. (1998). *The cooperative classroom*. Upper Saddle River, NJ: Prentice Hall.

Beckett, G. H., & Slater, T. (2005). The project framework: A tool for language content, and skills integration. *ELT Journal, 59*(2), 108–116.

Bejarano, Y., Levine, T., Olshtain, E., & Steiner, J. (1997). The skilled use of interaction strategies: Creating a framework for improved small-group communicative interaction in the language classroom. *System, 25,* 203–214.

Benesch, S. (1993). Critical thinking: A learning process for democracy. *TESOL Quarterly, 27,* 545–547.

Burks, J. (1999, June). Teaching peace in Okinawa. *Global Issues in Language Education Newsletter, 35,* 9–11.

Carter, G., & Thomas, H. (1986). "Dear Brown Eyes": Experiential learning in a project-orientated approach. *ELT Journal, 40*(3), 196–204.

Carter, R. (2003). Language awareness. *ELT Journal, 57*(1), 64–65.

Cates, K. A. (1990). Teaching for a better world: Global issues in language education. *The Language Teacher, 14*(5), 3–5.

Cates, K., Takayama, C., Lachman, A., & Perry. B. (2001) Hand in hand: Looking toward the 2nd Asian Youth Forum. *The Language Teacher, 25*(1), 15–20.

Crandall, J. A. (1987). *ESL through content-area instruction: Mathematics, science, social studies.* Englewood Cliffs, NJ: Prentice Hall Regents.

Derewianka, B. (1990). *Exploring how texts work.* Newtown, New South Wales: Primary English Teaching Association.

Dunayer, J. (2001). *Animal equality: Language and liberation.* Derwood, MA: Ryce Publishing.

Goodman, K. (1986). *What's whole in whole language.* New York: Scholastic.

Graman, T. (1988). Education for humanization: Applying Paulo Freire's pedagogy to learning a second language. *Harvard Educational Review, 58,* 433–448.

Greig, S., Pike, G., & Selby, D. (1987). *Earthrights: Education as if the planet really mattered.* London: Kogan Page.

Jacobs, G. M., & Farrell, T. S. C. (2001). Paradigm shift: Understanding and implementing change in second language education. *TESL-EJ, 5*(1). Retrieved September 1, 2005, from http://www.kyoto-su.ac.jp/information/tesl-ej/ej17/a1.html

Jacobs, G. M., & Loh, W. I. (2002). *Grammar in use* (Workbook 3). Singapore: Learners Publishing.

Kagan, S. (1994). *Cooperative learning.* San Clemente, CA: Kagan Publishing.

Kinsley, C. W., & McPherson, K. (Eds.). (1995). *Enriching the curriculum through service learning.* Alexandria, VA: Association for Supervision and Curriculum Development.

Lie, A., Jacobs, G. M., & Amy, S. (Eds.). (2002). *English via environmental education.* Jakarta: Grasindo.

Mattison, K. (2003, February). Volunteerism: Education beyond the classroom. *Global Issues in Language Education Newsletter, 49,* 12–14.

Mohan, B. (1986). *Language and content.* Reading, MA: Addison-Wesley.

Nagasaki, M. (2000, April). Our windows to the globe: Student essays on global issues. *Global Issues in Language Education Newsletter, 38,* 7–8.

Ribe, R., & Vidal, N. (1993). *Project work: Step by step.* Oxford: Heinemann.

Richards, J. C., & Rodgers, T. S. (2001). *Approaches and methods in language teaching.* New York: Cambridge University Press.

Robb, T. (2001). Extensive reading in an EFL environment. In J. Murphy & P. Byrd (Eds.), *Understanding the courses we teach* (pp. 218–235). Ann Arbor: University of Michigan Press.

Skutnabb-Kangas, T. (2000). *Linguistic genocide in education—or worldwide diversity and human rights?* Mahwah, NJ: Erlbaum.

Sny, C. (1980). *Global education: An implementation plan and research guide.* Madison: University of Wisconsin Press.

Tye, K. A. (1991). *Global education: From thought to action.* Alexandria, VA: Association for Supervision and Curriculum Development.

van Lier, L. (1996). *Interaction in the language curriculum: Awareness, autonomy and authenticity.* London: Longman.

Vegan Outreach. (n.d.). *Why vegan: Environmental destruction.* Retrieved May 7, 2005, from http://www.veganoutreach.org/whyvegan/environment.html

CHAPTER 11

KNOWING THE OTHER THROUGH MULTICULTURAL PROJECTS IN SCHOOL EFL PROGRAMS

Valerie Jakar
David Yellin College

INTRODUCTION

Don't judge your fellow man until you are in his place...
—Ethics of the Fathers, 2:5

In a multicultural, multiethnic country like Israel, where society is comprised of a potpourri of immigrants from numerous nations around the globe, understanding the other's perspective is a constant challenge. As a result of their experiences living and teaching in Israel, many teachers of English as a foreign language (EFL) have developed strategies for educating their students to understand their own world and the worlds around them (i.e., engaging in multicultural education) while experiencing and developing the use of English. In this chapter, I will examine instances of projects that I have observed in a school system where the national curriculum for EFL

Project-Based Second and Foreign Language Education, pages 181–193
Copyright © 2006 by Information Age Publishing
All rights of reproduction in any form reserved.

instruction does not merely acknowledge a role for project work within the regular textbook-driven program but actually encourages it. Examples will be given of the many pedagogical practices and language-learning opportunities made available by teachers who implement a project-based approach.

A place for project work in schooling today (in English-speaking nations) is well recognized, particularly in the field of science (see Roberts, 1999) and in elementary schooling across the curriculum (Goodrich, Hatch, Wiatrowski, & Unger, 1995; Ribe & Vidal, 1993). It is therefore reasonable and efficacious for EFL teachers in K–12 schooling contexts to adopt the use of projects as a pedagogical strategy.

It is acknowledged that, for EFL purposes, the project is more likely to be a curricular vehicle for enabling students to exercise and develop their newly acquired language skills via meaningful activities rather than for achieving a clear subject-matter goal. Nevertheless, it must be pointed out that English teachers, being known for their "citizens of the world kind of stereotype" (Medgyes, 2001), accomplish a good deal of general education while engaged in teaching their students to become proficient English speakers and users. Where they have a reasonable measure of autonomy regarding curricular issues, teachers will introduce and develop topics in which they have a particular interest or expertise. They will encourage their students to take an interest in issues that they believe to be vital for their students' well-being and development. It is for this reason that teachers of EFL are often at the vanguard of social action in their own schools and in school systems (see Shulman, 2004) and at national and international levels (see, e.g., Larson, 2003).

Programs observed by the author have utilized the freedom of choice that teachers in the Israeli education system are given to teach language skills using topics, themes, and texts according to their own preference. They are constrained by a requirement that every class use and cover the core material in a ministry-approved textbook, but there are no restrictions on the use of ancillary materials, other than the observance of moral and ethical propriety. Teachers have been encouraged to introduce issues of social welfare, global concerns, and education about self and the other (see Ministry of Education, 2001). Projects with titles such as *UNICEF, Lullabies*, and *Bread* are but representative of the range of subjects investigated by teachers and/or their students in school EFL classes in the Jerusalem area. They reflect the breadth of vision that characterizes the standards-based English curriculum that was instituted in 2001.

THE ENGLISH CURRICULUM

This new English curriculum, hereafter referred to as the EC, incorporates principles that "not only affirm the national need to set standards in order to equip students with the knowledge of English that the modern world demands but also serve as the basis for quality education" (Ministry of Education, 2001, p. 10). The curriculum committee explicitly left to textbook writers, schools, and teachers as much freedom as possible in choosing the methodology encouraging the teacher "to add the creative imagination that will bring the teaching of English alive" (p. 11). The EC goals state that at the end of 12th grade, students should be able to interact effectively in a variety of situations, obtain and make use of information from a variety of sources and media, present information in an organized manner, and appreciate literature and other cultures and appreciate the nature of language. The EC reflects a far more holistic curricular approach than that of previous curricula (Gefen, 1988), addressing the needs of today's learners and tomorrow's working population and acknowledging the necessity of making provision for diverse learning populations (see Ministry of Education, 2001, p. 33). While there is no explicit directive within the curriculum document that calls for teachers to include project work in their programs, there is an implicit understanding that projects be conducted. For example, the support for project work is reiterated and emphasized in the syllabus for the *bagrut* (graduation examination that is taken in the final years of high school). In the latest scheme of the final assessment, every student is required to produce at least two projects (or performance tasks, in the case of the weakest students) and will use one of these projects as a topic for presentation and discussion in the oral component of the final examination (Steiner, 2004).

The four core standards of the EC serve as a basis for project work (see Mann, Shemesh, & Shlayer, 2002). They are

- *Social interaction.* Pupils develop communication skills, both orally and in writing, enriching their vocabulary and improving their use of accurate language.
- *Access to information.* While researching their chosen topic, pupils are exposed to oral and written texts from a variety of sources: Internet, books, magazines, and experts in the field.
- *Presentation.* Pupils are given opportunities for presenting information and ideas on a wide range of topics in an organized manner, in a variety of formats in spoken and written English. The creative, multimedia oral presentation complements the written presentation.
- *Appreciation of literature, culture, and language.* Research and in-depth learning about the topic allows pupils to gain cultural, historical, and social insight.

There is, however, a concern regarding project work. It is posited that the introduction of a particular type of assessment tool (i.e., testing) creates a "washback" effect in school systems (Nazari, 2005). There is evidence of this occurring in schools around Israel, with projects being introduced in middle schools to prepare the students for their later "ordeal." Furthermore, more emphasis is being given to projects in elementary schools. At this level, topics are usually determined by the teachers and may, where there is harmony in the school and its curricular considerations, reflect an interdisciplinary approach, where two or more departments (or content teachers) collaborate.

PROJECTS IN MULTICULTURAL EDUCATION

Although multicultural education (ME) is not a professed subject for schooling in Israel, we see numerous instances of prevalent multicultural topics in the general curriculum and, frequently, in the EFL curriculum. In many schools in the public school system, classes are made up largely of Israeli born children who are native Hebrew or Arabic speakers. However, their cultural heritages, and hence their second (or even third) languages, are widely diverse. Indeed, in schools where the language of instruction is Hebrew, there may be as many as 20 different mother tongues or heritage languages represented (Ben-Rafael, Shohamy, Amara, & Trumper-Hecht, 2004). Students are encouraged to learn about their own and others' cultures, and about the world at large, engaging in personal studies on topics of interest and concern, often inspired by their teachers' passion for the subject. They may embrace global or universal issues (see Alan & Stoller, 2005), but they may begin by looking at issues that are much closer to home, to the contexts in which they live and survive.

Although many topics, such as *Children's Rights*, *Games People Played*, *The Olive Tree*, and *Local Folk Tales*, have grabbed the attention of enthusiastic students, two particular projects, *Bread* and *Peacefolks*, are discussed herein. While the individual projects vary in cognitive demands and student population (their socioeconomic status, age, and type of schooling), the overall stages of procedures are similar, as are the final outcomes (in terms of types of products and modes of presentation). Both projects are a result of the involvement of EFL teachers in the Jerusalem area in programs for mutual cooperation and understanding (MCU)—between teachers (in interdisciplinary professional development courses) and their students. In one MCU program, elementary school students from different ethnic groups (e.g., native Hebrew speakers, native Arabic speakers, native Amharic speakers) are brought together to celebrate their commonalities. A folklore specialist runs the program in paired elementary schools, working initially with the individual selected grades or classes in each school, then bringing them together for encounters and workshops (Lichman & Miller, 2002). The paired groups usually communicate in the dominant language (Hebrew) but also use Arabic or English (in cases where the

1. The topic is negotiated (teacher led).
2. Students and teachers seek, gather, and check resources.
3. Students investigate (by interviews and surveys) and gather further information.
4. Findings are shared and documented (in class).
5. Results of findings are represented and presented (replications are created, results are celebrated).

Figure 11.1.   Basic Elements of an MCU Program

native Arabic speakers are unable to converse in Hebrew). The basic procedures in that program are set out in Figure 11.1.

Realizing that this could be a useful way of promoting the use of English, EFL teachers developed a project to be conducted in English class. Thus was born the Folklore Project in which the rudiments of the (native-tongue) program (discussed previously) remained intact but the language of wider communication (LWC), namely English, was used as the *lingua franca*. The topics explored by various groups in grades 5 and 6 included street games, toys, clothes and utensils, proverbs, lullabies, and bread. In each case, the students investigated their own heritage via their friends, families, and neighbors. Their final presentations involved those same friends and family either in person or in the form of documented descriptive narratives, recipes, photographs, songs, or tales. The presentations took the form of an exhibition displaying final products or a "happening" where people came together to participate in activities (e.g., singing lullabies from different regions or playing street games that the elders of the communities taught to the students). The participants were given the opportunity to communicate about issues common to everyone in the assembly, issues about which they were the experts. They shared their observations—although some remained silent in the open mixed group, preferring to wait until they were in "friendly territory." The following is an account of one such project. It is a compilation of field notes taken by the author and reports by participant teachers who were involved in the Folklore Project program.

Bread

> im ein kemach ein torah *[if there is no flour, there is no law/lore]*.
> —Ethics of the Fathers, 3:21

The Bread Project was conducted in a number of elementary school classes (grade 6) in the Jerusalem area. Following an initial brainstorming exercise, the board was filled with observations and data about bread. The class reviewed the data and discussed how they could categorize them in terms of purpose and guiding principles. There followed a discussion on the essential ingredients and the basic types of bread. Names of breads were elicited, and lists were made. The homework assignment for that day was true to its name since the students were required to ask at home if and how bread was made in their (or their neighbors') homes or in their family homes when their parents were children. The students needed to write down the ingredients used and the method that the baker used to prepare his or her bread. The questions that the students were to ask were written down in English. Naturally, the data were collected in the native tongue, but the details were noted subsequently in English at the report-back session in the following lesson.

At a later stage, students were encouraged to seek aphorisms that related to bread. They began with their native languages, collecting and translating the data as they did in their initial "homework" assignment (see, for example, the well known expression at the beginning of this section). They were then exposed to texts and popular expressions connected with bread from the English-speaking world. Comparisons were made with the native-tongue findings.

In another lesson, students researched the topic of bread by reading recipe books and using library resources, Internet Web sites, and search engines. Some students also searched the Scriptures for allusions to bread. The teacher gave some guidelines for researching in different text types, using traditional and more current media.

Further into the Bread Project, the chemistry and physics of the process of preparing and baking bread was focused on, with a chart prepared by the teacher (who had previously consulted the science specialist in the school). Reference was made to the opening brainstorming session when an argument had ensued as to how many basic varieties of bread exist. Consensus had been reached when someone proposed that there are two basic types, flat bread and risen (containing yeast or another raising agent) bread. The issues of duration, time of day, temperature, and the need for patience were raised. Everyone was an expert—because they had all eaten bread and most had seen the making of bread. Students created their own charts (graphic organizers) representing one physical aspect.

Language-related components of the project included stories and rhymes that involve bread; well-known proverbs that relate to bread, in the native tongue and in English; and the traditions, blessings, and superstitions associated with bread—where students told their stories and shared their beliefs. Many culture-specific traditions exist regarding the preparation, consumption, and values held about bread and the stories that were related/narrated by the students were fascinating to hear.

On the final day of the project for two of the schools involved, the parents and grandparents were invited to celebrate together, though physically, socio-economically and culturally far removed from each other. But links were created, bonds were strengthened, and it may be asserted that the *staff of life* was the perpetrator (Henry, 1710). All were involved in preparing one of two types of bread, according to recipes written out by the students. The adults appreciated and lauded the students' work, which was on display in the classroom. Students had chosen between writing a recipe and guidebook about bread and making a poster advertising or promoting a bread product. They were able to use the aphorisms and proverbs that they had collected. Some students gave oral presentations along with their products, while others performed poems and songs associated with bread. The delight in their achievements was contagious and there was obvious joy in that classroom full of students "high" on self-esteem. The students viewed each others' work, asking and answering questions where possible. Those whose teachers had prepared checklists or charts of students' work logs displayed their self-evaluations and peer evaluations proudly next to their presentations. Finally, the whole group assembled to eat the breads they had made together earlier in the day.

In the Bread Project, not only do we see the advantages of the project approach, where content and motivation come together, where social interaction is emphasized, and where students are given opportunities to utilize their competencies, but we also see a valuable use of the LWC. The hegemony of the English language in the world today cannot be denied (Graddoll, 1999). It behooves us, therefore, to help our students function as well as possible in a society where the prestigious language is likely to be English, while still acknowledging, and even celebrating, the role of the native tongue. By incorporating the ethics and principles of a multicultural approach, we are ensuring that students do not lose their appreciation of their own cultural—and linguistic—heritage. This type of project work gives students the basis of practice and procedures needed to conduct any project in the future, thus standing them in good stead for their senior studies (in preparation for the *bagrut*) where they may choose the topic of their projects.

Peacefolks

This conflict is getting worse and worse. As teachers, we have to try our best to turn hatred into compassion and understanding. We have to teach our students how to listen to other people's perspectives. If we do this, we will help to create a better future for our children.

—S, 2004[1]

The second example of a multicultural project aimed at EFL learners is a literature-based program (see Duzzy, 2002; Wicks, 2000), which was an outcome of an MCU program titled "Teaching English Through Experiencing Cultures" (Jakar, 2005). When a high school teacher introduced colleagues to how he teaches the writing process and the concept of perspectives through the reading of a short novel, a teacher (S) became fascinated with the concept and was inspired to initiate a project with her 9th-grade class along with the novel *Seedfolks* (Fleischman, 1996). It consists of a series of first-person vignettes, told by different insular characters who come together as a community to create a lively garden out of a vacant lot full of trash.

S's students studied the book over a period of approximately 2 months, reading together in class and at home. They kept a journal of all the characters, detailing facts on age, ethnicity, and connection to the garden, plus their own personal reflections. Other tasks that all students were required to perform included a summary of the book, a cameo of their favorite character, and instructions on how to grow a specific plant that had some connection to their own family.

The final tasks of the project were, however, the most productive. Prompted and coached by S, the class wrote a book in the image of *Seedfolks*. They chose to investigate a neighborhood that was considered as multicultural; its population included Muslim and Christian Arabs, Palestinians and Israelis, European and Middle Eastern Jews, Europeans, native English speakers, French speakers, North Americans, and more. In that area was a forest, known as the Forest of Peace. It had originally been planted and developed as a place for communities to meet, but it was desolate. This was chosen as the central location for the "coming together" of the community.

The students' first assignment was to create their own vignettes of people who lived in the neighborhood. They interviewed residents, both young and old, using an outline format for interview questions. Most of the interviewing was conducted in English. After compiling information on age, ethnicity, relationships with neighbors, and time spent in the Forest of Peace, each student (or pair) wrote a character profile that became a chapter for the new book which they entitled *Peacefolks*. Students presented their drafts to be edited by the teacher who checked for grammatical and spelling accuracy. The teacher also read the chapters aloud in class to enable students to critique each other's work. Different students were chosen by the class for the various display tasks (illustrations, printing, and formatting). The book was completed by the end of the school year and copies were made for the whole class.

The EC states that students will show that they "are aware of the social and cultural framework within which the literary texts were written" (Ministry of Education , 2001, p. 31). *Peacefolks* is an excellent example of a project that was generated from an inspiring text, which, itself, clearly broadcasts awareness of social and cultural frameworks. The teacher, however, while displaying a strong awareness of social justice, did not allow her students to ignore the need for critical awareness and accuracy in presentation. She guided them rigorously through their project but also gave them a good deal of opportunity to be creative.

In assessing the efficacy of projects in the EFL context, it is not possible to use the same criteria of evaluation as one might, for instance, for a textbook series. The (possible) level and quantity of linguistic input that students obtain while conducting their projects, from process to product, are immeasurable. Similarly, once one allows self-determination regarding access to materials and media information, one cannot objectively assess levels of understanding or performance. It remains for the participants—the students themselves—to respond to checklists and advance organizers (see Andrade, 2000), to give their own evaluation of their achievement. This approach, as with the holistic nature of project work in general, reflects the precepts of the EC and responds to the influence of the benchmarks that are presently being embraced in the educational system (for EFL).

PEDAGOGICAL PRACTICES AND LANGUAGE-LEARNING OPPORTUNITIES

In considering particular features of the programs that show projects to be efficacious, I note three areas: pedagogical practices (teacher-led, contrived or directed activities) that encourage or generate language learning; language-learning opportunities (including skills and strategy development) that become available due to the nature of the activities; and content learning (information acquisition and personal development). Of this last feature, suffice it to say that the students gained in local and world knowledge through sharing, experiential learning, and investigation, motivated by clear incentives (set down by the teachers), personal and social interest, and a culture of inquiry and respect for others' ethnicities—or even existences. This element of the MC project in EFL is irrefutable, but not quantifiable. However, it is clear that students gain a good deal in a number of areas. This is evidenced in their subsequent levels of performance on standardized tests and in the classroom in general, particularly with regard to self-esteem and confidence in their abilities to perform. Teachers who act as examiners for the *bagrut* examination reported that students were able to speak fluently in a competent, extemporaneous manner when discussing their projects in which they had invested such considerable effort and interest. Junior high school students with whom I met at one school were delighted and confident to present to my English-speaking guests the fruits of their endeavors. Theirs was a term-long project on *The Olive Tree*, which comprised a biology display; a social history exhibition; a geographic chart, which they explained; and a collection of stories and poems, some of which were read aloud. Their language was fluent, reasonably accurate, appropriate in register, and certainly comprehensible.

We have witnessed that when teachers introduce projects, they invariably make comprehensible input available to the students through brainstorming (including elicitation from peers) and other induction activities and through presentation of text (printed, handwritten, or perhaps a film clip, song, or poem read by the teacher), engaging in reading comprehension activities, and reading strategy training. Brainstorming is a typical set induction strategy that gives rise to multiple opportunities for discussion and negotiation of meaning, two powerful means of acquiring and learning new vocabulary and terminology (Pica, 1996). In the Bread Project, the activities of categorization, sorting, and hierarchizing of the lexis were additional means of activating learners' vocabulary acquisition.

Teachers took the opportunities to focus on text types in both projects. In the Bread project, they focused on the form and structures used in recipes, posters, and narratives. In the Peacefolks project, focal texts were: types of narrative, the nature of an interview and the speaking styles preferred, the format of a questionnaire, and the structures used in question formulation.

In the middle stages of the projects (see Figure 11.1), students were guided toward developing their skills of reading for information, accessing information (on the Internet, in the encyclopedia, etc.), recognizing text types, and transforming information from one mode to another (e.g., reporting on narratives heard or performing a narrative that was heard from an elder). Study skills such as note taking, reporting, and report writing were introduced by the teachers as important tools to be acquired. A further skill, transformation of information from one mode to another, was introduced and practiced. Students needed to report on narratives heard or perform a narrative that was heard from an elder. They were required to prepare a graphic organizer based on data collected in note form. Remarkably, for both project groups, though disparate in age, there was adherence to one of the significant standards of the EC that requires students to appreciate (and become aware of) language differences and similarities. Within this realm, the two groups also engaged in translation—and sometimes interpreting—endeavors. These activities could be all the richer if the group were multilingual.

The final section of the project program, the preparation and presentation of a product, gives students motivation and opportunities for practice (rehearsal) and performance for an authentic purpose. This, too, is the stage where the students complete their final checklist and assess them-selves (and sometimes their peers). Use of the self assessment tool facili-tates cooperation and helps develop a sense of autonomy, something which language learners can continue to develop.

Reservations and Observations

Having given an account of exemplary projects and extolled the virtues of certain approaches, this writer must express certain reservations. They are on behalf of a number of beleaguered teachers who have toiled for hours preparing materials, checklists, and organizational charts to give their students sufficient materials, stimulus, and motivation to work through the process and conclude with a satisfactory product. Some of these teachers question whether a teacher should agree to engage in such endeavors if the burden of preparation is so heavy. They speculate whether the teacher should seek assistance or avoid the task entirely if a topic is cen-tered on an issue or discipline with which they themselves are unfamiliar. Is it not preferable that a teacher working with a project group be passionate about the subject(s) at hand? It has been seen (from the previous exam-ples) that where the teacher is really interested in the subject, the results are concomitant with that enthusiasm. But is the corollary true? How well can teachers conduct or facilitate a project-based program if the topics (possibly chosen by the students) are not appealing to them or if the teach-ers are neither knowledgeable nor competent in the area of investigation?

Sheppard and Stoller (1995) advocate the teacher taking on the role of guide (which we see in the cases discussed previously), which would obvi-ate the necessity of the teacher being expert in every field. It is my belief that teachers may certainly act solely as facilitators (given that they have educated their students in literacy skills), giving encouragement, technical assistance, linguistic guidance, and the benefit of their world knowledge, but no more than that. This approach is less likely to be seen as inspiring pedagogy, but it is also not suppressive. Since the teachers are primarily EFL specialists, it is not reasonable to expect them to function as interdisci-plinary experts, although they should be encouraged to exploit their own talents and interests where possible. Furthermore, there is evidence that, in the future, EFL specialists will be expected to display and utilize their expertise in some particular discipline in addition to their EFL expertise (see, e.g., IATEFL, 2005).

Another issue raised by teachers is whether students who are less cre-ative, less independent learners, or less literate should be expected to work on their projects as their more competent peers do. In the preceding examples, we see that different learning styles or abilities can be accommodated effectively, provided that the teacher is alert to students' difficulties and is creative enough to construct alternative resources or tasks. The students are given the opportunity to become the "experts" and are encouraged to use their literacy skills. Their teachers, while acting as guides, have the opportunity to pay special attention to those in need of assistance or coaching so that their language development is not impeded, but rather facilitated. In the growing climate of "inclusion" in schooling, teachers should not be disheartened by the burden of extra toil to accommodate a diverse group of learners. On the contrary, teachers should rejoice in the future opportunities that will permit many "others" to come together and share their varieties of linguistic expertise.

CONCLUSION

It has been a privilege to be able to observe every one of the students and their teachers taking the courses in multicultural education and producing such fine end products. It is hoped that the readers of this chapter will find some material, a few ideas, and a small amount of inspiration to encourage them to begin or continue developing their own projects. The state of the English language, the pace of the drive to maintain heritage languages, the technology race, and perhaps some yet unknown elements, all point to a possible need to start rethinking the EC yet again. However, due to the breadth of scope in project work and the opportunities that it provides, it will survive through the next round of innovations, enabling students to continue learning about themselves and others while developing their language skills and sensitivities.

NOTES

1.   S is a teacher who wishes to remain anonymous.
2.   I wish to thank Eleanor Satlow, Suzanne Sapir, and the TETEC group for their assistance in the preparation of this chapter.

REFERENCES

Alan, B., & Stoller, F. (2005). Maximizing the benefits of project work in foreign language classrooms. *English Teaching Forum, 43*(4), 10–21.
Andrade, H. G. (2000). Using rubrics to promote thinking and learning. *Educational Leadership, 57*(5), 13–18.
ben Azaria, Rabbi Elazar. (n.d.). *Mishna avot* [Ethics of the Fathers] 3:21, 3:5.

Ben-Rafael, E., Shohamy, E., Amara, M. H., & Trumper-Hecht, N. (2004). *Linguistic landscape and multiculturalism: A Jewish-Arab comparative study*. Tel Aviv: Steinmetz Center for Peace Research, Tel Aviv University.

Duzzy, R. (2002). Writing books: A project for seventh and eighth grades. *English Teachers' Journal, 54*, 50–55.

Fleischman, P. (1996). *Seedfolks*. New York: Harper Trophy.

Gefen, R. (1988). *English curriculum for state schools and state religious schools, grades 5–12* (new edition). Jerusalem: Ministry of Education.

Goodrich, H., Hatch, T., Wiatrowski, G., & Unger, C. (1995). *Teaching through projects: Creating effective learning environments*. Lebanon, IN: Dale Seymour Publications.

Graddoll, D. (1999). *The future of English?* London: The English Company.

Henry, M. (1710). Psalm 104. *Commentary on the whole Bible* (Vol. 3). Retrieved August 30, 2005, from http://www.ccel.org/h/henry/mhc2/MHC19104.HTM

IATEFL. (2005). Content and language integrated learning. *Proceedings of the International Association of Teachers of English as a Foreign Language, UK, 16*, 16–21.

Jakar, V. S. (2005, April). *Pickles and proverbs as a path to mutual understanding*. Paper presented at the annual conference of the Association for Supervision and Curriculum Development, Orlando.

Larson, D. (2003, March). *On being an observer at the United Nations*. Presentation at the annual conference of the Teachers of English to Speakers of Other Languages, TESOLers for Social Responsibility Caucus Meeting, Baltimore.

Lichman, S., & Miller, R. (2002). Showing different images with games. *The Coexistence Chronicle, 2*(1), 1, 4. Retrieved August 30, 2005, from http://www.coexistence.net/coexistence/library/V2Issue1.pdf

Mann, G., Shemesh, R., & Shlayer, J. (2002). Projects at work. *English Teachers' Journal, 39*, 21–33.

Medgyes, P. (2001, August 16). What unites us? Low esteem. *The Guardian Weekly*. Retrieved August 30, 2005, from http://education.guardian.co.uk/tefl/story/0,,537970,00.html

Ministry of Education. (2001). *English curriculum: Principles and standards for learning English as a foreign language for all grades*. Jerusalem: Ministry of Education. Retrieved August 30, 2005, from http://www.anglit.net/main/curriculum/rationale.html

Nazari, A. (2005). Washback effects on TEFL: A case study from Iran. *Voices, 185*, 9–10.

Pica, T. (1996). Do second language learners need negotiation? *International Review of Applied Linguistics in Language Teaching, 34*(1), 1–21.

Ribe, R., & Vidal, N. (1993). *Project work: Step by step*. Oxford: Macmillan Heinemann.

Roberts, D. (1999). The sky's the limit. *Science and Children, 37*(1), 33–37.

Sheppard, K., & Stoller, F. L. (1995). Guidelines for the integration of student projects in ESP classrooms. *English Teaching Forum, 33*(2), 10–15.

Shulman, A. (2004, December). Annual Report of the Education and Development Committee presented to the UNICEF Executive Board of Israel, Jerusalem..

Steiner, J. (2004, July). *On the changes for the new bagrut*. Paper presented to the English Teachers' Association, Jerusalem.

Wicks, M. (2000). *Imaginative projects*. Cambridge, UK: Cambridge University Press.

CHAPTER 12

L'IMMEUBLE

French Language and Culture Teaching and Learning Through Projects in a Global Simulation

Beatrice Dupuy
University of Arizona

Tell me and I will forget; show me, and I may remember; involve me and I will understand.

—Old Chinese proverb

INTRODUCTION

In recent years, foreign language (FL) scholars and practitioners have increasingly wrestled with the issue of communicative and cultural competence as goals of language instruction and how to reach them in the classroom, as mainstream curricular approaches and materials have proven to be rather ineffectual in supporting this endeavor. Finding sound, alternative, theoretically based and practical approaches that can help students acquire communicative and cultural competence in ways that can be meaningful and relevant to them has been a challenge.

Project-Based Second and Foreign Language Education, pages 195–214
Copyright © 2006 by Information Age Publishing
All rights of reproduction in any form reserved.

Global simulation (GS), a project-based learning approach, offers an alternative approach to achieve the goals stated above. GS is "reality of function in a simulated and structured environment" (Jones, 1984, p. 5). In other words, GS provides a way to create a representation of reality (e.g., an apartment building, a business, a village, a hotel, etc.) in which students function according to preselected roles as if they were actually these people. A variety of realia help construct the authentic setting (e.g., in the case of an apartment building, notifications left by the building manager in the elevator, "for sale" notices left by residents in the lobby area, local events posters, etc.) and enhance role fulfillment. Action in the realistic environment is built around a series of small projects that arise as life in the setting unfolds and feed into the large project of the GS (e.g., in the case of an apartment building, its life story and that of its residents). GS gives students integrated access to authentic input in the target language and culture and allows them to operate as if they were in the target culture, while being—through dramatic identification—affectively involved. It promotes students' metacognitive awareness through the use of debriefing sessions and it offers an environment where language and culture learning as a process can be emphasized through the use of multiple formative assessments. This chapter begins with an examination of the theoretical basis for GS and how it can accommodate the shifts that have recently occurred in foreign language teaching and learning. The stages for implementing Debyser (1996)'s creative GS workbook *L'Immeuble* are then described. Finally, student reactions to *L'Immeuble* are reported.

THE THEORETICAL BASIS FOR GLOBAL SIMULATION: A PROJECT-BASED LEARNING APPROACH

As an approach, GS has been around since the late 1970s, when it emerged from the BELC (*Bureau pour l'Enseignement de la Langue et de la Civilisation Française à l'Étranger*) research center as a response to a general dissatisfaction with the traditional language teaching and learning paradigm that drove instruction in L2 classrooms at the time (Caré, 1995; Debyser, 1973, 1974, 1996; Yaiche, 1996). In a seminal article entitled "La mort du manuel et le déclin de l'illusion méthodologique," Debyser (1973) strongly criticized textbooks and the structural approach to language teaching and learning they promoted. He called for recentering instruction on the student, encouraging more active learning, developing free expression and creativity, and fostering true communicative competence in culturally meaningful and relevant contexts.

Since the early 1990s, many L2 scholars and practitioners have shown renewed interest in GS as the majority of mainstream teaching university materials have, despite prefaces claiming otherwise, changed relatively little in form and content since the heyday of audiolingualism. Indeed, many textbooks continue to "be built upon the persistent assumption that the acquisition of a foreign language and its culture means studying discrete grammatical structures, vocabulary lists, and pieces of information" (Levine, 2004, p. 26), and as such fail to translate current theories of second language acquisition (SLA) and communicative language teaching and learning into practice. GS is certainly worth receiving a second look, but before examining its theoretical and empirical support, its key characteristics are first presented.

SIMULATION/GLOBAL SIMULATION: DEFINITION AND CHARACTERISTICS

Most people have heard of simulation. A well-known example is that of NASA's astronaut training simulator: a specifically modified four-engine jet aircraft designed to fly in parabolic arcs to produce brief weightless periods, giving the astronaut candidates a feel for space flight. Another example is OTIS, an online trading and investment simulator, which gives an opportunity for experienced investors to test new stock market strategies and for new investors to learn the basics of stock trading. Finally, an example more germane to foreign language instruction is a simulation[1] in which a group of students form a concerned citizens action committee and pitch their recycling plan to their city council.

Various conceptualizations of simulation exist. For the purpose of this chapter, however, Jones' (1984) three key elements of simulation are used:

- *Reality of function.* Even though a simulation is not reality, students must embrace their role (e.g., residents of an apartment building, stockbrokers, business people, diplomats, etc.) and behave and act within the simulation as if they actually were these people. As students bring life to a simulation, it takes on a reality of its own and "then the experiences of the participants become real, and the use of language becomes meaningful communication. Simulations thus encourage language participants to use their new language in the ways most people do in other (similar but real) situations" (Crookall & Oxford, 1990, p. 15).
- *Simulated environment.* A representation of reality is created around a single situation or premise (e.g., an apartment building, a stock trading room, an IT business, an international conference, etc.) to promote role acceptance and realization.

- *Structure.* Action is built around a set of small projects that are not invented but are rather generated as action progresses and contribute to the completion of a large project (e.g., the story of a building and its residents through the years, the advertising campaign of some new software, etc.).

Simulation is meant to be short term and is typically completed in a day or two. On the other hand, GS involves students in a long-term (a month or two, or an entire term) project. Global means:

- *Exhaustive.* Students are involved in inventing or (re)creating a part of the world, which has very clear and narrow borders so that spatial and chronological coherence and continuity can be more easily maintained. It is for this reason that one will want to choose a building rather than a neighborhood or an entire city. The steps involved in the invention/(re)creation of the part of the world students have chosen include setting and describing the stage and bringing it to life. For example, an apartment building will have a history that the residents can recall and tell to others. Once setting and describing the stage is done, a representative sample of the neighborhood's population moves into the building. The residents not only have an administrative identity but also a past and a future that feed into the exchanges with neighbors, local representatives, store owners, and so forth and shape the events and incidents that occur.
- *Integrated.* Opportunities for interpersonal, interpretive, and presentational communication, both oral (e.g., role plays and discussions for planning and evaluation) and written (e.g., students read a variety of documents, they write a wide range of documents, etc.), are available throughout a GS. These communicative exchanges naturally grow out of the needs that arise from the GS and are key to completing it successfully. Whether simulated, such as the exchanges that take place among the characters, or authentic, such as those that occur among students when sharing the results of individual or collective work or evaluating and negotiating the next move, all communicative exchanges are driven by the GS and the need to take it forward.
- *Multidisciplinary.* To complete a GS, a large spectrum of curricular areas (geography, history, art, music, literature, math, etc.) other than language are tapped into as needed. In the first stage of a GS, for example, a location needs to be chosen and its physical characteristics described (geography: drawing a map and the relief of the area; math: distance calculations, scales, etc.). Next, people move in (statistics: population sample, age pyramid, demography, etc.) and their biographies are written (geography: place of birth; history: date of birth, etc.). As they run into each other, they may talk about the

weather (geography: seasons, climate, etc.), their likings (art, music, etc.), and so on. Throughout a GS, students need to draw from multiple sources to work on the various projects it includes.

- *Multidimensional.* Academic and practical skills (taking pictures of residents with a digital camera, building the set of the GS, writing collaboratively using a wiki,[2] etc.) as well as cognitive and employability skills (goal setting, project planning, product archiving on a Web server, self-assessment, leadership, etc.) can be promoted, and affective behaviors such as self-confidence and risk-taking can be fostered.
- *Inclusive.* Teacher and students work in a tightknit partnership in which students no longer sit on the sidelines but play a central decision-making role. Students take control of their own destiny within a GS.

The key characteristics of GS clearly reflect a number of current teaching and learning principles both in and out of the field of second language learning and make GS a strong contender to answer the call from many FL scholars and practitioners for an alternative approach, one that can facilitate the development of communicative and cultural competence in ways that are meaningful, relevant, and motivating to students.

THEORETICAL AND EMPIRICAL SUPPORT OF GS

Experiential Learning and GS

GS finds strong support in learning theories in which cognitive, behavioral, and attitudinal changes are mostly the result of *experience* and fully integrates the principles of experiential learning theory.

Experiential learning, rooted in Dewey's (1938) view and that of his followers on learning and its relation to real experience, is effective in enhancing learner motivation and fostering higher cognitive skills as well as in enabling students to gain deeper understandings and valuable content knowledge. According to Kolb (1984), "Essentially, learning takes place through the experiences which the learner has; that is, through the reactions he makes to the environment in which he is placed" (p. 63). Like Kolb (1984), Joplin (1995) argues that "all learning is experiential" and goes on to explain that "this means that anytime a person learns, he must 'experience' the subject, significantly identify with, seriously interact with, form a personal relationship with, etc." (p. 15). However, both Kolb (1984) and Joplin (1995) insist that providing experience for students is not enough to be called experiential learning. It is reflection on that experience that turns experience into experiential learning. Besides the aspects of teacher feedback, debriefing, and focus, a fourth aspect is added by these later educators and others: emotional input. Maher (1987) indicates that "knowledge always has, and indeed should have, an emotional component, a feeling component, that comes from the student's sense of purpose, sense of connection to the material and the particular context" (p. 96). It is important to develop "a community of students," which gives them the opportunity to find their own voice in relation to the project in which they are engaged, thereby constructing knowledge from their individual and shared experience.

Recognizing the need to provide authentic use opportunities and foster positive affect for language acquisition, L2 scholars and practitioners have incorporated these experiential learning principles into recent approaches of language/culture teaching and learning. One example is the project-based learning (PBL) approach. A project can be defined as "A unit of work involving constructive thought and action in connection with learning, including a goal, a series of actions (activities or tasks) and a pre-defined sequence" (Tremblay, Duplantie, & Huot, 1990, pp. 58–59). The project defined at the outset of the unit

> creates the need to know certain language elements and the need to practice certain communicative situations to complete the final project successfully. It also provides an interesting and authentic context for the integration of cultural and general language education content related to the project. The activities or tasks of the units are sequenced in such a way as to lead the students step-by-step to the final project. (Turnbull, 1999, pp. 549–550)

The initial phase of the project involves students pooling their preexisting (linguistic and content) knowledge about the topic and agreeing on the final project. The last phase of the project involves them in presenting their final product and reflecting on learning: what they accomplished, instead of what they did not accomplish.

Experiential learning holds much promise for SLA in terms of communicative and cultural competence, motivation, and engagement, which are examined next.

Communicative Competence and GS

In the mid-1960s, Chomsky's (1965) notion of competence was expanded to a broader notion of communicative competence, which refers to the ability to function in a communicative setting by using not only grammatical knowledge but also gestures and intonation, strategies for making oneself understood, and risk-taking in attempting communication (Bachman, 1990; Canale & Swain, 1980; Celce-Murcia, Dörnyei, & Thurrell, 1995; Hymes, 1972).

One major question that was raised then and is still raised today is whether the classroom can provide the type of experience students need to develop communicative competence. In the traditional teacher-centered language classroom, the teacher controls communication and genuine conversation is generally absent, which consequently prevents the full range of registers found in the real world to be available to students.

Watson and Sharrock (1990) see in GS an opportunity to "declassroom" the classroom which involves "1) restructuring relations between teacher and learner and 2) reconstructing the relevance of educative tasks" (p. 233). GS rectifies the teacher-learner imbalance in the language classroom in two ways. It does so by placing "the onus on the students to do things for themselves and to discover what they need to know, where guidance displaces instructions" (Watson & Sharrock, 1990, p. 234). Furthermore, it provides a whole range of conversational models between different types of speakers in different types of speech situations, which allows students to be exposed not only to various registers but also to verbal and nonverbal cultural behaviors that accompany discourse, all of which would not be possible in the traditional language-teaching paradigm.

GS builds on the principles that language use and language learning are facilitated when students collaborate on projects that (1) are challenging, communicative, worthwhile, and absorbing and (2) provide opportunities for student ownership and participation in their own language learning. Both principles can trigger powerful intrinsic motivation, which leads to better learning. One theory of intrinsic motivation that is well suited to GS is that of "flow," which Csikszentmihalyi (1990) represents as an experiential state characterized by intense focus and involvement that leads to improved performance on the task in which one is currently engaged.

The conditions associated with "flow" can be characterized along four dimensions: (1) a balance exists between *challenge and skills* that prompts students to be totally engaged in the task; (2) students notice that their *attention* is entirely focused on the task; (3) students find the task *interesting* and *relevant*; and (4) students perceive a sense of *control* over the task.

Student reactions to the GS examined in this chapter seem to indicate that many of them encountered these conditions and experienced "flow". A student wrote, "It was great to work in a group on creative writing in another language. It increases the complexity of talking about creative writing, sort of doubling the difficulty and putting extra emphasis on word choice and expression" (conditions 1 and 2). One student confided, "I have to say that I have enjoyed having the chance to practice my French outside of the box, outside the normal frame of learning a language. It was great to assume the role of my character and take all the characteristics that I believe she should have from seeing characters like her in movies, and from stumbling upon real-life ones in Paris" (condition 3). Another student indicated, "The most fun aspect of the project was the opportunity to be creative; we are not often afforded opportunities like this in the university setting. I think that the more opportunities students have for personal input on a project, the more ownership of it they will take" (condition 4). Given its principles and features described earlier in this chapter, GS can provide a learning environment in which students are very likely to experience flow as indicated above.

Cultural Competence and GS

In 1996, Grittner offered the following historical overview of the teaching and learning of culture in the L2 classroom:

> Earlier approaches tended to view culture as a means to some end....As for method, the student was to receive and store information about the target culture....More recent approaches have placed the emphasis on content... more emphasis has been put on having students discover cultural data rather than having it "fed" to them as static information. (p. 18)

In other words, culture learning has come to be perceived as "the process of acquiring the culture-specific and culture general knowledge, skills and attitudes required for effective communication and interaction with individuals from other cultures. It is a dynamic, developmental, and ongoing process which engages the learner cognitively, behaviorally, and affectively" (Paige, Jorstad, Siaya, Klein, & Colby, 2000, p. 50).

Culture learning as a process is grounded in experiential learning theory and can best be promoted by implementing pedagogies congruent with the theory in which it is rooted. In each phase of GS, students work closely with a variety of authentic documents rich in information about the target language and culture. As they do, they can perceive certain aspects of the target culture and form hypotheses about its behaviors, attributions or expectations, which they confirm or disconfirm by looking at additional documents. Students also examine related features in their own culture. For example, students note that in French birth announcements, time of birth, weight, and size are traditionally omitted. The parents, whose names figure prominently, usually announce the birth of the child, rather than the child or his or her siblings. However, they also note that in French birth announcements today, time of birth, weight, and size are increasingly included, and siblings often announce the birth rather than parents. French birth announcements are increasingly more like birth announcements from the native culture. Students make hypotheses on why certain information would be included or omitted, why the layout would be what it is, and what this reveals about the target culture. As Kramsch (1993) indicates "understanding a foreign culture requires putting that culture in relation to one's own ... an intercultural approach to the teaching of culture is radically different from a transfer of information between cultures. It includes a reflection both on the target and the native culture" (p. 205). Students convey their new learning in the artifacts they create and archive and the self-reflection in which they engage, which provide the basis for systematically assessing their learning about culture as a discovery process.

An assessment tool in keeping with language and culture learning as process rather than product is the use of portfolios (Abrams, 2002; Allen, 2004; Jogan, Herdia, & Aguilera, 2001; L. Lee, 1997; Moore, 1994; Wright, 2000). Delett, Barnhardt, and Kevorkian (2001) indicate that "Portfolios provide a portrait of what students know and what they can do, offer a multidimensional perspective of student progress over time, encourage self-reflection and participation, and link instruction and assessment" (p. 559). A portfolio is naturally embedded in GS as students need to (1) archive over the course of the simulation their artifacts, which reflect the new insights and understandings they gain in the process; and (2) self-reflect on their own learning over time. As such, GS, as a format, can facilitate teaching culture and assessing students' cultural learning process. GS is a powerful approach in language teaching with considerable theoretical and empirical support. Furthermore, many practical features, detailed in the following section, make it an appealing curricular approach to language and culture teaching.

L'IMMEUBLE: AN IMPLEMENTATION MODEL

In this section, a semester-long GS implemented in a third-year (intermediate-high intermediate) French course at a large university in the southwest United States is examined. This course is part of a set of required courses for French majors and minors and focuses on reading and writing in a cultural context.

To promote both communicative and cultural competence, in ways that can meet and accommodate student needs and interests, an alternative to the approach in place then was sought and implemented. A number of considerations came into play when deciding to adopt and implement a French apartment building GS for which *L'Immeuble*, a creative workbook written by Francis Debyser (1996), would serve as the point of departure. Several steps were taken to ensure its success.

Selecting *L'Immeuble* as a GS

When choosing a project topic, I. Lee (2002) suggests that the following points be taken into account: learner background, interest and relevance of topic under consideration, ability of topic to spur learner imagination and creativity, appropriateness of topic for long-term work, and link between topic and previously acquired language and culture knowledge. In this case, it was also essential to find a topic that would make it possible to meet the goals and objectives set for the course by the department.

In third-year courses at the institution where this study took place, students are typically majoring or minoring in French, and they have usually had a short immersion experience in France (Paris for the most part) or another French-speaking country. They are often preparing themselves for a longer immersion experience, generally in France, during which they will often renew the experience of living in a dorm or with a family.

Given this set of factors, *L'Immeuble* was a good candidate as it could offer the kind of context and experiences that would allow these students to tap into their acquired linguistic and cultural knowledge/experiences and would also meet their future needs. It also provided a framework in which the departmental course goals and objectives could be met, namely, extensive reading of various genres of literature and extensive writing of various styles (portrait, description, critical review, correspondence, narration, etc.) to improve students' reading comprehension and writing ability in French.

L'Immeuble has been conceived to offer a realistic approach to French urban culture. In this GS, students "move" into an apartment building as residents and live, by proxy of the simulation, their lives. Like most GSs, *L'Immeuble* follows a five-phase development sequence. In each of the five phases, students carry out a number of tasks, which all lead to an artifact that can later be integrated in the final project.

Integral to GS, each phase includes a briefing and debriefing session. In the briefing session, students are initiated into the simulation in a way that will activate their content, linguistic, and cultural background knowledge. "Accessing background knowledge before launching an activity helps enrich the learning experience by preparing the groundwork for new experiences to build on top of old ones" (Knutson, 2003, p. 57). It is during briefing that students understand the pedagogical purpose and rationale for the simulation, which "can lead to greater learner awareness of, and involvement in, their own learning process" (Knutson, 2003, p. 57). In the briefing session, Jones (1984) cautions against overdoing the language briefing in particular as this may bring students to see themselves as students again, which would prevent the GS from being genuine, and reiterates that "the aim of the simulation is not to produce correct words, grammar, or pronunciation, but to communicate effectively according to roles, functions and duties" (p. 38). Once the simulation has ended, students reflect in the debriefing session on their own learning and critique their own performance.

Phase 1: Choosing a location. Selecting the setting is the responsibility of the students and no one else. Students, as they looked for an address for their apartment building, considered the particular location to select, the various neighborhoods, their history, their population makeup, their local economy, their local landmarks, and so forth. Students researched and read a variety of authentic materials (history articles, surveys, phone books, maps, etc.) that would help them decide. In this phase, students created the following artifacts:[3]

- An address with number and street name plate, which they drew
- A description of the neighborhood, of the exterior and interior of the apartment building
- A meaningful name for the store at the foot of the apartment building as well as a plate design, description of signs, small ads, etc. posted in the window

Phase 2: Populating the location and creating identities. The residents and their pets move into one of the fourteen units available in the apartment building. The identity of the residents is created in three distinct stages: (1) the administrative identity; (2) the biographical identity, which fleshes out the residents by giving them a past; and (3) the portrait, which integrates the information developed in the two previous stages and gives residents a psychosocial dimension that will later be used as a reference in the role plays and novel. In the first stage, students considered the age, nationality, and socioprofessional category of the residents who would move into their apartment building. They also reflected on the first names they would give residents on the basis of their birthday, the schools they attended, the degrees they received and the professional preparation they got, the schools and grade level attended by school-age residents, and so on. In this phase, students produced an ID card with a photo, a first and last name, a birthplace, an age, a nationality, a profession, and a family status; an outgoing message on an answering machine; a biography; a portrait; a description of a favorite room; and a description of the vehicle the resident drives

Phase 3: Interactions. Now that the setting is in place, that the residents have moved in, it is time to bring life to the apartment building by imagining the types of everyday conversation residents would strike, or not strike (depending on the nature of their relations), as they meet in the stairwell, in the elevator, in the neighborhood stores, and elsewhere. These interactions offer a range of affective situations that promote the development of both communicative and cultural competence. In this phase, students engaged in small talk about the weather; asked for a favor; gossiped; received phone calls; and exchanged recipes, books, music, and the like.

Phase 4: Writings. Students considered different kinds of writings residents might leave on a door, post on the apartment building blog, send or receive in their mailboxes, and so forth. In this phase, students produced personal notes, announcements, small ads, postcards and letters, invitations, drawings, and recommendations.

Phase 5: Events and incidents. Students develop their capacity to react accordingly to an event such as a love story involving two residents or an incident like a crime in the apartment building. It is in this phase that the final project comes together in the form of a romance or detective novel centered around the apartment building and its residents, and in which many of the artifacts created in earlier phases or dialogues exchanged throughout the GS will be inserted as needed. To present their final project to the class, several options can be entertained. For this GS, three were retained: a short movie, a photo novella, and a short puppet show (this option was retained by one of the groups as one of their characters, a 6-year-old girl, was the narrator in the novel on which the show would be based, and this medium they thought would be appropriate for her to tell her story).

Gathering the Materials and Resources Needed

While *L'Immeuble* includes some targeted quality input that can help students fulfill the various tasks included in the GS project by presenting useful models for later production, the input provided certainly does not meet Krashen's (1983) criteria of "quantity" necessary for students to develop communicative competence and cultural literacy. For this reason, books, Web resources, video excerpts, and references were included as they would provide students with the kind of integrated language and culture exposure that would be useful in achieving a more authentic GS. In GS, authentic documents are selected and used for their content but they also happen to be a great source of linguistic and cultural data students can tap into when creating artifacts.

Novels

Over the course of the semester, for the purpose of the GS, students engaged in extensive reading by selecting six novels representing four genres: romance/coming of age, adventure/mystery, life narrative, and detective. Primarily selected for their content and interest, these novels also offered excellent linguistic and cultural models for neighborhood and room descriptions, portraits, biographies, dialogues, letters, and romance or detective novels that students would later write. In addition to the novels, excerpts from Pérec's (1978) *La Vie Mode d'Emploi* and (1983) *Espèces d'Espaces* provided additional models. They can also help enhance students' literary sense both as readers and as writers.

Web Resources

Web resources gathered by the teacher and students were available at various stages of the GS. They helped students set the décor, decide who the residents would be, assign them names and jobs (or not), name the store at the foot of the apartment building, to name a few.

Since students needed to decide on an address for their apartment building, they consulted a variety of online resources about Paris that gave them an overview of Paris today: the various *arrondissements*, the divide between northeast and southwest Paris and its meaning both socially and economically, the *bobozation* of the French capital, the increasingly multi-ethnic and multicultural face of Paris. Students used this information to make informed decisions as to what the population makeup of their building would be; the marital and employment status of the residents; the type of apartments they would live in; the décor of their apartment; and their leisure activities, their reading, music, and food preferences. Once they had settled on a possible address, they made use of the search engine Voila to input it and get a picture of the actual apartment building; a view of the neighborhood and local stores; and a map of the area with its landmarks, parks, schools, and nearby metro stations.

To more authentically name the residents, students used a number of Web sites to find out about popular first names at the times their residents were born, about last names, their origin, and where they are most commonly found in France. To decide where the residents were most likely to vacation and from where they would send parents, relatives, and friends living in the building postcards and letters, students read surveys about the 35-hour work week and what the French think and say about it; French people's preferred destinations, lodgings, and activities on vacation; and so on. This information would help shape the content of the correspondence residents would receive.

To decide on which vehicle a resident would drive, students looked at statistics about brand preferences among the French, visited the Web sites of the three main French car makers, and chose a vehicle based on a resident status, lifestyle, and the like.

Besides providing useful cultural information, the Web resources also provided good writing models for announcements of many kinds (births, weddings, bar and bat mitzvahs), invitations, notices, small ads (vehicles for sale in *La Centrale du Particulier*), and so forth that residents would send or post on their door, on the apartment building blog, in their hallway, or in the entrance of their apartment building. In addition, the Web proved useful to find pictures and maps to illustrate the artifacts as well as to give students free access to online bilingual dictionaries, lexicons, and grammars.

Video Excerpts

Once students had decided on the address of their apartment building, defined its surroundings, populated it with residents, developed the interpersonal relationships between family members and between neighbors, they started playing the role of the residents. They called each other on the phone, met in the stairs, exchanged greetings, inquired about how they were doing, talked about the weather, asked favors, borrowed items they needed, gossiped, exchanged recipes, and attended the annual apartment owners' meeting.

To get a feel for the way these kinds of interactions would take place between residents and help students notice the differences and similarities between conversations in their culture and the target culture, they watched segments of *Forum Images*, a video that features the daily interactions of several residents in an apartment building in Paris. It gave them a visual image of what apartment building life in Paris looks like and what facial expressions and body language the French use when engaged in conversations. Furthermore, it gave them an opportunity to hear how conversational language differs from written language and to be exposed to the use of intonation in real conversations.

All these additional materials were gathered in order to increase the amount of the input students would need to develop the communicative and cultural competence required for later use in their creative productions in French.

DEPLOYING APPROPRIATE AND MEANINGFUL TECHNOLOGY TOOLS

While *L'Immeuble* does not mention the use of new technologies, it is clear that they can provide key assistance not only in giving access to resources and models for completing the GS project, but also in promoting collaboration among peers inside and outside of the classroom. Caré (1995) discusses the role technology can play in archiving in GS, but I believe that the use of technology in GS can be pushed beyond that.

For the purpose of *L'Immeuble*, a Web site was created to post guidelines, list rubrics, and archive learner productions as they were completed. Having easy access to completed productions is important in GS as they serve as references for later productions. Tools that could facilitate collaboration among students were integrated. Students had access to a forum, which they used to discuss their reactions to materials they had read or heard; a chat room, which they used to organize the completion of future tasks; and a wiki, which they used as a collaborative writing space.

In addition, online technologies assisted in creating an atmosphere that would closely reflect real-life contexts. In the past couple of years, focused blogs have sprung up everywhere, and neighborhood or apartment building blogs have become a popular means of giving a voice to a community in Paris and elsewhere (e.g., *Eiffel/Suffren*, *Paris-Marais*, and *Montparsud* are neighborhood blogs; *le blog de Mouchotte* is an apartment building blog). So a blog was integrated in the class Web site for the purpose of providing residents with a news outlet. On the blog, students posted greetings and/or a short introduction as they moved into the apartment building, small ads, restaurant recommendations, and so on, activities that people regularly engage in real life in the "blogosphere."

DETERMINING TEACHER AND LEARNER ROLES

In a GS environment, the teacher-learner relationship takes on a different form than the one we are accustomed to seeing in the traditional teaching-learning paradigm, where the learner's access to knowledge necessarily goes through the teacher who takes on the sole responsibility for all that happens in the classroom.

A GS is not taught. "The teacher is on the outside, not in the inside; he or she does not participate in the interaction, has no powers or responsibilities for the decision-making" (Jones, 1995, p. 11). In *L'Immeuble*, the major roles that the teacher assumes are those of resource person and architect. As a resource person, the teacher directs students to appropriate resources only if students request it, as the purpose is to lead students to become autonomous, to develop strategies to learn on their own by using sources other than the teacher. As an architect, the teacher divides and organizes the work in such a way that it would be easier for students to tackle.

When the roles of the teacher change, so do the roles of the learner. "Just as there is no teacher... neither are there... students" (Jones, 1995, p. 11). In *L'Immeuble*, the role of the learner is no longer to listen and regurgitate information but to pull content together, negotiate meaning, reflect on learning, and come up with an appropriate final product.

DECIDING HOW STUDENTS WILL BE ASSESSED

Formative assessments and debriefing sessions are an integral part of GS since the focus is more on the process than on the product. Not only do students receive ongoing feedback from their teacher and peers, they are also involved in evaluating their performance and progress, which gives them a voice and promotes autonomy as well.

Within the framework of *L'Immeuble*, three sources of assessment are included: teacher peers, and students. The teacher provides measurable criteria related to each project objective, makes sure students know and understand the criteria before working on a task, and evaluates and makes suggestions. Students are involved in evaluating the teamwork of their peers. They evaluate their writing and offer suggestions for revision. For oral work, they make suggestions for improvement and show support. Students also evaluate their peers in terms of participation, ability to follow through, and respect given to other team members in collaborative work. To develop learning strategies and build learner autonomy, students also have a chance to reflect on their own work in class.

The GS learning environment is one in which students are active participants in situations where they use authentic language to accomplish particular objectives, assess their performance and progress, and are in charge of their own learning process. In the following, student reactions to these features are discussed.

STUDENT REACTIONS TO GS

At the end of the GS, students reflected on what they had learned, highlighted the positive and negative aspects of the GS to improve it for classes to come. Beckett (2002) reviewed the literature on L2 student evaluations of PBL and found that students had mixed feelings about this approach to learning. While students in this GS shared a couple of the concerns echoed by students in the studies Beckett (2002) reviewed, their evaluation of the project was overwhelmingly positive.

Many students particularly appreciated the collaborative aspect of the GS. One learner wrote,

> This project was a great way to get involved in group work. It helped facilitate our learning and understanding of the French language because we had other people besides the teacher to help us with questions and doubts regarding grammar, sentence structure, and the basics many of us tend to forget over the years. This project was very versatile and it ranged in a variety of things that in my opinion helped us all achieve a great ending.

Another said, "What I liked best was collaborating with my group and being able to use my creativity to invent and actually write the story of a building and its residents in French." These students highlight the importance of having a collaborative, holistic approach to language teaching and learning in which more knowledgeable peers can be sought for help. Collaborative learning also leads to more positive attributions for learning success, greater self-perception, and increased confidence with the target language.

Students also enjoyed having the opportunity to engage in creative writing, they appreciated having a say in the direction and shape of the project, it made it more meaningful and engaging, and, therefore worth the effort it required. Students also realized how they could tap into the knowledge they had acquired in previous and current classes and experiences. One learner stated,

> I really enjoyed many aspects of L'Immeuble project. It allowed me to write in different ways that I had not tried before. I especially enjoyed writing the chapters of the novel after having read our class texts. This allowed me to internalize a lot of what I had learned through reading the books.

Another indicated,

> The most fun aspect of the project was the opportunity to be creative; we are not often afforded opportunities like this in the university setting. I think that the more opportunities students have for personal input on a project, the more ownership of it they will take.

Contrary to some of the student reactions reported in Beckett's (2002) literature review, here students welcomed having autonomy from the teacher, having control on the direction and shape of the GS, and learning in a nontraditional way.

Students attested that this project was more interesting and engaging that any other they had before. One learner volunteered,

> I do want you to know that the apartment project has probably been my favorite thing in college to do in a class. I graduate next December too, so I've had MANY classes.... Practically all of my friends and family were updated weekly on the latest from our *immeuble.*

While it is disheartening to read that this was one of the few projects deemed worthwhile by this student during 4 years of college, it is encouraging to see that GS, a PBL approach, can generate this type of interest and involvement.

A few students made negative comments and complained that, "It was a LOT of work, combined with all of the assignments in [their] other classes." However, it is interesting to read that they do not ask to get rid of GS but rather to rethink the schedule of its implementation, given the limited number of contact hours of the course: "Sometimes, I didn't have the time to dedicate to the creative writing project that I would've liked, and that was disappointing." This student clearly enjoyed the GS but could not devote to it the necessary time due to school pressures and this led to frustration and disappointment. Students wholeheartedly endorsed GS, especially stressing the importance of collaborative work, student input in the project, and student autonomy.

CONCLUSION

In this chapter, an implementation model for *L'Immeuble*, a GS designed for a French setting, was presented. While it is set in Paris, the premise is easily transferable to another city in the French-speaking world and elsewhere for that matter and the phases of the project can be readily transferred to other L2 contexts.

GS is a viable alternative approach, one that, as rightly described by Levine (2004), "allows [one] to move away from a linear, sequential, formulaic approach to learning about the target language and cultures" (p. 34) and ties well with current thinking in the field of second language acquisition. It promotes the use of language for real communication in a real cultural context and helps students achieve the goals of communicative and cultural competence. However, its implementation has yet to become a widespread reality in university foreign language classrooms.

NOTES

1. According to Jones (1984), simulation differs from role play on two levels: reality and power. Simulation is reality and role play is a play, pretence, or game. "In a business simulation, the business may be conducted by people who have never been in business in their lives, but their thinking and talking and decision-making are absolutely genuine.... The participants are not imitating businessmen, they *are* businessmen because they are functioning as businessmen" (Jones, 1984, p. 21). Participants in a simulation cannot shape the world the way they want to. In addition, simulations are participant owned. In role plays, personalities and actions are often prescribed by the instructor, which reduces participant ownership and therefore takes away a major feature of simulation.
2. A wiki is a Web application that enables documents to be written collectively in a simple markup language using a Web browser.
3. To see artifacts created by students, please visit http://frenchgateway .coh.arizona.edu/F04/FREN320.

REFERENCES

Abrams, Z. (2002). Surfing to cross-cultural awareness: Using Internet-mediated projects to explore cultural stereotypes. *Foreign Language Annals, 35*(2), 141–153.

Allen, L. (2004). Implementing a culture portfolio project within a constructivist paradigm. *Foreign Language Annals, 37*(2), 232–239.

Bachman, L. (1990). *Fundamental considerations in testing.* Oxford: Oxford University Press.

Beckett, G. (2002). Teacher and student evaluations of project-based instruction. *TESL Canada Journal, 19*(2), 52–65.

Canale, M., & Swain, M. (1980). Theoretical bases of communicative approaches to second language teaching and testing. *Applied Linguistics, 1*(1), 1–47.

Caré, J.-M. (1995). Inventer pour apprendre: Les simulations globales [Inventing for learning: Global simulations]. *Die Neueren Sprachen, 94*(1), 69–87.

Celce-Murcia, M., Dörnyei, Z., & Thurell, S. (1995). Communicative competence: A pedagogically motivated model with content specifications. *Issues in Applied Linguistics, 6*(2), 5–35.

Chomsky, N. (1965). *Aspects of the theory of syntax.* Cambridge, MA: MIT Press.

Crookall, D., & Oxford, R. (1990). Linking language learning and simulation/gaming. In D. Crookall & R. Oxford (Eds.), *Simulation, gaming, and language learning* (pp. 3–23). New York: Harper House.

Csikszentmihalyi, M. (1990). *Flow: The psychology of optimal experience.* New York: Harper & Row.

Debyser, F. (1973). La mort du manuel et le déclin de l'illusion méthodologique [The death of the textbook and the decline of the methodological illusion]. *Le Français dans le Monde, 100,* 58–66.

Debyser, F. (1974). Simulation et réalité dans l'enseignement des langues vivantes [Simulation and reality in the teaching of modern languages]. *Le Français dans le Monde, 106,* 16–19.

Debyser, F. (1996). *L'Immeuble* [The apartment building]. Paris: Hachette.

Delett, J., Barnhardt, S., & Kevorkian, J. (2001). A framework for portfolio assessment in the foreign language classroom. *Foreign Language Annals, 34*(6), 559–568.

Dewey, J. (1938). *Experience and education.* New York: Macmillan.

Grittner, F. (1996). Introduction to special issue on culture. *Foreign Language Annals, 29*(1), 17–18.

Hymes, D. (1972). On communicative competence. In J. P. Pride & J. Holmes (Eds.), *Sociolinguistics* (pp. 269–293). Harmondsworth, UK: Penguin.

Jogan, M., Herdia, A., & Aguilera, G. (2001). Cross-cultural e-mail: Providing cultural input for the advanced foreign language student. *Foreign Language Annals, 34*(4), 341–346.

Jones, K. (1984). *Simulations in language teaching.* Cambridge, UK: Cambridge University Press.

Jones, K. (1995). *Simulations: A handbook for teachers* (Rev. ed.). London: Kogan Page.

Joplin, L. (1995). On defining experiential education. In K. Warren, M. Sakoffs, & J. S. Hunt (Eds.), *The theory of experiential education* (3rd ed., pp. 15–22). Dubuque, IA: Kendall/Hand.

Knutson, S. (2003). Experiential learning in second-language classrooms. *TESL Canada Journal, 20*(2), 52–64.

Kolb, D. (1984). *Experiential learning: Experience as a source of learning.* Englewood Cliffs, NJ: Prentice Hall.

Kramsch, C. (1993). *Context and culture in language teaching.* Oxford: Oxford University Press.

Krashen, S. (1985). *The input hypothesis: Issues and implications.* New York: Longman.

Lee, I. (2002). Project work in second/foreign language classrooms. *Canadian Modern Language Review, 59*(2), 282–290.

Lee, L. (1997). Using portfolios to develop L2 cultural knowledge and awareness of students in intermediate Spanish. *Hispania, 80*(2), 355–367.

Levine, G. (2004). Global simulation: A student-centered task-based format for intermediate foreign language courses. *Foreign Language Annals, 37*(1), 26–36.

Maher, F. (1987). Toward a richer theory of feminist pedagogy: A comparison of "liberation" and "gender" models for teaching and learning. *Journal of Education, 169*(3), 91–100.

Moore, Z. (1994). The portfolio and testing culture. In C. Hancock (Ed.), *Teaching, testing, and assessment: Making the connection* (pp. 163–182). Lincolnwood, IL: National Textbook Company.

Paige, R., Jorstad, H., Siaya, L., Klein, F., & Colby, J. (2000). Culture learning in language education: A review of the literature. In R. Paige, D. Lange, & Y. Yershova (Eds.), *Culture as the core; Interdisciplinary perspectives on culture learning in the language curriculum* (pp. 47–113). Minneapolis: Center for Advanced Research on Language Acquisition.

Pérec, G. (1978). *La Vie mode d'emploi: Romans* [Life: A user's manual]. Paris: Le Livre de Poche.

Pérec, G. (1983). *Espèces d'espaces* [Species of spaces]. Paris: Galilée.

Tremblay, R., Duplantie, M., & Huot, D. (1990). *National core French study: Communicative-experiential syllabus.* Ottawa: Canadian Association of Second Language Teachers.

Turnbull, M. (1999). Multidimensional project-based teaching in French Second Language (FSL): A process-product case study. *The Modern Language Journal, 83*(4), 548–568.

Watson, D., & Sharrock, W. (1990). Realities in simulation/gaming, In D. Crookall & R. Oxford (Eds.), *Simulation, gaming, and language learning* (pp. 231–238). New York: Harper House.

Wright, D. (2000). Culture as information and culture affective process: A comparative study. *Foreign Language Annals, 33*(3), 330–341.

Yaiche, F. (1996). *Les Simulations globales: Mode d'emploi* [Global simulations: Instructions]. Paris: Hachette.

CHAPTER 13

FRENCH GASTRONOMY THROUGH PROJECT WORK IN COLLEGE CLASSES

Becky Brown
Purdue University

INTRODUCTION

Postsecondary target language curricula centered on the practice of the four skills exploit a broad array of techniques to promote a truly communicative environment (Ellis, 1987; Hadley, 1979, 2001). One underexplored technique that, by design, forces a real-life communicative context is project work. When a class is conducted in the target language, students working on group projects must manage the project in that language. The result is an assignment constructed in the target language with reinforcing language practice. Consequently, this chapter lends support to Beckett and Slater (2005) who demonstrate in the English as a second language (ESL) domain the way in which project work promotes simultaneous acquisition of the four skills as well as meaning.

The model illustrated in this chapter is a French project or *dégustation* embedded in a larger themed-based course entitled, French Gastronomy. The course was originally conceived as part of a larger curriculum overhaul

Project-Based Second and Foreign Language Education, pages 215–224
Copyright © 2006 by Information Age Publishing
215

to explore innovative approaches to the teaching of the four skills of French at the intermediate and advanced levels. Higher level target language (TL) courses customarily use review grammars with short texts incorporated within each chapter. The texts are often topic- and culture-based and span the francophone world. Usually, more emphasis is on expository writing at these levels as compared to the introductory level. The proficiency-based model is perpetuated, and student-centered activities are the purported norm. Complex grammar exercises and lengthier writing assignments continue to be predominantly individual pursuits assigned as homework. These tenets are still maintained in the innovative French course illustrated in this chapter; however, it is theme based. Furthermore, the theme, it was felt, had to be highly culturally based for maximum authenticity. Thus, for France, possible semester themes could be high fashion, the Tour de France, or gastronomy. For this course, gastronomy was chosen. In effect, the design could be characterized as a four-skills culture course thematically centered on French gastronomy. The larger goals of the course were to find creative ways to teach the four skills of the target language, to draw students to French studies, and to encourage students to continue taking French beyond the fourth college semester.

CONTENT-BASED INSTRUCTION

In the second language acquisition (SLA) literature, theme-based courses are termed content-based instruction (CBI). Although CBI is becoming more widespread in practice, it still falls short of its theoretical potential. Brinton, Snow, and Wesche (1989) define CBI as "the concurrent study of language and subject matter, with the form and sequence of language presentation dictated by content material" (p. vii). This orientation toward a focus on meaning has found support in the general SLA research of Swaffar, Arens, and Byrnes (1991) and Ryan (1994) who found improved language acquisition when meaning was central.

In practice, CBI curricula have been designed around job-oriented topics (Leaver, 1997; Stryker, 1997; Vines, 1997) and academic subjects (Beckett, Gonzalez, & Schwartz, 2004; Fein & Baldwin, 1986; Reid, 1984; Straight, 1997). The French gastronomy example illustrates that CBI may be enhanced further by choosing even more meaningful contexts—a theme or topic that is a prominent cultural trait intricately linked to that country's identity. Similarly, a CBI course for a Spanish curriculum could center on bullfighting; a Japanese language CBI course could explore the popular anime media, interior design, or landscape architecture. A CBI ESL course in an American curriculum could focus on African American history and the civil rights movement or the American West.

Thus far, if culture is included in CBI instruction, it is often through authentic texts on current events as related to contemporary target language societies (Klahn, 1997; Klee & Tedick, 1997). The French gastronomy course takes this practice one step further and establishes a goal of deepening the cultural experience by centering each of the four skills on only one theme. For example, the course (taught in the target language) includes a historical perspective, descriptions of regional cuisine, cultural traditions and festivals related to gastronomy, contemporary problems in the food industry, authentic menus and culinary vocabulary, prominent historical and contemporary chefs, food shopping, and relevant texts from literature and films. Furthermore, the gastronomy course illustrates that while CBI is about learning to make meaning, it can also promote four skills as Fried-Booth (2002) claims. The four skills are exercised using theme-appropriate feature-length films and contemporary music, staging in-class food tastings by student groups and guest chefs, writing critiques, and completing interactive Web exercises. In essence, although the course is generally a CBI approach, a variety of methodologies are incorporated to create the most meaningful contexts. Furthermore, the cultural experience is given superior relevance with the integration of a study abroad trip to a French cooking school during semester break.

COURSE MATERIALS FOR THE
FRENCH GASTRONOMY COURSE

The first problem a teacher will encounter with a CBI culture course on French gastronomy is that there is no available course text. Noteworthy, teachers of genre literature classes confront this perennial dilemma by constructing a reading list of authors and/or creating spiral-bound short texts. The teachers are crucially dependent on an introductory literature prerequisite for the content foundation. Because no such prerequisite exists for French gastronomy, the instructor is required to amass and compile an in-depth array of materials and then create activities and exercises around them. This daunting task may be facilitated by the creation of a course Web page with Internet links to an abundance of resources. Consequently, a certain amount of responsibility is shifted to the student who must browse links to find rudimentary concepts normally found in a course text. Although the instructor's content knowledge is a commonly reported dilemma in CBI literature, the vast and ever-increasing Internet resources abate the problem considerably. In effect, while the library may be the standard resource for tomes on the history of alimentation in human civilization, in general, and culinary movements in Europe and France, in particular, the Internet remains the best resource for information on contemporary topics such as food festivals, celebrity chefs, and genetically modified produce.

The course Web page also facilitates the incorporation of cutting-edge computer-assisted language learning (CALL) techniques as a site for customized interactive exercises. For example, dialogues can be enhanced with audio files, regional foods can be "dragged" to specific regions on a French map, and names of foods can be "dragged" to the appropriate images. Traditional methods for teaching culture rely on a textbook of essays on contemporary issues and established traditions. Common teaching tools are slide presentations, physical artifacts, and documentary shorts. To complement these group-paced materials, the gastronomy interactive activities promote individually paced learning. The students regulate the repetition of the audio segments, the visual imagery, and the tactile movement of clicking the mouse. Traditional exercises such as dialogues, matching drills, and the memorization of cultural traits take on a whole new meaning when recast in the form of interactive educational tools. In turn, students may become more motivated to learn about French culture.

THE FRENCH GASTRONOMY PROJECT WORK: *DÉGUSTATIONS*

Noting that college students often eat and drink in class, the author was led to design a course in which students were *required* to eat during class time to minimize the intrusion. Thus, not only would the students learn about French gastronomy, but they would also participate in the appreciation of French cuisine. Methodologically, this is total physical response (TPR) at its best. Learning through actions, the essence of TPR (Asher, 2003), is still widely believed to motivate learners. The bonus of actually nourishing the human system while involving the total physical being only maximizes the TPR instructional tool.

As a result, casual eating was methodologically formalized into semester-long group projects as part of the requirements for the French gastronomy course. Hence, the groups performed a series of in-class food tastings and critiques or *dégustations*. The dégustations were held every 2 weeks and complemented the other activities that typically occur in four-skills classes, such as the reading and discussion of texts, theme-based vocabulary building, and small group role playing. The class met in a seminar classroom with conference tables that could be transformed into dining tables for the presentations. The optimal setting, however, would be in a campus "French House," if available. The class enrollment was capped at 12 students for a division of 4 groups of 3 students. Each group conducted two dégustations, the first of which served as a dry run for the final dégustation, which constituted the final exam. The presentations ranged from the simple (such as chocolates, cheeses, breads, pastries, tea biscuits, salads, quiches, and soups) to the complex (such as *bûche de Noël, crème brûlée*, and *mousse au chocolat*). The dégustation experience was further enhanced by guest chefs who typically exhibit more exotic fare. Their presentations included *gougères*, chocolate éclairs, *vichyssoise*, and Alsatian *bäckeoff* and *kugelhopf*. The Alsatian dégustation was prepared by Paul Chamness Miller (co-editor of this volume) and was enhanced in cultural authenticity by his use of regional ceramics and genuine glassware.

The students remained in the same groups for the duration of the semester to foster a lab-group approach much like in the sciences. The activities were conducted "lab-group" style with group members working together toward one goal, and the groups were responsible for setup and cleanup. At the beginning of the semester, the instructor conducted the first dégustation to demonstrate the model for the students to emulate. Moreover, they were encouraged to consult the instructor regularly during the conceptual stage since this type of project is unusual in the typical foreign language classroom.

The students were asked to pay a small "lab fee" at the beginning of the term. A $15 lab fee per student sufficed for eating supplies and the instructor's dégustations, as the total was matched by the department's teaching supply fund. The students' dégustations were at their own expense and a budget of $15 per presentation was advised. In the absence of a course text to buy, the students' cost for the course totaled about $25 ($15 course fee, $5 first dégustation, $5 second dégustation). In keeping with the spirit of a food tasting as opposed to a full lunch, it was quite possible to stay within budget.

Before the day of the presentation, the students met outside of class to select their group's item for dégustation (which then was approved by the instructor), prepared the display of the item or the item itself (if necessary), and conducted and recorded the cultural research in report form. With the exception of the highly motivated student, these pre-presentation tasks were, no doubt, not conducted in the target language. On the day of the presentation, the group submitted a report to both the instructor and the class, an example of which is shown in the sample lesson plan that follows. The students were later responsible for the cultural content and culinary vocabulary from these reports for the course quizzes.

At the beginning of the semester and during periodic reminders, the students were informed that evaluation of the project would be based on cultural significance and not culinary exoticism. In other words, a dégustation featuring crème brûlée would not necessarily be evaluated higher than one on varieties of cheese. Students were, by all means, encouraged to be adventuresome, but the project was not meant to be intimidating. It was helpful for the instructor to emphasize that the class was, afterall, a culture class and not a cooking class.

One outstanding example that captured the essence of the French gastronomy project is illustrated by a group who uncommonly chose the apple for its presentation. The students spoke of cultivation and varieties in the Normandy region, economic import, nutritional value and composition, and manufacturing for alimentary by-products (juice, *Calvados*). While the traditional *tarte aux pommes* recipe was described in the cultural context of the afternoon tea, the group opted out of making it and, instead, settled for an ingeniously simple pastry-style dessert. Using 3" × 3" flat squares of store-bought phyllo dough as a "dish," the students arranged cooked apple slices topped with a drizzle of honey. This creatively simple, yet elegant presentation captured the true spirit of the intended design of the French project.

LESSON PLAN FOR A FRENCH GASTRONOMY PROJECT

Dégustation: Salade Niçoise and Vinaigrette

I. Introduction

In this particular dégustation, the group has chosen an important cultural specialty and decides to involve the class in the creation of the final product, in addition to the actual tasting and critique. Since the choice of a salad and dressing lends itself to this outcome, the instructor approves the creative bent on the assignment. The class is conducted in a regular classroom with seminar tables arranged in a square so everyone has eye contact with each other. The dégustations last 45 minutes of a 75-minute class, which allows for a small amount of pre-dégustation time for the instructor's business and some post-dégustation time for cleanup. Picnic-style plasticware supplies are kept in a department cabinet for the duration of the semester. The group brings the supplies to classroom the day of presentation and cleans and returns them to the cabinet at the end.

II. Pre-Prepared Materials

    A. Food supplies: chopped and cooked niçoise salad ingredients in plastic containers; vinegars, oil, salt, pepper, and French mustard for vinaigrette.

    B. Report for instructor and class members.

Report Guide for Dégustation

    1. Members of dégustation team.

    2. Type of dégustation.

3. Explanation of the importance of the food item in the French culture.

4. Descriptive TL vocabulary pertinent to this particular food (i.e., "sparkling" water, "shortbread" cookies, "medium-rare" or "well-done" meat).

5. Descriptive TL vocabulary pertinent to the preparation of the food item (i.e., "bake in the oven at 250 degrees," "bring water to a boil," "garnish with rosemary").

6. Suggested dishes to make with this food as well as complementary menu items.

7. Description and discussion of at least two recipes, including historical notes and contemporary variations.

8. Some interesting facts or details uncovered during research.

III. Oral Presentation

The group has chosen to make the historically original version of salade niçoise and presents it as such within the cultural context of the region of France where it is a specialty (Nice, southeastern France). Recipes are distributed and explained. Historical recipes are compared to contemporary variations. Information from the report is presented. Once the class members learn the original components of salade niçoise, they are advised to create their own contemporary version. The same steps are followed for the vinaigrette, after which it is put on the salad.

IV. Dégustation

The group that has decided to make the historically original version serves small portions to individual class members (if it is a cheese dégustation, portions are placed on platters and labeled for reference). The class members then taste their own versions for comparison.

V. Discussion and Critique

The group leads a discussion and critiques and encourages the use of new vocabulary and full participation of other class members. The instructor may, at this point, assign a brief written critique for homework as a follow-up.

VI. "Lab" Cleanup

Tables are wiped. Trash is disposed of. Supplies are returned to the storage cabinet.

EVALUATING THE QUALITY OF THE FRENCH GASTRONOMY PROJECT

Noting the varied nature of project work across the curriculum, Alan and Stoller (2005) promote several much-needed standards (culled from an array of earlier research) to maximize the student's experience. For example, rather than focus on visual attractiveness, they suggest that the projects should strive for richness in content. The instructor for the French project emphasizes cultural significance over culinary acuity or exoticism. Also, the report guide serves as an evaluation rubric for the instructor and points the students in the right direction by setting them up for success. Furthermore, instructors should also find a balance between too much control and too little feedback. In the French project, once the dégustation item gains instructor approval, the students work autonomously with the report guide steering them through the process. Thus, the instructor's guidance is present to maintain quality work, but only indirectly. However, the instructor may also be approached voluntarily at any stage of the project, if necessary.

Alan and Stoller also advocate time-depth projects, disfavoring single-class projects while favoring lengthier unit projects. The French example is optimal in its repetition, embodying "practice makes perfect" and spanning the entire semester. Overall, the French project follows their recommended multistep process for maximizing the potential benefits of the task. Stoller (see Chapter 2) rearticulates these standards into components of a definition for effective project-based learning.

CONCLUSION

The French gastronomy model illustrates how projects can "actively construct meaning" (Beckett, 2005) in a college setting. Since the French project is situated within a theme-based course, the stage is set for a fertile learning environment and forces a real-life communicative context. Consequently, the students become an active part of their own literacy socialization. Furthermore, the design of the dégustation involves all five senses, promoting maximal long-term learning.

Culturally prominent themes enmeshed in a country's identity offer several noteworthy advantages in four-skills L2 learning. First, given the real-world connection, this project ensures a highly meaningful contextualization and significance with rich L2 input. Second, the continuous recycling of culinary content in a myriad of forms throughout the semester fosters increasing fluency in that content area. Third, content can be easily manipulated to move students to higher levels of language processing. And finally, choosing high-interest themes may revitalize the often-noted lagging motivation of advanced students.

ACKNOWLEDGMENTS

I gratefully acknowledge the help of several colleagues throughout the inception, design, compilation of materials, and implementation of this extremely rewarding French course: Thomas Broden, Juliette Cherbuliez, Katharine Conley, Philippe Dubois, David Dulle, Renée Gosson, Marianne Gupta, Kathleen Hart, Julia Hebert Perceval, Sandra Hebert Perceval, Karine Henault, Garrett Heysel, Ken Knight, Elizabeth Knutson, Kathy Krause, Yannick Lallement, Tat Yen Lee, Susan McCready, Paul Chamness Miller, John Niendorf, Sidney Pellissier, Elizabeth Reeve, Charlotte Scarcelli, Deborah Houk Schocket, Marcia Stephenson, Allen Wood, and Ute White. I extend singular thanks to René Dorel and his École des Trois Ponts for his specialized French culture curriculum adapted to complement this American course for the study abroad component. Finally, I am indebted to the three anonymous reviewers of this chapter for their insightful critique.

REFERENCES

Alan, B., & Stoller, F. (2005). Maximizing the benefits of project work in foreign language classrooms. *English Teaching Forum, 43*(4), 10–21.

Asher, J. (2003). *Learning another language through actions* (6th ed.). Los Gatos, CA: Sky Oaks Productions.

Beckett, G. H. (2005). Academic language and literacy socialization through project-based instruction: ESL student perspectives and issues. *Journal of Asian Pacific Communication, 15,* 191–206.

Beckett, G. H., Gonzalez, V., & Schwartz, H. (2004). Content-based ESL writing curriculum: A language socialization model. *NABE Journal of Research and Practice, 2,* 161–175.

Beckett, G. H., & Slater, T. (2005). The project framework: A tool for language, content, and skills integration. *ELT Journal, 59,* 108–116.

Brinton, D., Snow, M., & Wesche, M. (1989). *Content-based second language instruction.* Boston: Heinle & Heinle.

Ellis, R. (1987). *Second language acquisition in context.* Englewood Cliffs, NJ: Prentice Hall International.

Fein, D., & Baldwin, R. (1986). Content-based curriculum design in advanced levels of an intensive ESL program. *English for Foreign Students in English-Speaking Countries: Interest Section Newsletter, 4,* 1–3.

Fried-Booth, D. L. (2002). *Project work* (2nd ed.). New York: Oxford University Press.

Hadley, A. O. (1979). *Games and simulations in the foreign language classroom*. Arlington, VA: Center for Applied Linguistics.

Hadley, A. O. (2001). *Teaching language in context: Proficiency-oriented instruction*. Boston: Heinle & Heinle.

Klahn, N. (1997). Teaching for communicative and cultural competence: Spanish through contemporary Mexican topics. In S. Stryker & B. L. Leaver (Eds.), *Content-based instruction in foreign language education: Models and methods* (pp. 203–221). Washington, DC: Georgetown University Press.

Klee, C., & Tedick, D. (1997). The undergraduate foreign language immersion program in Spanish at the University of Minnesota. In S. Stryker & B. L. Leaver (Eds.), *Content-based instruction in foreign language education: Models and methods* (pp. 141–173). Washington, DC: Georgetown University Press.

Leaver, B. L. (1997). Content-based instruction in a basic Russian program. In S. Stryker & B. L. Leaver (Eds.), *Content-based instruction in foreign language education: Models and methods* (pp. 30–55). Washington, DC: Georgetown University Press.

Reid, J. (1984). *TTT Review: Teachers, texts, and technology in EFL/ESL training*. Fort Collins: Colorado State University.

Ryan, F. (1994). Languages across the curriculum: More than a good idea. In H. S. Straight (Ed.), *Language across the curriculum: Invited essays on the use of foreign languages throughout the postsecondary curriculum* (pp. 47–54). Binghamton: Center for Research in Translation, State University of New York.

Straight, H. S. (1997). Language-based instruction. In S. Stryker & B. L. Leaver (Eds.), *Content-based instruction in foreign language education: Models and methods* (pp. 239–260). Washington, DC: Georgetown University Press.

Stryker, S. (1997). The Mexico experiment at the Foreign Service Institute. In S. Stryker & B. L. Leaver (Eds.), *Content-based instruction in foreign language education: Models and methods* (pp. 174–202). Washington, DC: Georgetown University Press.

Swaffar, J., Arens, K., & Byrnes, H. (1991). *Reading for meaning: An integrated approach to language learning*. Englewood Cliffs, NJ: Prentice Hall.

Vines, L. (1997). Content-based instruction in French for journalism students at Ohio University. In S. Stryker & B. L. Leaver (Eds.), *Content-based instruction in foreign language education: Models and methods* (pp. 118–140). Washington, DC: Georgetown University Press.

CHAPTER 14

INTEGRATING SECOND LANGUAGE STANDARDS INTO PROJECT-BASED INSTRUCTION

Paul Chamness Miller
University of Cincinnati

INTRODUCTION

One of the biggest challenges that teachers of the 21st century face is integrating state and national standards into their curriculum. This is no exception in the case of foreign and second language instruction. In fact, the American Council on the Teaching of Foreign Languages (ACTFL) notes that the *Standards for Foreign Language Learning* do not represent what is currently occurring in American foreign language education. ACTFL also argues that "while they [the standards] reflect the best instructional practice, they do not describe what is being attained by the majority of foreign language students" (p. 24).

Another challenge exists for English as a second language (ESL) classrooms, as there are more than 3.5 million English language learners (ELLs) enrolled in U.S. schools (Fillmore, 2000). Teachers of English to Speakers of Other Languages, Inc. (TESOL) has noted that the number of

Project-Based Second and Foreign Language Education, pages 225–240
Copyright © 2006 by Information Age Publishing

homes where a language other than English is spoken has increased by more than 68% over the last 10 years. This change in the population of American classrooms is coupled with significant diversification in terms of language, culture, proficiency level, and academic needs (TESOL, 1997a). These national standards attempt to bring ELLs closer to the educational mainstream by setting high expectations (TESOL, 1997b).

As language teachers address these issues, they must also consider how to integrate the standards into their curriculum. While there are many approaches and methods to help language teachers achieve the standards in their language classrooms, one way to do so is by using project-based instruction (PBI). As this chapter will describe, PBI lends itself to meeting many of the standards set forth by ACTFL and TESOL.

THEORETICAL BACKGROUND

Language standards have been influenced by theories of second language acquisition:

1. Language is functional.
2. Language varies.
3. Language learning is cultural learning.
4. Language acquisition is a long-term process.
5. Language acquisition occurs through meaningful use and interaction.
6. Language processes develop interdependently.
7. Native language proficiency contributes to second language acquisition.
8. Bilingualism is an individual and societal asset. (TESOL, 1997a, General Principles of Second Language Acquisition section, ¶1)

Second language acquisition theories have been instrumental in shaping standards and accepted teaching practices in the second language classroom. It is, therefore, important to understand from where these principles have come.

Language Is Functional

Language serves a purpose, to communicate. To counter such methods of language teaching as grammar translation, Richards and Rodgers (1986) have proposed the communicative language teaching (CLT) approach, which was influenced by research on communication from such scholars as Savignon (1983) and Finocchiaro and Brumfit (1983). Hadley (2001) sums up CLT as possessing the following characteristics:

1. Teaching occurs through meaning and in context.
2. Communication is encouraged from the start.
3. Language is learned through negotiation of meaning via interaction with others (see Hatch, 1992; Long, 1983; Pica, 1994).
4. Content, activities, and strategies are selected based on students' interests.
5. Teaching stresses minimal use of one's native language.
6. The goal of language learning is communicative competence.

Teaching through meaning and in context helps make language learning functional because it gives language learning a purpose. Encouraging communication early in the language process also sends a message that communication is important and meaningful.

Language Varies

Another important part of language learning is that the language learner moves along a continuum between the native and target languages (Hadley, 2001). Selinker (1972) describes this system as the language learner's "interlanguage." Second language learners, then, will be at various places along this continuum, depending on their unique situation and background. In addition to this continuum, Ellis (1985) proposes that the language learner has a variety of styles of language from which to choose, depending on the individual, the context, the individual's emotional or physical condition, and the nature of various rules that operate in free variation, such as sex, age, social class, and dialect group (Carter & McCarthy, 1997). It is, therefore, important that a language instructor and other speakers understand that communication comes in many forms and varieties.

Language variation can also be viewed from another lens, that of World Englishes. Historically, the notion of a "standard" English for which a nonnative speaker of English should strive has been debated by many; perhaps the most famous debate was between Quirk (1985) and Kachru (1985) who argued for and against a standard form of the English language. It is now widely accepted among English language teachers that there is no "norm" by which to teach English (Rajagopalan, 2004). What becomes important in this case is for the language teacher to distinguish between what may be language creativity and what is simply an error in the student's utterance (Bamgbose, 1998). It is also crucial for native speakers of the language to be more receptive to other varieties of the second language (see Lippi-Green, 1997).

Language Learning Is Cultural Learning

It is widely accepted that language and culture must be integrated in the language classroom (see Galloway, 1985; Lafayette & Strasheim, 1981), where culture is embedded in language instruction and language instruction is embedded in cultural lessons. Seeley (1993) argues that what is needed is to foster in students an interest in the target culture(s) and an understanding of the connection between the way people speak and their social and cultural setting. On the other hand, Lafayette (1988) suggests that what is important is to focus on factual information of the target culture (e.g., geographical information, popular culture, etc.). Hadley (2001) argues that, in fact, what is important is both what Seeley and Lafayette propose. She maintains that "language is one of the primary means used to express one's perspectives of the world and to participate in social interaction" (p. 351). To achieve interaction, language should be accessible and contextualized in a sociocultural setting (van Lier, 1996). Successful interaction is based on three principles: awareness, autonomy, and authenticity (see van Lier, 1996).

Language Acquisition Is a Long-Term Process

Bialystok (1994) argues that language acquisition occurs through the processes of analysis and control. That is, "proficiency increases as the mental representations become more analyzed and attentional control more selective" (p. 162). Along with the notion of these processes, Selinker's (1972) theory of interlanguage also suggests that language learning does not occur overnight. Instead, language learners move along a continuum as they are exposed to comprehensible input (Krashen, 1982), "noticing the gap" between their interlanguage and a "native" form of the target language (Schmidt, 1990; Schmidt & Frota, 1986), interacting with others (Hatch, 1992; Long, 1983; Pica, 1994; Savignon, 1983; van Lier, 1996), having opportunities to produce output, and repairing their errors (Oliver, 1995; Swain, 1985). As is clearly evident here, language acquisition cannot occur quickly. As students begin to acquire language and their proficiency develops, they are able to become more analytical about the language-learning process and pay more attention to those aspects of the target language that matter.

Language Acquisition Occurs Through Meaningful Use and Interaction

It is believed that learning in general is best achieved through meaningful instruction. From a cognitive psychological perspective, Ausubel, Novak, and Hanesian (1978) argue that meaningful learning occurs when new knowledge is associated with preexisting knowledge through meaningful tasks and activities. This is in contrast to rote learning, which is merely memorization and regurgitation of information with no connection to prior knowledge. In the context of second language acquisition, meaningful learning is also deemed important. Specifically, Brown (2002) notes that "meaningful learning will lead toward better long-term retention than rote learning" (p. 13), especially in the context of content-based learning.

One method of providing meaningful instruction is through the communicative approach. When one learns *about* the language (i.e., through methods such as grammar translation or audiolingual instruction), one learns for reasons such as passing an exam. However, when one learns through the communicative approach, one is learning the language (Lightbown & Spada, 1999). As Finocchiaro and Brumfit (1983) note, meaning is central to CLT, and Richards and Rodgers (1986) also maintain that in order for learning to occur, it is important for language learners to be engaged in meaningful tasks. Lee and VanPatten (2003) call this "informational-cognitive purposes" where "learners exchange information for a common purpose" (p. 54).

Language Processes Develop Interdependently

Language instruction has focused for many years on the "four skills" (listening, speaking, reading, and writing), and helping students achieve proficiency in these skills is still central to foreign language education (Hadley, 2001). It is important, however, to note that these four skills are not separate; rather they are developed interdependently in order for language learners to attain communicative competence (Phillips & Draper, 1999). What is more, Hadley (2001) maintains that language teachers establish goals that will help students develop "functional skills" in the target language (p. 462).

Native Language Proficiency Contributes to Second Language Acquisition

In contrast to what was believed in more behaviorist views of language learning, it is now believed that language transfer is not to blame for all the difficulties associated with second language acquisition (Lightbown & Spada, 1999). It is also now widely accepted that language learners draw on knowledge of their first language as they learn their second language. But as Brown (2002) has pointed out, the "native system will exercise both facilitating and interfering (positive and negative transfer) effects on the production and comprehension of the new language" (p. 13). For example, Schachter (1974) suggests that language learners avoid those aspects of a target language that appear to be very different from their first language. White (1989) also found that when language learners' first language and interlanguage are similar, the learner tends not to notice the gap. Therefore, first language ability can be beneficial when carefully monitored, but there are potential hindrances.

Bilingualism Is an Individual and Societal Asset

Bilingualism is a highly debated topic, but before discussing this topic, it is important to distinguish between the two primary categories of bilinguals: sequential bilinguals and simultaneous bilinguals. Simultaneous bilinguals are those who learn two (or more) languages at the same time (usually from birth), while sequential bilinguals begin learning one language after having learned a previous language. It has been suggested that learning two languages at the same time slows down the learner's development of linguistic and cognitive skills (Lightbown & Spada, 1999); however, this claim has not been backed by sufficient research. What is more interesting to note is that when sequential bilinguals are placed in a situation of subtractive bilingualism (where the learner begins to lose first language abilities prior to mastering the second language), there may be serious consequences. The primary concern is that such language learners often end up failing to develop their first language and never really mastering the second. In fact, studies show that students who learn the second language while maintaining (and further developing) their first language achieve a valuable goal by becoming bilingual (see Miller & Endo, 2004). In addition, research shows that subtractive bilinguals or those who are only allowed to speak English have a greater risk of dropping out of school than those who are encouraged to be bilinguals (Rong & Preissle, 1998).

WHAT ARE STANDARDS?

In light of the theoretical basis for the standards, it is important to consider what the standards are and their purpose in the process of acquiring a second language. The primary purpose of standards is to "describe the language skills necessary for social and academic purposes" (TESOL, 1997a, Why ESL Standards Are Needed section, ¶5). That is to say, standards are meant to "specify the language competencies" (¶5) that students need for proficiency in the target language. ACTFL (1996) cautions, however, that standards should not be used as a curriculum guide nor should they dictate what content a course will contain. Based on the national standards established by TESOL and ACTFL, most individual states have established their own set of standards for foreign and second language learning. This chapter will focus on national standards in consideration of the general readership of this volume.

The standards developed by ACTFL are based on what is commonly known as the *five Cs*: communication, cultures, connections, comparisons, and communities (1996). At the center of language learning is *communication*, regardless of its form. Communicative competence is not fully achieved without gaining the knowledge and understanding of the *cultures* that use the target language (see Lee & VanPatten, 2003). It is also recognized that knowledge of other languages affords individuals with *connections* that a monolingual individual does not have. Students are able to recognize that there are many ways to view the world through *comparisons* and contrasts between the target and native languages. Last, studying another language provides the student with ways to establish multilingual *communities* both locally and around the world. Table 14.1 presents the standards of each of the five Cs.

As TESOL (1997a) has noted, there is a series of common principles on which both the TESOL and ACTFL standards are based: (1) language is communication; (2) language is learned through meaningful and significant use; (3) there is recognized value in bi- and multilingualism; (4) language learning occurs through cultural, social, and cognitive processes; and (5) assessment must respect language and cultural diversity.

From these principles, TESOL (1997a) established three goals with three broad standards for each of these goals; these basic goals and standards were developed for all ELLs at all age levels. The first goal indicates that ELLs will use English to communicate not just at school but outside of school as well. The second goal is to help ELLs use English to succeed academically. The third goal focuses on teaching ELLs "to use English in socially and culturally appropriate ways" (TESOL, 1997a, Goals for ESOL Learners section, ¶6). The standards that correspond to these three goals are summarized in Table 14.2.

From these goals and general standards, TESOL developed standards for Pre-K–12 ESL students. For each group of ELLs, Pre-K–Grade 3, Grades 4–8, and Grades 9–12, TESOL developed descriptors and objectives based on the standards for each of the goals described previously.

Table 14.1. ACTFL Five Cs and Standards

Communication: Communicate in languages other than English.	**Standard 1.1:** Students engage in conversations, provide and obtain information, express feelings and emotions, and exchange opinions.
	Standard 1.2: Students understand and interpret written and spoken language on a variety of topics.
	Standard 1.3: Students present information, concepts, and ideas to an audience of listeners or readers on a variety of topics.
Cultures: Gain knowledge and understanding of other cultures.	**Standard 2.1:** Students demonstrate an understanding of the relationship between the practices and perspectives of the culture studied.
	Standard 2.2: Students demonstrate an understanding of the relationship between the products and perspectives of the culture studied.
Connections: Connect with other disciplines and acquire information.	**Standard 3.1:** Students reinforce and further their knowledge of other disciplines through the foreign language.
	Standard 3.2: Students acquire information and recognize the distinctive viewpoints that are only available through the foreign language and its cultures.
Comparisons: Develop insight into the nature of language and culture.	**Standard 4.1:** Students demonstrate understanding of the nature of language through comparisons of the language studied and their own.
	Standard 4.2: Students demonstrate understanding of the concept of culture through comparisons of the cultures studied and their own.
Communities: Participate in multilingual communities at home and around the world.	**Standard 5.1:** Students use the language both within and beyond the school setting.
	Standard 5.2: Students show evidence of becoming lifelong learners by using the language for personal enjoyment and enrichment.

© 1996 American Council on the Teaching of Foreign Languages. Reprinted with permission.

Table 14.2. TESOL Goals and Standards

Goal	Standards
1. To use English to communicate in social settings	1. Use English to participate in social interaction.
	2. Interact in, through, and with spoken and written English for personal expression and enjoyment.
	3. Use learning strategies to extend their communicative competence.
2. To use English to achieve academically in all content areas	1. Use English to interact in the classroom.
	2. Use English to obtain, process, construct, and provide subject matter information in spoken and written form.
	3. Use appropriate learning strategies to construct and apply academic knowledge.
3. To use English in socially and culturally appropriate ways	1. Use the appropriate language variety, register, and genre according to audience, purpose, and setting.
	2. Use nonverbal communication appropriate to audience, purpose, and setting.
	3. Use appropriate learning strategies to extend their sociolinguistic and sociocultural competence.

© 1997 Teachers of English to Speakers of Other Languages. Reprinted with permission.

WHAT IS PROJECT-BASED INSTRUCTION?

Project-based instruction has been defined by Stoller (see Chapter 2) as: (1) having a process and product; (2) giving students (partial) ownership of the project; (3) extending over a period of time (several days, weeks, or months); (4) integrating skills; (5) developing students' understanding of a topic through the integration of language and content; (6) collaborating with other students and working on their own; (7) holding students responsible for their own learning through the gathering, processing, and reporting of information from target language resources; (8) assigning new roles and responsibilities to students and teacher; (9) providing a tangible final product; and (10) reflecting on both the process and the product. Stoller also maintains, however, that project-based instruction is more than merely engaging students in projects; rather, it has taken on a variety of forms, depending on the teacher, the students, and the situation. In addition to the projects themselves, students are engaged in many types of learning, including experiential and negotiated learning, problem solving, and research. Projects often elicit collaboration among students; they can be simple assignments or very intricate, multiphase tasks that take weeks or even months to complete. There are many other definitions of projects, and it is important to keep in mind that projects come in many different forms, but for the purpose of this chapter and to maintain uniformity with the rest of this book, this chapter will follow Stoller's definition.

INTEGRATING PROJECT-BASED LEARNING WITH STANDARDS

From this definition of project-based instruction, there are several ways that projects can help second and foreign language teachers address national standards. To facilitate the discussion in this section, examples will be provided based on the idea of a thematic, project-based unit about French gastronomy.

To consider how PBI can be used in the foreign language setting, let's start with the five Cs developed by ACTFL (1996) (see Table 14.1 for a summary). As was discussed in the theoretical section, *communication* is central to second language acquisition (see Finocchiaro & Brumfit, 1983; Richards & Rodgers, 1986; Savignon, 1983). Projects lend themselves well to communication in its various forms. To address the first communication standard, which focuses on engaging in conversation and exchanging information and opinions, as a technique for activating students' background knowledge about food, students could interview each other about their likes and dislikes concerning food (in French, of course). To address the second standard of interpreting written and spoken language, students could take the information obtained in the interview to write a biography about the interviewee's eating habits. To promote interpretation, students should be encouraged to put the information into their own words and synthesize the information as well as make inferences. To address the third standard of presenting information to an audience, the students could then present orally their classmate's biography to the class as well as create a poster presentation to be displayed in the classroom. Obviously, this type of project could be adapted to fit a variety of themes or topics (e.g., hobbies and interests, plans for future careers, what they would do if they inherited a large sum of money), as well as adaptations for a variety of linguistic levels or foci (e.g., specific verb tenses).

As previously discussed, *culture* and language are integrated (see Galloway, 1985; Lafayette & Strasheim, 1981; Seeley, 1993). The unit on French gastronomy can also easily lend itself to the study of culture. To address the first standard of understanding the relationship between the practices and perspectives of the culture, one portion of the unit could include a project that investigates customs of the meal table and how these customs fit into the French culture (e.g., the importance of having the evening meal as a whole family, the importance of saying *bon appétit*, etc.). Students could also explore the different perspectives on nutrition (e.g., prepackaged food, fast food, organic food, etc.). To address the second standard where students are expected to make connections between products (i.e., literature, film, and other products) and the culture, students could locate authentic poetry, music, literature, films, art, or other artifacts that relate to the practices and perspectives of the culture. The project could focus on drawing inferences from the authentic materials as well as the students creating their own products (e.g., their own poems, stories, films) that pertain to the same issues.

In the theoretical background, the language processes were described as being developed interdependently of each other (see Hadley, 2001; Phillips & Draper, 1999). This connection among the processes ties to the third of the ACTFL goals, *connections*. The first connections standard emphasizes the integration of language and content. This gastronomy unit would not only help students develop their skills in the target language and their knowledge of the target culture but would also help reinforce their knowledge of other topics. One particular project that would emphasize this connection would be asking students to research recipes for their assigned region of France (or assigned francophone country). Students could actually prepare the recipes and thus develop their skills in consumer and family sciences (or perhaps team up with students enrolled in a cooking class so that both groups learn from each other). Along with learning about the regional cuisine, students could also begin making connections in geography by learning about the various regions of France or other francophone countries from around the world, the history of these regions and countries as it pertains to gastronomy, and even mathematics by learning how to convert metric measurements and measure dry ingredients by weight rather than by volume. The second connections standard emphasizes the connection between information in the target language and how that information portrays unique viewpoints of the target culture and its language(s). By completing the projects on the various topics proposed above, along with exposure to authentic materials and the final products of these projects, students may begin to make connections between the acquired information and the language and culture studied.

Making *comparisons* is also achieved through project-based instruction and is also strongly tied to second language theories (see Brown, 2002; Lightbown & Spada, 1999). The emphasis of the first standard is on making comparisons between the students' native and second language in order to understand the nature of language. The unit on gastronomy can help address this standard in several ways. First, if students were to complete a project where they compare recipes from their native culture and recipes in the target culture, their task could be to make comparisons about the language used in recipes. Other authentic materials such as poems and songs related to gastronomy could also be used to make such comparisons. These same projects could also be used to help students make comparisons of interaction patterns between one's native and target culture. By engaging the students in a project with interviews as discussed previously (inquiring about one's likes and dislikes with food), the students have opportunities to demonstrate their ability to apply their knowledge of the differences in interaction between their first and second language through the interviews themselves and the written and oral presentations.

Last, *communities* can also be addressed through project-based instruction. It is also important to note that establishing communities encourages meaningful interaction (see Brown, 2002, Lee & VanPatten, 2003; Lightbown & Spada, 1999; Richards & Rodgers, 1986). One emphasis of this aspect of language learning is that in addition to using the language in the classroom, the student must also demonstrate the ability to use the language outside of the classroom. Keeping with the unit on gastronomy, perhaps part of this project might be to contact restaurants in the target culture to conduct an interview. Another part of the project might be to visit a French restaurant in the community and use the target language to communicate in the restaurant (with the assumption that there are people in the restaurant who speak French), and then perhaps write a critique of the meal following examples of critiques from the *Michelin Guide*. The project on gastronomy could also be taken further to address the second standard, which focuses on using the language for personal enjoyment and enrichment. The nature of project-based instruction, especially when implemented in a very student-centered manner, would help to meet this standard. Giving students autonomy in selecting topics and determining how to complete a project would also encourage enjoyment. Designing a unit around a theme that interests students also promotes personal enjoyment, especially when tasks make connections to students' personal ideas, opinions, and interests.

As previously noted, the TESOL standards are organized differently than the ACTFL standards (see Tables 1 and 2); however, because both sets of standards on based on similar principles of language learning, there is significant overlap between the two.

The first goal, *to use English to communicate in social settings*, is met through project-based instruction in a variety of ways and is also supported by the theories presented earlier (see Finocchiaro & Brumfit, 1983; Richards & Rodgers, 1986; Savignon, 1983). First, project-based instruction commonly requires students to communicate when working on a project in collaboration, and when communication occurs in the target language, this goal is achieved. Projects can also contain components that deliberately require students to communicate, usually on a specific topic. In the case of the gastronomy unit (although perhaps in an English setting, rather than a French setting), and using the interview project, students would be encouraged to interact socially on a subject that involves personal expression and enjoyment (standards 1 and 2) with each other through the interview. If students are asked to write a biography about the interviewee or present the biography to the class, the students would also be encouraged to use learning strategies to develop communicative competence by being engaged in meaningful activities that have a purpose (standard 3).

The second goal, *to use English to achieve academically in all content areas*, is also supported by the theories presented earlier (see Hadley, 2001; Phillips & Draper, 1999). This goal can also be achieved through project-based instruction. As Stoller (see Chapter 2) described, project-based instruction strives to integrate language and content, thus encouraging language learners to use the target language across subject areas. As previously discussed with the ACTFL standards, this gastronomic unit could easily lend itself to integrating language and content, provided the target language is used and the projects implemented focus on various aspects of gastronomy that incorporate other disciplines. What is more, since projects also require the gathering, processing, and reporting of content, students are further able to interact in the classroom (standard 1) with the teacher, group mates, and other classmates. Students are also ultimately expected to develop a final product as part of the project, which would typically involve providing content information either in spoken or written form (or both) (standard 2). With the assistance of a well-planned project, students will learn to use appropriate learning strategies to help them develop and apply academic knowledge (standard 3), once again by being engaged in meaningful activities or tasks.

The third goal, *to use English in socially and culturally appropriate ways*, is also supported by the theories of second language acquisition discussed previously (see Galloway, 1985; Lafayette & Strasheim, 1981; Seeley, 1993). This goal can also be met through the use of projects, especially when completed with certain final products (e.g., oral presentation, written report, etc.). We once again turn to the gastronomy unit and the interview project. By engaging the students in interviews, students are required to use the appropriate language variety, register, and genre to conduct the interview (standard 1). Then if students are asked to write a biography about their interviewee, another register, genre, and language variety might be used (academic language). An oral presentation might once again require a different register, variety, or genre of language. The interview and oral presentation would also require students to use nonverbal communication appropriate to the audience and based on the different styles of communication (standard 2). Once again by engaging the students in meaningful activities, the students will have opportunities to develop appropriate learning strategies for developing sociocultural competence (standard 3).

While this chapter has provided a very specific project that would address each of the ACTFL and TESOL standards, this is merely one example. But as is demonstrated by this one interview project as part of a unit on gastronomy, even one project can address all of the necessary standards in multiple ways.

CONCLUSION

In light of the potential that projects have for helping students meet the standards for language learning, it is important to consider how language teachers can achieve a connection between the standards and PBI. It is important to note that the focus of language instruction should not be on the projects themselves. Instead, projects should help meet the goals and standards that have been set forth by individual teachers, schools, state departments of education, and organizations such as TESOL and ACTFL. As this chapter has demonstrated, project-based instruction can help language teachers achieve important instructional goals such as promoting communication, integrating the study of culture with language, making connections between language and content, making comparisons between the students' first and second languages, and establishing communities both inside and outside the school walls.

It is also important to remember that projects are not a magical fix to instructional difficulties. As this volume has demonstrated, project-based instruction is a significantly beneficial approach to language instruction, but like any other approach (or method), it requires careful planning. The instructor must determine the goals and objectives of the course and decide how projects may help achieve these goals. Then language instructors must continually act as guides, ensuring students are communicating in the target language and working on the tasks at hand, as well as answering questions and helping students be successful learners.

It is also important to note here the challenges that may arise when dealing with projects and the standards. To consider the challenges, we once again turn to the gastronomy unit and the interview project. The ACTFL standards (see Table 14.1) encourage the understanding of various cultures. This unit is very specific and focuses on one particular culture; to develop an understanding of other cultures, several projects that focus on other cultures would be required. In the foreign language setting, it is also challenging to encourage the use of the target language outside of the classroom, and in some settings (e.g., rural middle America) it is virtually impossible. The Internet and other current technology have made access to target languages and cultures more feasible. Another significant challenge pertains to the linguistic level of the students. In the foreign language setting, novice learners have little linguistic knowledge, which makes achieving the goals of the standards more difficult. It is important to remember, however, that the standards are further broken down into appropriate linguistic levels. One final challenge to consider is that the TESOL standards (see Table 14.2) heavily emphasize the use of learning strategies. While projects do not overtly teach students learning strategies, they do provide opportunities for students to engage in the use of strategies. Explicit strategy instruction could be included as a pre-project activity, which is then reinforced with the project.

As this chapter has demonstrated, projects can play an integral part in the development of a sound curriculum. Instruction should be based on pedagogically sound curriculum, grounded in second language acquisition theories and in alignment with state and/or national standards. As the examples presented here and those found in the other chapters of this volume have demonstrated, project-based tasks can achieve these goals.

REFERENCES

American Council on the Teaching of Foreign Languages (ACTFL). (1996). *Standards for foreign language learning: Preparing for the 21st century*. Yonkers, NY:

ACTFL. Retrieved September 1, 2005, from http://www.actfl.org/files/public/execsumm.pdf

Ausubel, D. P., Novak, J. D., & Hanesian, H. (1978). *Educational psychology: A cognitive view* (2nd ed.). New York: Holt, Rinehart, & Winston.

Bamgbose, A. (1998). Torn between the norms: Innovations in world Englishes. *World Englishes, 17*(1), 1–14.

Bialystok, E. (1994). Analysis and control in the development of second language proficiency. *Studies in Second Language Acquisition, 16*(2), 157–168.

Brown, H. D. (2002). English language teaching in the "post-method" era: Toward better diagnosis, treatment, and assessment. In J. C. Richards & W. A. Renandya (Eds.), *Methodology in language teaching: An anthology of current practice* (pp. 9–18). Cambridge, UK: Cambridge University Press.

Carter, R., & McCarthy, M. (1997). *Exploring spoken English*. Cambridge, UK: Cambridge University Press.

Ellis, R. (1985). *Understanding second language acquisition*. Oxford: Oxford University Press.

Fillmore, L. W. (2000). Loss of family languages: Should educators be concerned? *Theory Into Practice, 39,* 203–210.

Finocchiaro, M., & Brumfit, C. (1983). *The functional-notional approach: From theory to practice*. New York: Oxford University Press.

Galloway, V. B. (1985). *A design for the improvement of the teaching of culture in foreign language classrooms*. Yonkers, NY: ACTFL.

Hadley, A. O. (2001). *Teaching language in context* (3rd ed.). Boston: Heinle & Heinle.

Hatch, E. (1992). *Discourse and language education*. Cambridge, UK: Cambridge University Press.

Kachru, B. B. (1985). Standards, codification and sociolinguistic realism in the English language in the outer circle. In R. Quirk & H. G. Widdowson (Eds.), *English in the world: Teaching and learning the language and literatures*. Cambridge, UK: Cambridge University Press.

Krashen, S. (1982). *Principles and practice in second language acquisition*. New York: Pergamon Press.

Lafayette, R. (1988). Integrating the teaching of culture into the foreign language classroom. In A. J. Singerman (Ed.), *Toward a new integration of language and culture* (pp. 47–62). Middlebury, VT: Northeast Conference on the Teaching of Foreign Languages.

Lafayette, R., & Strasheim, L. (1981). Foreign language curricula and materials for the twenty-first century. In *Proceedings of the National Conference on Professional Priorities*. Hastings-on-Hudson, NY: ACTFL.

Lee, J. F., & VanPatten, B. (2003). *Making communicative language teaching happen* (2nd ed.). Boston: McGraw-Hill.

Lightbown, P. M., & Spada, N. (1999). *How languages are learned* (Rev. ed.). Oxford: Oxford University Press.

Lippi-Green, R. (1997). *English with an accent*. London: Routledge.

Long, M. (1983). Does second language instruction make a difference? A review of the research. *TESOL Quarterly, 17,* 359–382.

Miller, P., & Endo, H. (2004). Understanding and meeting the needs of ESL students. *Phi Delta Kappan, 85,* 786–791.

Oliver, R. (1995). Negative feedback in child NS-NNS conversation. *Studies in Second Language Acquisition, 17,* 459–481.

Phillips, J. K., & Draper, J. C. (1999). *The five Cs: The standards for foreign language learning work text.* Boston: Heinle & Heinle.

Pica, T. (1994). Research on negotiation: What does it reveal about second language acquisition? *Language Learning, 44,* 493–527.

Quirk, R. (1985). The English language in a global context. In R. Quirk & H. G. Widdowson (Eds.), *English in the world: Teaching and learning the language and literatures.* Cambridge, UK: Cambridge University Press.

Rajagopalan, K. (2004). The concept of "World English" and its implications for ELT. *ELT Journal, 58*(2), 111–117.

Richards, J. C., & Rodgers, T. S. (1986). *Approaches and methods in language teaching: A description and analysis.* Cambridge, UK: Cambridge University Press.

Rong, X. L., & Preissle, J. (1998). *Educating immigrant students.* Thousand Oaks, CA: Sage.

Savignon, S. J. (1983). *Communicative competence: Theory and classroom practice.* Reading, MA: Addison-Wesley.

Schachter, J. (1974). An error in error analysis. *Language Learning, 24,* 205–214.

Schmidt, R. W. (1990). The role of consciousness in second language learning. *Applied Linguistics, 11*(2), 129–158.

Schmidt, R. W., & Frota, S. N. (1986). Developing basic conversational ability in a second language: A case study of an adult learner of Portuguese. In D. Richard (Ed.), *Talking to learn: Conversation in second language acquisition* (pp. 237–326). Rowley, MA: Newbury House.

Seeley, H. N. (1993). *Teaching culture: Strategies for intercultural communication.* Lincolnwood, IL: National Textbook Company.

Selinker, L. (1972). Interlanguage. *International Review of Applied Linguistics, 10,* 209–231.

Swain, M. (1985). Communicative competence: Some rules of comprehensible input and comprehensible output in its development. In S. Gass & C. Madden (Eds.), *Input in second language acquisition* (pp. 235–253). Rowley, MA: Newbury House.

Teachers of English to Speakers of Other Languages, Inc. (TESOL). (1997a). *ESL standards introduction: Promising future.* Alexandria, VA: TESOL. Retrieved September 1, 2005, from http://www.tesol.org/s_tesol/sec_document.asp?CID=113&DID=310

Teachers of English to Speakers of Other Languages, Inc. (TESOL). (1997b). *ESL standards for Pre-K–12 students.* Alexandria, VA: TESOL. Retrieved September 1, 2005, from http://www.tesol.org/s_tesol/seccss.asp?CID=95&DID=1565

van Lier, L. (1996). *Interaction in the language curriculum: Awareness, autonomy, and authenticity.* New York: Longman.

White, L. (1989). *Universal grammar and second language acquisition.* Amsterdam: John Benjamins.

CHAPTER 15

ASSESSING PROJECTS AS SECOND LANGUAGE AND CONTENT LEARNING

Tammy Slater
University of British Columbia

Gulbahar H. Beckett
University of Cincinnati

Carolyn Aufderhaar
University of Cincinnati

BACKGROUND

Although project-based instruction has been gaining popularity in the field of second language acquisition (SLA) as an approach to teaching language and subject matter content simultaneously (e.g., Beckett, 1999; Beckett, 2002; Kobayashi, 2004; Stoller, 1997), the critical issue of how to assess students' progress meaningfully within this model has remained a challenge. One reason for this may be that participants do not always agree on just what learning should be the focus of assessment during project-based instruction, yet research has suggested that more than language learning

Project-Based Second and Foreign Language Education, pages 241–260
Copyright © 2006 by Information Age Publishing
All rights of reproduction in any form reserved.

takes place through the implementation of projects. Beckett (1999), for example, reported success in teaching not only the English language, but also critical thinking, cooperative work skills, and academic and social culture by Canadian high school English as a second language (ESL) teachers, although many of the students in the project-based classes she investigated focused on their language-learning experiences only. Beckett's study suggested that students and parents often have difficulty seeing progress when project-based approaches are being used (see also Guo, 2001, for similar findings). Kobayashi (2004) documented English language learning through projects carried out in junior and sophomore classes in a Canadian university exchange program, showing that the students in his study also appeared to increase their content understanding and improve their presentation skills. This multiple acquisition raises the question of whether it is adequate to assess only language through these projects, or whether there exists ways to examine the broader integration of language, skills, and content. This chapter examines these issues by looking at the formative assessment of project work by learners and teachers to address the following question: How can teachers assess students' work so that the total curricular goals of project-based instruction—developing language, content, and skills simultaneously—are clear to all involved?

Before we begin to examine the above question, it is important to clarify what we mean by projects and project-based teaching and learning. As pointed out by Beckett (1999) and Stoller (see Chapter 2), project-based learning has been defined differently in the general literature and the SLA literature, ranging from short-term projects such as writing a letter to ones that take several weeks to accomplish. In this chapter, project-based learning is defined as a social practice into which students are socialized through a series of individual or group activities that involve the simultaneous learning of language, content, and skills. Project-based learning as a social practice requires language and content learning through planning, researching (empirical and/or document), analyzing and synthesizing data, and reflecting on the process and product orally and/or in writing by comparing, contrasting, and justifying alternatives (Beckett, 1999). As such, projects require various formative and summative evaluations. Depending on the purpose of the assessment, teachers can evaluate discrete aspects of projects such as the vocabulary and grammar used in a given project report, the progress students made throughout a 14-week research project, the overall achievement of language and subject matter goals in an ESL social studies project, and/or general curricular goals.

Our discussion of the assessment of project-based learning concerns what Hancock (1994) defined as "formative" assessment: "an ongoing process involving the student and teacher in making judgments about the student's progress in language using non-conventional strategies" (p. 2),

Leung and Mohan (2004) offered a useful example of formative assessment in a multiethnic and multicultural elementary school classroom, which we will discuss in more detail later. Reif (1995) stated that the strategies of relearning, synthesizing, and applying—frequently absent in traditional evaluation instruments—should be the goal of any assessment. Higher order thinking, differentiated learning styles, the cooperative process, and real-world application are inherent in activities such as case studies, Web pages, slide shows, revisions of previously done work, brochures, student-generated newsletters, and student-written curricula and tests, which lend themselves to the formative assessment that we are addressing in this chapter.

Like any assessment model, formative assessment is not free of concerns, particularly regarding its reliability (consistency of the measurement) and validity (consistency in the replication of the results). Huerta-Macias (1995) cited triangulation as a means of ensuring reliability. Triangulation in assessment refers to the collection of three or more different perspectives or sources. The perspectives might be those of the teacher, the student, or the student's project group members. The sources might come from examining the variety of tasks that the student carries out during the course of the project.

The notion of validity brings us back to the key question we want to address in this chapter: How can we assess the learning of language, content, and skills in a way that is easy for teachers and transparent for students and their parents? The broad theoretical framework that informs our discussion is systemic functional linguistics (SFL), which sees language and content as being intrinsically related and language learning as expanding one's resources for making meaning in the various contexts one encounters (for a full discussion of SFL, refer to Halliday, 1994). We also bring in Mohan's Knowledge Framework, or KF (Mohan, 1986, 1989, 2001), which is based on this theoretical framework, as a useful model for exploring the assessment of projects as a social practice. Through this lens, we will respond to the above questions and offer practical suggestions for such assessment.

ASSESSING THE DEVELOPMENT OF LANGUAGE AND CONTENT: AN ILLUSTRATION

The following scenario illustrates some of the issues addressed in this chapter. Imagine you are the teacher of a project-based, multilevel ESL class and there are several groups of students working around the room. Each group is composed of three students who are discussing how they should present what they have learned to the class. Two groups catch your interest because they are talking about the same content as follows:

Group 1

> A1: Shall we put "To stop the brain's aging, we can use our bodies and heads"?[1]
> B1: Yes. That sounds good. (Student C makes no comment.)

Group 2

> A2: Shall we put "We can prevent our brains from getting weak by being mentally and physically active"?
> B2: That's a good idea. It's one of our main arguments.
> C2: And if we have it on an overhead, it will help everyone understand our point.

These students are participating in the social practice of planning a presentation about content that they have been studying, and it is obvious that they have good control over the grammatical form needed to construct these short excerpts, although it is difficult to say much about B1 and impossible to assess C1 as this student did not participate in the exchange. From this imaginary data, we cannot tell how Group 1 and Group 2 have developed their language and content knowledge over the course of the project as we would need to compare these examples to earlier discussions. Intuitively, however, we can see that there are differences in language use between these two groups with regards to their ability to construct and participate in the types of academic discourse that the project-based instruction is attempting to develop. Clearly, there is a difference in how Students A1 and A2 construct the "same" knowledge linguistically, but just how can we go about assessing these differences? How can assessment within a project-based course be carried out in a way that reflects the instructional goals of simultaneously acquiring language, content, and skills? We can begin by looking at how we can use the learners' own formative assessment.

MAKING USE OF LEARNERS' FORMATIVE ASSESSMENT

Formative assessment is a process that occurs not only when teachers evaluate progress made by students during particular learning tasks, but also when students assess what they are learning through the assigned tasks. With regards to project-based instruction in SLA, however, research has shown how learners have frequently evaluated the use of projects negatively (see, for example, Beckett, 1999; Eyring, 1989; Moulton & Holmes,

2000). The reasons for student dissatisfaction with project-based instruction in ESL classes are complex, reflecting potentially different philosophical, cultural, and linguistic beliefs held by students and teachers (Beckett, 1999), but a recurring view by these students is that ESL class is for learning language components such as vocabulary, grammar, speaking, and writing, rather than for building skills in such areas as research and cooperative work. Students with this view, therefore, will assess the use of projects negatively as they work through them because they do not agree with the teacher on *what* is to be taught.

To guide the students to understand and assess what they are learning through projects, Beckett and Slater (2005) developed the Project Framework, a tool that shows the students how language, content, and skills development occur simultaneously through the process of carrying out project work. Based on SFL and influenced by Mohan's KF, the Project Framework has two key components: the planning graphic and the project diary. Beckett and Slater revealed how second-year university exchange students, who had until this experience been learning English in a context where language, content, and skills were seen as separate subjects and thus taught separately, found the Project Framework useful in helping them to see the value of doing projects to develop their ability to perform in an English-speaking academic context. They reported in their project diaries what they were learning during their project-based course, and many proudly discussed in interviews that they felt they had learned a considerable amount about their chosen topics as well as the language and skills needed to demonstrate this knowledge. Moreover, the students' views about learning language through project-based learning changed by using the Project Framework as a heuristic to guide them.

If we were to imagine that the students in Group 2 from our project scenario had initially talked about their topic using language such as *bodies* and *heads* and then learned that they could recast these words in sentences as *mentally* and *physically,* these latter terms would have likely appeared at some point in their project diary as new language items. Later, you would have heard the students use these new terms, providing support that they have acquired them. During the student presentation (which these groups are planning), these terms would likely have been used again. The final written project would again show evidence of acquisition. In other words, the students' formative assessment guidelines (the project diary), while indicating to the student what was learned, also provide the teacher with necessary information for his or her assessment.

From a formative assessment perspective, then, the use of the Project Framework allows the students to see the value of project-based instruction by making explicit the various components (content, language, and skills development), thus providing a valuable tool to the students to guide the formative assessment of their own learning of these components. This use, in turn, offers the teachers a perspective other than their own to enhance the reliability of their summative evaluation and therefore helps to make the assessment of the curricular goals of content, language, and skills through projects more transparent for students and parents alike.

FORMATIVE ASSESSMENT OF PROJECTS AS SOCIAL PRACTICES

Earlier, we defined project-based learning as a social practice into which students are socialized through a series of individual or group activities that involve the simultaneous learning of language, content, and skills. In using the term *social practice*, we follow Mohan (2001) with regards to the Knowledge Framework, which is considered to be a "basic starting point for analysis, a heuristic," which is "a view of language as discourse in the context of social practice" (p. 110), thereby connecting social practice to the language that constructs and is constructed by it. According to Mohan, every social practice is a combination of knowledge (theory) and action (practice), meaning that students participating in a social practice are required to *know* something and to *do* something. The theory aspect of a social practice typically includes knowledge structures such as *classification, principles*, and *evaluation*, whereas the practice aspect includes *description, sequence*, and *choice*. These knowledge structures, which are "means of representing...the abstract logical patterns of experience" (Mohan, 1989, p. 104) and can therefore be considered as thinking skills, pattern into three theory/practice sets, as shown in Figure 15.1.

Mohan argued that each knowledge structure has specific language associated with it; thus, the assessment of a knowledge structure (or thinking skill) is an assessment of the language used to construct it. It is also important to note that often a phase of project work will focus naturally on one of the three pairs of knowledge structures in the KF. For example, when the students first gather into small groups to discuss which topic to choose, they will be likely working primarily with the discourse of choice and evaluation, the same knowledge structures that are apparent as they discuss which information should be put on slides for their presentation, as we have captured in our short scenario. When the students discuss their research methodology, they will likely be using sequence discourse along

| Social Practice | Theory | classification | principles | evaluation |
| | Practice | description | sequence | choice |

Figure 15.1.   The Knowledge Framework (Mohan, 1986, 2001)

with principles, in the form of the steps they plan to take and the general rules for conducting research. This pair of knowledge structures will also surface in relevant explanations of how and why, both in the write-up of their project and in the presentation. Classification and description will likely appear as the students work with the organization and definitions of concepts within their topic area. All six knowledge structures appear in the social practice of *knowing* and *doing* projects.

The Knowledge Framework, therefore, is a powerful heuristic for the assessment of project-based learning as a social practice. The KF reinforces the connections between language and content and provides us with an organizational framework for planning integrated assessment tools. Before we can discuss the assessment of different theory/practice sets, however, we need to explain the term *grammatical metaphor*, as this plays a key role in academic language and content development.

GRAMMATICAL METAPHOR: PATHS OF DEVELOPMENT AS ROADS TO ASSESSMENT

The notion of grammatical metaphor is critical when discussing the development of academic, and particularly scientific language (Halliday & Martin, 1993; Slater, 1998). Because of the differences in resources between learners and experts, the meanings that learners construct are often very different in complexity and accuracy than their teacher's, and SFL can help illuminate these differences using discourse analysis. One key concept is the idea of grammatical metaphor, defined as being similar to lexical metaphor, but "instead of being a substitution of one *word* for another ... it is a substitution of one grammatical class, or one grammatical structure, by another" (Halliday & Martin, 1993, p. 79, italics in original). For example, the clause *He persisted*, in which the process of *persisting* is realized as a verb (the typical or congruent pattern), can be changed to the grammatically metaphoric noun phrase *His persistence*, which deviates from the congruent pattern by realizing the process of *persisting* as a noun. If we look again at the imaginary scenario presented earlier, we can see that the sentences uttered by Students A1 and A2 are different with regards to grammatical metaphor. Student A1 uses a congruent construction, "we can use our bodies and heads." As Mohan and Beckett (2001) argued, "being physically and mentally active" is much more grammatically metaphoric, realizing the noun *bodies* as the adverb *physically* and *head* as *mentally*. Concepts of *bodies* and *heads* are much more related to everyday talk than are *physically* and *mentally*, which are grammatically metaphoric terms associated with academic discourse. This is a developmental path that speakers of English as a first language also go through; they do not gain full control of this grammatical metaphor until they are well into high school (see Derewianka,

Relators ⟶ circumstances ⟶ processes ⟶ qualities ⟶ entities
(conjunctions)   (prepositions)   (verbs)   (adjectives)   (nominal groups)

Figure 15.2.   Halliday's general drift of grammatical metaphor

1995; Gibbons, 1998; Halliday & Martin, 1993; Mohan & Slater, 2004). Halliday (1998) described "the 'general drift' of grammatical metaphor" (p. 211) to illustrate how language evolves as it constructs science knowledge. As Figure 15.2 shows, the movement of grammatical metaphor, from the more congruent forms to the more metaphoric ones, progresses from the use of conjunctions toward more metaphoric constructions of circumstances (prepositional phrases), processes (verbs), qualities (adjectives), and entities (nominal groups), or in Halliday's terms, from the clause complex to the clause, to the nominal group, which is considered to be the most metaphoric construction. This move plays an important role in the assessment of academic language and content learning.

ASSESSING KNOWLEDGE STRUCTURES: IMPLICATIONS FOR PROJECTS

Sequence and Principles

Much has been done on the analysis of sequence and principle discourses (e.g., Halliday & Martin, 1993; Mohan & Beckett, 2001; Mohan, Slater, Luo, & Jaipal, 2002; Slater, 2004; Veel, 1997), but we will focus here on work that has implications for assessing the development of language for talking about sequence and principles. Mohan and Beckett (2001) discussed functional recasts made by a teacher as she listened to a presentation in which her ESL students talked about factors that lead to maintaining a healthy brain. The following data excerpt from Mohan and Beckett (2001, pp. 145–146) helps to illustrate this:

1. S: (a) To stop the brain's aging, *we can use our bodies and heads.* (b) Like walking make the circulation of blood better. (c) If we supply nutrition to our brain cells, we can prevent the destroy of the cells. (d) It is said that the more we use our heads, the better our brain get. (e) The painting, knitting clothes, and keeping our diary make use of prevention of our brain.

2. T: [RECAST] So, we can prevent our brain from getting weak *by being mentally and physically active?*

Notice that the knowledge structure being constructed here is that of principles, and in particular, cause-and-effect relationships. The student is attempting to show five different causal relationships in the five sentences she utters, as paraphrased here:

(a) Using our minds and bodies can *cause* our brains to stop aging.
(b) Walking *makes* circulation better.
(c) *If* we supply nutrition to our brain cells, *[then]* we can prevent cell destruction.
(d) *If* we use our brain more, *[then]* it'll become stronger.
(e) Doing things will *make* our brains work longer.

As we can see, the teacher recast the student's initial causal statement (a), proposing a less congruent and more grammatically metaphorical utterance, while maintaining the causal relationship that was core information in this student's presentation. Observations of students learning more grammatically metaphoric ways of constructing sequential and causal language were also made by Kobayashi (2004) in his study of oral academic presentations. Such observations suggest that the language of sequence and principles can play a major role in project work, at least during the presentation stage. The teacher's recasts in Mohan and Beckett's article also show how the teacher is making judgments about—assessing—the students' ability to use this type of discourse as well as helping them develop a more academic way of constructing these relationships.

Slater (2004) examined the developmental path present in the oral causal explanations of ESL and mainstream students at two grade levels as they talked about their learning of science knowledge. She noted that the use of grammatical metaphor by the primary students in her study was low, and that the high school ESL students had more difficulty using metaphoric constructions than did their mainstream peers, supporting the idea that there is a developmental path in the acquisition of these types of linguistic features. This developmental path, proposed initially through an analysis of written science text (see Mohan et al., 2002), provides a useful guide for assessing the academic maturity of language characteristic of sequence and principles knowledge structures.

Mohan and Slater (2004) showed how a functional discourse analysis could be used to show critical differences between two explanations of the water cycle, one a sequential explanation and the other causal. The authors argued that these differences could not be distinguished using assessment rubrics from traditional linguistic approaches. Their analysis demonstrated how the causal text was more linguistically sophisticated than the sequential text while also demonstrating a deeper knowledge of the topic. By highlighting and comparing the types of linguistic features used in both texts, including the use of grammatical metaphor, the authors demonstrated how assessment from an SFL discourse analysis perspective could be reliably carried out on sequence and principles discourse.

Description and Classification

Mohan (2001) revealed the differences in classification texts written by a basic ESL writer and a skilled non-ESL writer. He stated that while both used the same information, their writing differed in the variety of lexical choices and grammatical patterns, with the ESL writer relying on a few devices repetitively, an observation also made by other researchers (e.g., Flowerdew, 1998; Schleppegrell, 1998, 2002). Tong (2004) examined the language features present in Chinese and English classification texts written by 12 ESL students at three points in a time series design. Between the first and second try at writing a classification text, the students were given a model text in Chinese. After the second try at writing, the students were given a 1-hour lesson in Chinese on how to write classification texts. Tong's analysis for looking at the linguistic features of classification texts as suggested by Collerson (1994), Derewianka (1990, 1995), and Halliday (1999) revealed that although the students' texts did not change much with regards to linguistic features between the first try and the second, their classifications showed a shift from a commonsense understanding to a scientific one, showing an increase in scientific content understanding. Between the second and third effort, Tong found a statistically significant difference in both the Chinese and the English texts. The participants had produced more elaborate discourse using more sophisticated and complex grammatical constructions. In other words, teaching students the linguistic features that characterize sophisticated classification texts helped the students construct more complete and complex discourse. For other similar studies, see Huang and Morgan (2003) and Mohan and Huang (2002). Note that there are striking similarities between the language features revealed in Mohan and Slater's (2004) and Slater's (2004) work on causal explanations and work on classification and description texts as described by Huang and Morgan (2003) and Mohan and Huang (2002). Both concern the use of grammatical metaphor, and in particular, the creation of nominal groups. These findings offer a potential for assessment charts that can target these features, as we will show later.

Choice and Evaluation

Little has been done on the SFL discourse analysis of evaluation and choice as it relates to assessment. The exception is Leung and Mohan

(2004), which looked at the evaluation of student participation and language use in two multilingual, multiethnic elementary (grade 4) classrooms. The authors examined the linguistic processes of joint decision making by groups of students as they carried out tasks with and without their teacher's help. The authors' functional discourse analysis, based on Halliday (1994) and Eggins and Slade (1997), focused on revealing examples of *offers* of answers, *reasons* supporting or rejecting the offered answers, and *responses* to the offered answers, whether acceptances or rejections. The goal of the teacher was to guide students to reason out answers through discussion instead of simply guessing and accepting the guess.

Leung and Mohan's findings showed that the groups of students they examined gave few reasons in their discussions, opting instead for offers and responses, thus denying themselves opportunities to develop the thinking skills and language needed to reason successfully within an academic context. Moreover, the authors noted that several students did not participate at all. The teacher, however, attempted to elicit offers, reasons, and responses and provided models for the students.

The findings of the Leung and Mohan study are of great importance to the assessment of project-based learning, where students are often expected to work cooperatively. What are the patterns of language use that appear when students make decisions and discuss their projects, and do these patterns change over the course of the project? What kinds of tasks might teachers incorporate into their project-based classes to help facilitate the development of the deep thinking and language that students need in order to state and support their arguments? Leung and Mohan's work has offered a valuable framework for analyzing choice and evaluation discourse in the context of project-based instruction, as we shall see.

DRAWING RESULTS

The literature presented above offers various ideas for assessing project-based learning. We have offered ways to involve learners in formative assessment that will support teacher assessment of a project, thereby making the overall evaluation more transparent. We have also suggested potential ways to assess particular knowledge structures in pairs, but it is important to keep in mind, however, that the *combination* of knowledge structures comprises a social practice, represented in the heuristic of Mohan's Knowledge Framework. This suggests that when using the KF to assess project-based learning—which is a particular social practice carried out by the students and into which they are becoming socialized—it would be valuable to target each of these knowledge structures to compile a variety of discourse types for assessment (see Celce-Murcia & Olshtain, 2000, for a brief discussion of what research can tell teacher-evaluators). Moreover, if each structure is targeted on at least two occasions over the course of the project, development can be tracked and made evident for students and parents to see.

From the research we have presented, then, we would like to propose ways that can take the formative assessment of project-based learning further. We will begin with Leung and Mohan's work on choice and evaluation. The authors recorded a section of a lesson in which students were given a decision-making task. They transcribed the interactions, then examined the data for offers, reasons, and responses, as described previously. These were quantified and placed in tables to show both how often the students participated and—considering the deeper thinking skills and greater language requirements needed for reasoning—how well they did with regards to their participation.

Although the analysis in Leung and Mohan's article was done by language researchers subsequent to the classroom interactions, the authors proposed that teachers could use decision-making charts as a formative assessment tool in the classroom to see what and how participation is being carried out. The table they presented in the article has been adapted in Figure 15.3 to create a generic model.

Let us look again at our imaginary scenario. We see Student A1 making an offer to which B1 responds with an acceptance. Student C1 does not participate, and there are no reasons proposed. In other words, no deeper thought has gone into Group 1's brief discussion, and only one offer and one response (accept) would be marked in the chart. The students in Group 2, however, have a much richer discussion with regards to language use and participation. Student A2 makes an offer just as A1 had done, but B2 goes beyond a simple response of acceptance; he proposes a reason for accepting. Student C2 also responds and proposes a reason. Even from this short example, we can see that Group 2 has exhibited greater language use, deeper reasoning, and more participation in the discussion than did Group 1 (one offer, two reasons, and two responses). Ongoing tallies of this type can offer evidence of how individual students are participating in

Name	Offers	Reasons	Responses	Totals
Totals				

Figure 15.3.   A scoring rubric for decision-making (based on Leung & Mohan, 2004)

and adding to the group discussions, and how these patterns may be changing over time. They may also reveal strengths and weaknesses of individual students with regard to specific content areas.

There are numerous decision-making tasks that can be assigned in project-based instruction at the high school or college level, and we offer a variety of these in Table 15.1. These tasks follow the general process of designing, carrying out, and presenting the results of research projects on social studies topics such as "The Impact of Illegal Immigration on the California Economy," "Race Relationships in Cincinnati," or "Immigration and ESL Education in British Columbia."

Table 15.1. Tasks for Promoting Decision-Marking in Project-Based Instruction

Tasks to elicit decision-marking discourse from project work groups

- Decide on the project topic and focus.
- Decide what you want to learn about the topic.
- Decide how to keep track of language, content, and skill development using the Project Diary.
- Decide how the project should be carried out (methods and strategies).
- Decide which resources and literature to use (Internet/books/articles).
- Decide what population to survey/interview/observe.
- Decide how many people should be surveyed/interviewed/observed.
- Decide how to locate the people who will be surveyed/interviewed/observed.
- Decide what questions to ask.
- Decide who in the group does what/how to proceed.
- Decide how to make sense of what was researched.
- Decide how to present the findings orally and visually.

A chart that targets knowledge structures and grammatical metaphor (Figure 15.4) can be used to note the language the students are using to talk about what they know or have learned. A self-evaluation form (see Appendix A) targets the same types of knowledge structures; students can use this to document the language they are acquiring as they learn to talk about their topics. The teacher can then compare the self-evaluation forms to what they are noting in Figure 15.4.

The focus in the use of these scoring charts is on how the students construct causal and taxonomic relationships among the concepts they have for the topic they are studying. Content knowledge involves more than simply the concepts the students have within a topic; it includes the relationships among these concepts. Concept maps (see Novak, 1998) are useful

	Students appear to have a variety of ways to construct relations, offering elaborations and examples where necessary or with little prompting. Consistent effort at using grammatical metaphor, usually successfully.	Students are attempting more complex elaborations and grammatical metaphor, but often require help when attempting these. Ways of meaning, while not always correct, show some variety and indication of expanding linguistic resources.	Students show fairly simplistic ways of talking about what they know. Limited use of grammatical metaphor. Turns may be short and a lot of prompting is needed to elicit more elaborate responses.	Students appear to need a lot of scaffolding. The relations are constructed using limited, somewhat repetitive language features with obvious problems using grammatical metaphor.
Definitions				
Classifications				
Sequences				
Causes and effects				
Justifications				
	Many	**Several**	**Some**	**Few**
Technical terms				
	Definition language	**Classification language**	**Sequence language**	**Causal language**
Examples of language variation	Be, means, refers to	Is a kind of, Is a type of Is divided into, There are X types of … Are classified into.	First, second, then, initially, finally, is followed by, in the beginning	Because (of), so, if, hence, consequently, make, cause, lead to, produce, generate

Figure 15.4.   Evaluating language as it constructs content

graphic illustrations of both the concepts and the relationships and can therefore easily show what the students know. We recommend learning how to construct these from interviews as two maps drawn over time can offer evidence of learning. In fact, the use of a variety of resources in constructing the relationships can determine the difference between deep and shallow understandings of the content as well as between expert and novice speakers or writers. Note that Figure 15.4 offers examples of language variation within four of the knowledge structures, although the list is by no means exhaustive.

Teachers can use Figure 15.4 by simply checking the appropriate box as they elicit examples of the various knowledge structures, but it would be more valuable to note the variety (types and tokens) of the language features used within each knowledge structure. In other words, teachers should note the types of conjunctions the student is using to construct classifications or causal relationships as well as the types of prepositions, verbs, and nominal groups. Are there a wide variety of these features? Or is the student relying heavily on particular forms or knowledge structures? This is important in that good classification discourse includes more than the classification of terms; it defines and describes these terms as well, as our literature review suggested. Similarly, causal language includes both cause-and-effect relationships as well as features of sequence. Note that contrary to other scoring rubrics for project-based instruction (e.g., Luongo-Orlando, 2001), Figure 15.4 and Appendix A highlight the different knowledge structures being attempted, thereby making connections between the knowledge of the topic and the language used to construct that knowledge.

Halliday (1998) argued that learning science involves two types of patterning: creating new technical taxonomies and relating the participants (concepts) in these taxonomies. These two types appear in all academic texts that aim to classify and explain. With regards to constructing taxonomic texts, Tong (2004) and Huang and Morgan (2003) offered two related lists of language features and suggested that as classification texts become more elaborate and sophisticated, the numbers of each feature apparent in the discourse increase. Figure 15.5 combines information from these two articles and offers a list of features that teachers can look for as they read their students' classification texts.

Generic reference
- Nouns/noun phrases which create nodes in the classification tree
- Noun phrases that define generalized participants
- Examples given to exemplify generalized participants

Transitivity
- Linking verbs (relational processes): Linking the subject to its larger group
- Linking verbs (relational processes): Linking the subject to its characteristics (attributes)
- Linking verbs (relational processes): Linking the subject to its parts/components (possessives)
- Existential processes: Stating what exists
- Action verbs (material processes): Describing behavior

Conjunctions (additive)
Lexis
- Verbs/verb phrases (e.g., *are, are classified as*)
- Nouns/noun phrases (e.g., *kind, class, group*)
Nominal groups: Expansion of the head noun by use of pre- and post-modification

---

Figure 15.5.   The key language features of classification

Time
- Sequences of events.
- Time markers (e.g., *then, until, subsequently*)
- Dependent clauses of time (e.g., *when X, then Y; as X happens, Y happens*)
- Time as process (e.g., *begins, finishes*)
- Time as participant (e.g., *the start, the finish, the end*)

Cause
- Actions of one thing on another
- Causal conjunctions (e.g., *thus, consequently*)
- Dependent clauses of cause (e.g., *if X, then Y; X in order to Y*)
- Cause/means as circumstance (e.g., *through X; by X*)
- Cause as process (e.g., *produce, cause, bring about*)
- Cause as participant (e.g., *the cause, the effect, the result*)
- Causal metaphor

Figure 15.6.   The key language features of explanation

To explore how students are constructing causal meanings in academic projects, teachers can analyze their explanations to find examples of how concepts are being related to each other using the language features presented in Figure 15.6. Notice how the construction of cause involves features of sequence as well as principles, as we suggested earlier. Explanations that are more highly valued academically are those that go beyond sequence to exhibit features of cause. As with Figure 15.5, teachers can use Figure 15.6 on multiple occasions to show progress. The use of both Figure 15.5 and Figure 15.6, based on Halliday's argument, allows for a detailed analysis of students' explanations of their topics, and the use of these figures over time can help show the development of their language and content over the course of the projects.

CONCLUSION

It was the aim of this chapter to introduce a new way of thinking about the assessment of project-based instruction. Space limitations prevent us from providing all the tools needed to help the reader become an expert functional discourse analyst, but we hope this chapter offers a useful starting point. By synthesizing existing literature on the assessment of individual knowledge structures, we have shown how we can assess the social practice of doing a project. Moreover, by focusing on the linguistic features of knowledge structures, assessment can reveal connections among language, content, and thinking skills. This discussion should be continued theoretically, empirically, and pedagogically.

We invite theorists to extend our ideas regarding the potential of SFL for constructing assessment models appropriate for the simultaneous learning of language, content, and skills through project-based learning. We encourage test makers and curriculum designers as well as teachers to incorporate these ideas in their work. Test designers need to understand that assessing social practices such as project-based learning is a complex undertaking that cannot be accomplished through traditional multiple-choice instruments for vocabulary and reading comprehension. Project work needs to be evaluated holistically through sound research-based assessment models like the one we have proposed in this chapter. The model should be made appropriate for age and context as well as transparent for teachers, students, and parents.

We urge researchers and teachers to field-test the assessment model we have proposed in various contexts and make suggestions for improvement. For example, research should be conducted to investigate at what level (e.g., secondary- or university-level ESL classes) and in what contexts (e.g., ESL social studies, ESL science) this model works best and why. Researchers in foreign language education may also explore how the proposed model may be applied to the assessment of language, content, and skills learning in their area. Action research should also be conducted to identify the training that teachers need to implement assessment models like the one we have introduced in this chapter. With continued research on and dialogue about this focus-on-meaning approach to evaluation, we can meet the challenge of holistically and transparently assessing the social practice of project-based language learning.

NOTE

1. The sentences about the brain uttered by A1 and A2 in this imaginary scenario are from Mohan and Beckett (2001, p. 145).

REFERENCES

Beckett, G. H. (1999). *Project-based instruction in a Canadian secondary school's ESL classes: Goals and evaluations.* Unpublished doctoral dissertation, University of British Columbia, Vancouver.

Beckett, G. H. (2002). Teacher and student evaluations of project-based instruction. *TESL Canada Journal, 19*(2), 52–66.

Beckett, G. H., & Slater, T. (2005). The Project Framework: A tool for language, content, and skills integration. *ELT Journal, 59*(2), 108–116.

Celce-Murcia, M., & Olshtain, E. (2000). *Discourse and context in language teaching: A guide for language teachers.* Cambridge, UK: Cambridge University Press.

Collerson, J. (1994). *English grammar: A functional approach*. Newtown, Australia: Primary English Teaching Association.

Derewianka, B. (1990). *Exploring how texts work*. Newtown, Australia: Primary English Teaching Association.

Derewianka, B. (1995). *Language development in the transition from childhood to adolescence: The role of grammatical metaphor*. Unpublished doctoral dissertation, Macquarie University, Australia.

Eggins, S., & Slade, D. (1997). *Analysing casual conversation*. London: Cassell.

Eyring, J. L. (1989). *Teacher experience and student responses in ESL project work instruction: A case study*. Unpublished doctoral dissertation, University of California, Los Angeles.

Flowerdew, L. (1998). Integrating "expert" and "interlanguage" computer corpora findings on causality: Discoveries for teachers and students. *English for Specific Purposes, 17*(4), 329–345.

Gibbons, P. (1998). Classroom talk and the learning of new registers in a second language. *Language and Education, 12*(2), 99–118.

Guo, Y. (2001). Chinese parents and ESL teachers: Understanding and negotiating their differences. Unpublished doctoral dissertation, University of British Columbia, Vancouver.

Halliday, M. A. K. (1994). *An introduction to functional grammar* (2nd ed.). London: Edward Arnold.

Halliday, M. A. K. (1998). Things and relations: Regrammaticising experience as technical knowledge. In J. R. Martin & R.Veel (Eds.), *Reading science: Critical and functional perspectives on discourses of science* (pp. 185–235). New York: Routledge.

Halliday, M. A. K. (1999). The notion of "context" in language education. In M. Ghadessy (Ed.), *Text and context in functional linguistics* (pp. 1–24). Philadelphia: Benjamins.

Halliday, M. A. K., & Martin, J. (1993). *Writing science: Literacy and discursive power*. Pittsburgh: University of Pittsburgh Press.

Hancock, C. R. (1994). Alternative assessment and second language study: What and why? *ERIC Digest* (ED D00 036).

Huang, J., & Morgan, G. (2003). A functional approach to evaluating content knowledge and language development in ESL students' science classification texts. *International Journal of Applied Linguistics, 13*(2), 234–262.

Huerta-Macias, A. (1995). Alternative assessment: Responses to commonly asked questions. *TESOL Journal, 5*(1), 8–11.

Kobayashi, M. (2004). *A sociocultural study of second language tasks: Activity, agency, and language socialization*. Unpublished doctoral dissertation, University of British Columbia, Vancouver.

Leung, C., & Mohan, B. (2004). Teacher formative assessment and talk in classroom contexts: Assessment as discourse and assessment of discourse. *Language Testing, 21*(3), 335–359.

Luongo-Orlando, K. (2001). *A project approach to language learning: Linking literary genres and themes in elementary classrooms*. Markham, ON: Pembroke.

Mohan, B. A. (1986). *Language and content*. Reading, MA: Addison-Wesley.

Mohan, B. A. (1989). Knowledge structures and academic discourse. *Word*, *40*(1–2), 99–115.

Mohan, B. (2001). The second language as a medium of learning. In B. Mohan, C. Leung, & C. Davison (Eds.), *English as a second language in the mainstream* (pp.107–126). London: Pearson.

Mohan, B., & Beckett, G. (2001). A functional approach to research on content-based language learning: Recasts in causal explanations. *Canadian Modern Language Review, 58*(1), 133–155.

Mohan, B., & Huang, J. (2002). Assessing the integration of language and content in a Mandarin as a foreign language classroom. *Linguistics and Education, 13*(3), 407–435.

Mohan, B., & Slater, T. (2004). The evaluation of causal discourse and language as a resource for meaning. In J. Foley (Ed.), *Functional perspectives on education and discourse* (pp. 255–269). London: Continuum.

Mohan, B., Slater, T., Luo, L., & Jaipal, K. (2002, July). *Developmental lexicogrammar of causal explanations in science.* Paper presented at the International Systemic Functional Linguistics Congress (ISFC29), Liverpool, UK.

Moulton, M. R., & Holmes, V. L. (2000). An ESL capstone course: Integrating research tools, techniques, and technology. *TESOL Journal, 9* (2), 23–29.

Novak, J. D. (1998). *Learning, creating, and using knowledge: Concept maps as facilitative tools in schools and corporations.* Mahwah, NJ: Erlbaum.

Reif, M. (1995). Alternative assessment for adult learners. *Adult Learning*, 6(3), 12–14.

Schleppegrell, M. J. (1998). Grammar as resource: Writing a description. *Research in the Teaching of English, 32*(2), 182–211.

Schleppegrell, M. J. (2002). Challenges of the science register for ESL students: Errors and meaning-making. In M. J. Schleppegrell & M. C. Columbi (Eds.), *Developing advanced literacy in first and second languages* (pp. 119–142). Mahwah, NJ: Erlbaum.

Slater, T. J. A. (1998). *Evaluating causal discourse in academic writing.* Unpublished master's thesis, University of British Columbia, Vancouver.

Slater, T. J. A. (2004). *The discourse of causal explanations in school science.* Unpublished doctoral dissertation, University of British Columbia, Vancouver.

Stoller, F. L. (1997). Project work: A means to promote language and content. *English Teaching Forum, 35*(4), 2–9, 37.

Tong, E. K. (2004). *Science register across Chinese and English: The relation between learners' language production of scientific classification discourse in Chinese and English.* Unpublished master's thesis, University of British Columbia, Vancouver.

Veel, R. (1997). Learning how to mean—scientifically speaking: Apprenticeship into scientific discourse in the secondary school. In F. Christie & J. R. Martin (Eds.), *Genre and institutions: Social processes in the workplace and school* (pp. 161–195). London: Continuum.

APPENDIX A
Student Self-Evaluation Checklist

	Yes	Kind of	No	Examples
I learned about my topic.				
I learned new words and concepts related to my topic.				
I can define the key terms related to my topic.				
I can use my key terms in many forms (word taxonomies).				
I learned new ways of classifying things.				
I learned new ways of sequencing events.				
I learned new ways of talking about causes and effects.				
I can provide examples to support my argument and conclusions.				
I learned new ways to show my ideas through graphics.				
My ability to carry out a research project has improved.				
I increased my overall ability to interact with people about my topic.				

PART III

FUTURE DIRECTIONS

CHAPTER 16

LINKING INTERPRETIVE RESEARCH AND FUNCTIONAL LINGUISTICS

From Learning Projects to Teaching Projects

Bernard Mohan and Grace I-chia Lee
University of British Columbia

Central themes of Project-Based Learning (PBL) research that underlie many of the chapters of this book are: the learner as active agent; the learner as reflective inquirer; interpretive approaches to research; and a holistic view of language and discourse that relates them to their context of meaning and culture. How do these themes link together? We believe that answers can be found if we view PBL as a process of learning social practices and of acting and reflecting on them. We will examine these themes and their links through a case study of a graduate course for teacher researchers and of the experience of a graduate student taking this course. At a more general level, moving beyond the case study, we will describe a model that makes a bridge between functional linguistics and interpretive research. We will argue that by linking interpretive research with functional linguistics we can offer a more unified approach to PBL that offers linguistic tools that can provide significant insights and can foster action and inquiry that is more situated and agentive. We believe that this unified

Project-Based Second and Foreign Language Education, pages 263–280
Copyright © 2006 by Information Age Publishing
263

approach is specially important in PBL work because learners often need to become more conscious of the value of the content and language of their projects.

It is important to relate our work to the tradition of John Dewey. Our exploration of these themes will draw upon a number of interconnected strands from Dewey's thought that have continued to be influential. PBL is based on the problem method of teaching (see Beckett in Chapter 1), and the problem method is closely connected with Dewey's theory of reflection or 'inquiry' (see Tiles, 1988, p. 104ff.), which models reflective experience as a problem-solving cycle of reflection and action applied to the situation of the inquirer. Dewey's concept of inquiry embodies his view of the knower as a reflective agent rather than mere spectator. The cycle of reflection and action also embodies Dewey's concern to relate theory and practice rather than to treat them in isolation from each other. This concern underlies Dewey's respect for informal learning and his stress on "the importance of keeping a proper balance between the informal and the formal, the incidental and the intentional, modes of education" (Dewey, 1916, p. 9) in order to avoid the danger that the subject matter of the schools will be isolated from life experience and everyday practices. Finally, Dewey's view of language was based on how language functions in a context of shared human activity or social practice (Dewey, 1916, pp. 15–16; Tiles, 1988, pp. 98–103).

CASE STUDY: FROM LEARNING PROJECTS
TO TEACHING PROJECTS

Bernard Mohan was the instructor of a graduate course entitled "Research in Language Curriculum: Social Practice Perspectives." Part of this case study will describe his understanding of the course. The course is for researchers and teachers who are interested in both language as a medium of learning and teaching and language as a focus of learning and teaching. ("Language curriculum" is understood broadly to mean both language as a medium of learning and language as a focus of learning: learning language, learning through language, learning about language). It is a research course, not a teaching methodology course. The course explores the idea of social practices (or human activities), action and reflection discourse and relevant theory of discourse and social context based on Systemic Functional Linguistics, using the methodology of discourse analysis. It emphasises student analysis of discourse data along with student participation. Many of the students are teachers of English as a Second Language working towards a graduate degree.

Grace was a graduate student who took this course. She is an English teacher from Taiwan, and Mandarin is her first language. Part of this case study will narrate her experience with the course, starting from her reflection on her informal learning project and ending with a description of her term paper project. It will describe how she developed insights about her informal learning and then applied them to her usual patterns of teaching. It will describe how she used the model of social practice and the discourse analysis associated with it to make a connection between her informal learning and her formal teaching.

The course begins with a discussion of social practice. This is followed by an exercise where students describe one of their recent informal learning projects, identifying the social practice being learned. Next are a series of structured exercises with discourse analysis where students play a card game as an example of a social practice and analyse their game discourse accordingly. For the term paper for the course, they were encouraged to create an inquiry relevant to social practice, collect a sample of discourse as data, and use discourse analysis to discuss useful understandings of social practice. They could put greater emphasis on research issues or on curriculum questions, as they wished.

At the beginning of the course, the instructor discussed the notion of social practices with the students. It was mentioned that education can be defined in social terms as the initiation of learners into a culture, but that because "culture" is a very broad and general idea, it is often more helpful to think of culture in terms of social practices or activities, and education as the initiation of learners into the social practices or activities of society. Traditionally, each new generation has had to learn to take over the practices of adults. Future artisans had to learn their craft, and future priests had to learn their role. The students were introduced to a basic model of a social practice as including theory (i.e., knowledge) and practice (i.e., action). The discourse of theory was called reflection discourse and the discourse of practice was called action discourse. When people talk to get things done in a social practice, they engage in the discourse of action, and when they talk to reflect on a social practice they engage in the discourse of reflection.

The first exercise asked the student to choose a social practice she/he had learned independently and informally and to describe how she/he had learned it. We discussed the simple example of informally learning to type, and we noted how a social practice was a larger unit of analysis than the text or discourse, which was a typical unit of analysis in language education. Two main aims of the exercise were to introduce the students to the analysis of social practices (sometimes termed "activities") and to help them reflect on their experiences with informal learning as opposed to learning in school. In preparation, students read about adult learning projects and about teachers as action researchers. We will now discuss the background to these themes.

INFORMAL ADULT LEARNING PROJECTS

There is evidence that many adults have extensive but largely hidden experience with informal learning projects. (This is true for younger learners also, but we are not aware of any studies which measure how frequently they engage in projects.) This has major implications for PBL research and education: if learners have extensive experience with informal projects, they should be able to build on it to achieve successful formal project work in schooling. However, this will often require that learners be helped to reflect on and appreciate the informal experience they have.

In a landmark study, Tough (1971) described and researched the informal learning projects that adults engage in. Tough defined a learning project as a "sustained, highly deliberate effort to learn." Tough (1978) summarized a wide range of studies in the 1970s: "The typical learner conducts five quite distinct learning projects in one year. He or she learns five distinct areas of knowledge and skill. The person spends an average of 100 hours per learning effort—a total of 500 hours per year" (p. 252). In a more recent review of research on adults' informal learning, Livingstone (2001) speaks of "the still largely hidden informal dimensions of the iceberg of adult learning" and comments that "the empirical research to date has at least established that adults' intentional informal learning activities are both very extensive and warrant continuing documentation and assessment" (p. 22). An extensive body of relevant research is available at New Approaches to Lifelong Learning (NALL), a research network coordinated by Livingstone at http://www.nall.ca/.

Livingstone defines (ibid) self-directed learning versus formal schooling on two graded dimensions, one ranging from where there is dominant learner control to where there is dominant teacher control, and the other ranging from where learners learn from learning situations which are more incidental and spontaneous to situations where the learners learn from a curriculum taken from a pre-established body of knowledge. Clearly, some PBL, like informal learning projects, is closer to self-directed learning in this sense, and some PBL, like projects conducted in educational institutions, is closer to formal schooling. Livingstone also notes (ibid) two different knowledge traditions in the study of adult informal learning, a cognitive knowledge tradition "which emphasizes recordable theories and articulated descriptions" and a practical knowledge tradition which stresses "direct experience in various situated spheres" (p. 3). We will draw attention to the practical knowledge tradition when we discuss Charles Taylor's ideas below.

ACTION RESEARCH

How can learners be helped to become aware of the experience they have of informal learning projects and to reflect on what they have done in these projects? One way is for them to see themselves as action researchers, studying and analysing their own learning. Action research can provide a frame of reference for reflective learners that is consistent with the Dewey tradition. We have seen in previous chapters that second language learners can be reluctant to engage in project work in educational institutions because they do not recognise the value of their projects for language development, a reluctance that may be related to their prior experiences with language education that overemphasise formal memorisation of language items. Yet learners can be helped to recognise this value by analysing the discourse and language they use in their projects (Beckett & Slater 2005). In effect, teachers need to help learners inquire into their own learning by engaging in action research on projects. More broadly, this suggests that future developments in PBL should study learners as reflexive inquirers more intensively.

The students in the course read sections from Altrichter, Posch, and Somekh (1993) who use this definition of action research "the study of a social situation with a view to improving the quality of action within it" (p. 6). Their list of features which distinguish action research includes:

- Action research is carried out by people directly concerned with the social situation that is being researched.
- Action research starts from practical questions arising from everyday educational work...It aims to develop both the practical situation and knowledge about the practice of the participants.
- Action research "is characterised by a continuing effort to closely interlink, relate and confront action and reflection, to reflect on one's conscious and unconscious doings in order to develop one's actions, and to act reflectively in order to develop one's knowledge. Both sides will gain thereby: reflection opens up new options for action and is examined by being realised in action" (p. 6).

Thus students researching projects can be action researchers studying their social practices with a view to improving their action and knowledge (or practice and theory). Action research offers a frame to guide their reflections.

NARRATIVE OF AN INFORMAL LEARNING PROJECT

Here is Grace's narrative that reflects on her informal learning project:

Exercise A: Learning to Take the Bus in Vancouver

> I moved to Vancouver three weeks ago. Since I don't have a BC driver's
> license, the only way for me to move around the city is taking bus rides. How-
> ever, my first try was a disaster. I received some general oral instruction from
> my landlady, hopped on the bus, but ended up being carried away to a wrong
> destination. As a result, I decided to get online studying the Great Vancouver
> Translink website carefully. Then I realized why I made the blunder—Bus 49
> ships students to UBC only during peak hours. In addition to that, the two lit-
> tle signs of a bike and a wheelchair on the website made sense to me, because
> on the first ride I had seen people transport their bikes, and those who move
> by wheelchair can travel with ease at courtesy seats. Therefore, I started to
> observe how people fixed their bikes on the rack so that I could take my bike
> with me to UBC campus. Of course I still make mistakes from time to time.
> For example, once a bus driver yelled at me simply because I stood at the
> rear door, not knowing I should push the bar on it to get off. That negative
> experience urged me to stay alert as soon as I got on board, and I would
> inquire of other passengers as long as something looked strange to me. After
> practicing for a couple of weeks, I acquired all the "bus taking techniques"
> here, and I now could finally sit back and enjoy every ride. It was a valuable
> process for me to go through because I hadn't learned anything with such a
> keen spirit ever since I left campus. Not only have I got to survive better in
> Vancouver, but also I have improved my problem-solving competence
> through reflection and action. It's certainly worth it.

We have noted that the class had been introduced to the concept of a
social practice as a combination of knowing and doing (or theory and practice), and were asked to view their project as learning a social practice.
Although it was unfamiliar at first, Grace found that she could do this. In
her learning diary she wrote "I never viewed taking the bus as learning a
social practice before. *I am surprised to learn there is this difference between
'knowing' and 'doing.'* I never looked at a learning process in such pattern
(theory/practice), although they are always there." As a social practice, taking the bus is obviously a matter of doing, but it also requires a background
of knowledge and assumptions, and she had to acquire some local knowledge to use the bus system. Transitivity analysis of her narrative shows
doing and knowing in this social practice quite clearly. There are processes
of doing: "[I] *hopped* on the bus but ended up being carried away to a
wrong destination." And there are mental processes related to knowing:

"Then I *realized* why I made the blunder—Bus 49 ships students to UBC only during peak hours."

In the week following the first exercise, the class discussed the relation of the social practice concept to culture and ethnography and Grace found the discussion provided helpful insights. She wrote in her learning diary:

> It is very true that within each social context we are placed there is a particular norm or frame that nurtures our knowledge systems and governs our behavior. To be socialized into that culture, one needs to learn about the cultural knowledge, cultural artifacts and develop cultural behaviour.

In effect, Grace now saw a social practice as a semantic unit of culture, with 'doing' related to cultural action and agency and with 'knowing' related to cultural knowledge and consciousness. Her reflection illustrates the characteristics of an informal adult learning project and shows how she is a very active learner with strong *agency*. It clearly talks about a sustained, highly deliberate effort to learn. It is a learning process where the learner is in control and it is a learning situation which is rather incidental and spontaneous, though it is based on an organised and pre-established body of knowledge. There was a strong element of practical knowledge involving direct experience in a situated sphere, but this did not exclude cognitive knowledge of articulated descriptions, and Grace was careful to note that she learned both from "making inquiries, observations and mistakes" and "from surfing the Greater Vancouver translink website."

Grace's reflection also illustrates her work as an action researcher, and shows how she has developed her *consciousness* of her informal learning. She has studied a situation that she is directly concerned with. The nature of her own informal learning is a practical question with implications for her everyday educational work. She is reflecting on her actions, and she will act on her reflections, as we will see later.

Many in the class found it initially difficult to recall their own learning projects. Nevertheless, everyone was eventually able to write about a project of their own and share it with the class. Grace writes: "I could have taken it for granted if we were not asked to view it as an 'adult learning project.'" This suggests that learning as an engaged agent is so much part of everyday living that learners have difficulty even recognizing it, never mind reflecting on its special qualities. Drawing on the adult learning project research and on action research provides general lenses to bring it into view, but much more is required to address more adequately the nature of engaged learning.

TAYLOR, SOCIAL PRACTICE,
AND INTERPRETIVE RESEARCH

The deeper significance of Grace's reflection cannot be fully appreciated until we have a clearer view of the relations between social practice and interpretive research. Charles Taylor is an influential philosopher whose views address these relations. Across its rich variety of approaches, interpretive research (by contrast with positivism) is an attempt to understand and explain human social world in its cultural and historical context. "The interpretivist approach looks for culturally derived and historically situated interpretations of the social life world" (Crotty, 1998, pp. 66–67). A central characteristic of interpretative research is the inclusion of the interpretations, reflections or "perspectives of the participants and their diversity" (Flick, 1998, p. 5). Another characteristic is reflexivity, most obviously the self-reflection of the researcher upon her/his activities in the research process. Grace's reflection can be seen in the broad tradition of interpretive research.

A rich view of an approach to interpretive research is provided by Taylor in his critique of the social sciences and his defence of interpretive phenomenology for the social sciences. For Taylor, a social practice includes action and reflection. It provides a context that can mutually relate social action and social interpretation. For example, an act such as raising the hand can be interpreted as a vote within the social practice of voting. A social practice is a locus of shared activity and ideas, where ideas include moral ideals and values:

> The kinds of ideas I'm interested in here—moral ideals, understandings of the human predicament, concepts of the self—for the most part exist in our lives through being embedded in practices. By "practice" I mean something extremely vague and general: more or less any stable configuration of shared activity, whose shape is defined by a certain pattern of dos and don'ts, can be a practice for my purposes. The way we discipline our children, greet each other in the street, determine group decisions through voting in elections, and exchange things through markets are all practices. And there are practices at all levels of human social life... The basic relation is that ideas articulate practices as patterns of dos and don'ts. That is, the ideas frequently arise from attempts to formulate and bring to some conscious expression the underlying rationale of the patterns. (Taylor, 1989, p. 204)

Taylor sees language resources as embedded in larger contexts of social practice, which could not exist without these linguistic resources to both reflect and shape them (see Abbey, 2000, p. 192). In sum, social practices are the context and background of human action and reflection.

With respect to the importance of human action, Taylor draws on the thinking of Heidegger, then later Wittgenstein and Merleau-Ponty. Taylor points to the inadequacy of disengaged and abstract concepts of instrumental reason to define the totality of our lives as agents:

> We note that the ideal of disengaged reason must be considered precisely as an ideal and not as a picture of human agency as it really is. We are embodied agents, living in dialogical conditions, inhabiting time in a specifically human way, that is making sense of our lives as a story that connects from the past from which we have come to our future projects. (Taylor, 1991, pp. 105–106)

Taylor says that human knowing flows from our engaged embodied agency in the world as purposeful beings located in physical and moral space trying to find out what is worth doing and that human knowing depends on a tacit background of the assumptions and abilities that underlie social practices. This everyday being in the world is a precondition of disengaged abstract reason (see Abbey, 2000, p. 155ff.). Taylor's agentive view of knowing has major implications for education, since views of learning and teaching depend on views of knowing.

Basic as it is, Grace's narrative has many of the features of Taylor's view of the agent: Grace appears as fundamentally an engaged, embodied, purposeful agent trying to cope in the world as she sets out to achieve her goals. She dialogues with her landlady, a bus-driver, and other passengers. As she tries to travel to university and to learn about the bus system, she literally exemplifies how agents try "to make their way around and make sense of their world" and how "the embodied self's orientation in space is directly related to its ability to cope in the world around it" (Abbey, 2000, p. 186). Her agency appears clearly at the outset in "I moved" and all the other first person action verbs in the text. (We will comment on the linguistic analysis of agency later in this chapter). In "...the only way for me to move around the city," agency ("me to move"), purpose ("for me to move") and orientation ("around the city") appear together. Her coping (and decision-making/problem solving) comes to the fore when, after her disastrous first try, she decides to learn more about her world: "As a result, I decided to get online studying the Great Vancouver Translink website carefully."

With respect to reflection, Taylor believes that articulating the tacit knowing embedded in practices is important personally because it can deepen self-knowledge and heighten awareness of the complexity of the understandings: "human beings are self-interpreting animals; our understandings of ourselves play a crucial ...role in shaping who we are and what we do" (Abbey, 2000, p. 40). This needs to be understood in the complex context of Taylor's magisterial work on the development of the modern self (Taylor, 1989). Articulation is also important interpersonally and publicly in communication with others interested in the practice, for this sharing can provide a practice with recognition of its value and a more adequate public language. One strand of the tacit knowing which is particularly desirable to articulate are the moral ideals, or "visions of the good" embedded in practices.

In the last two sentences of her narrative, which form a brief epilogue, Grace articulates the good she sees in her learning project experience. "It was a valuable process for me to go through because I hadn't learned anything with such a keen spirit ever since I left campus. Not only have I got to survive better in Vancouver, but also I have improved my problem-solving competence through reflection and action. It's certainly worth it." Her values of survival and resourcefulness as they relate to notions of good in the social practice appear where she uses the language of appraisal (see Martin & Rose, 2003, p. 22ff.): "a *valuable* process," "such a *keen* spirit," "I got to survive *better*," "*improved* my problem-solving *competence*," "*worth* it." In her Learning diary, Grace also comments on her values: "In recalling and analyzing the experience of learning to take a bus in Vancouver, I got a strong sense of achievement." This sense of strong achievement and agency was shared by other members of the class who contrasted their strong agency in their informal learning projects to the weak agency of learners in classrooms where they noted that students waited for the teacher to take the lead. Some felt that projects reminded them of all the active learning things they did *naturally* (their emphasis) outside the classroom that they could apply to learning inside the classroom. In a similar vein Grace wrote: "I am very excited because somehow I know if I grow to be more aware of which level a learner dwells on, it will make their learning more efficient and effective."

Benner (1994) provides a striking illustration of a study that follows Taylor's lead and articulates the good embedded in practices. She examines the knowledge embedded in the clinical and caring practices of nursing and the experiences of suffering and comfort central to that practice. She relates how in recent history domestic caring practices have been extended to public institutions, but have been marginalised because modern commodified health care highly values only what can be made into scientific and technical procedures that fit with concepts of instrumental reason. She therefore examines the notions of good embedded in caring practices. Analysing narratives by nurses in intensive care units, for example, she notes how nurses describe their work with the patients' and families' worlds, humanising the technology, domesticating the alien environment and supporting the patient to be an agent in the recovery process. She thus provides the humane quality of these practices with greater recognition and public language. This leads us to an interesting comparison. Where Benner critically contrasts the humane caring practices of the nurses with the commodified practices of modern health care, Grace and the students in the graduate class were beginning to critically contrast the active learning embedded in their informal learning projects with the passive learning that can be found in public institutions of formal education.

SOCIAL PRACTICE AND DISCOURSE

But how does social practice relate to language and discourse? For Grace this was now an urgent question: "I am still quite puzzled about the idea of the social practice/activity. What has it to do with language education? What is its connection with ESL teaching?" With the help of the model in Figure 16.1, the class discussed how discourse in a social practice could be linked to the contrast between doing and knowing, and how discourse of doing the social practice could be called "action discourse" and discourse of knowing about the social practice could be called "reflection discourse." To learn how to apply these types of discourse to learning situations Mohan arranged for the class to work in small groups and learn a simple card game (called "Blackjack" or "Twentyone"). They then did a discourse analysis of their own speech in a series of exercises. They worked to see how they used action discourse when playing the game and how they used reflection discourse when talking about the game in the process of learning about the game. Towards the end of the exercises, the group explored the discourse analysis of the decisions they made during the game and how they discussed them. Analysis of decision discussions showed that they were important places where action and knowledge were brought together. Grace's diary records:

> We started playing the card game Black Jack in class in order to study it as a social practice through collecting and analyzing the discourse during our play. This is the first time I tried to collect discourse data and analyze it by labelling nouns and verbs. It is a refreshing experience for me to pay attention to our own speech within three different stages of the card game. I feel a new sensitivity to language is being awakened. I never learned that a classroom activity (or even any human activity) can be divided into three layers: General Reflection (when S. was talking about the card game rules), Specific Reflection (when she started to ask us play by ourselves and gave comments to support our learning), and our using language to do the Action of playing the card game.

Figure 16.1 is a basic heuristic model of the relation between social practice, discourse, and interpretive research, simply illustrated using the card game of bridge. We can apply it to any project that can be viewed as learning a social practice (e.g., learning to vote). The present case study illus-

Field: Bridge			
Social Practice	Discourse	Card Game	Example
Theory	Reflection—generic	Rules	1. "The dealer has the right to make the first bid."
	Reflection—specific	Advice on play	2. "Say 'I bid three clubs.'"
Practice	Action	Actual play	3. "I bid three clubs."

Figure 16.1.   A model of social practice and discourse.

trates how it can be applied to other examples of projects and social practices. The model uses social practice as the hinge between interpretive research and discourse analysis. It assumes a view of interpretive research (e.g., that of Charles Taylor) that recognises social practices and views a social practice as including the distinction between ideas and activity or knowing and doing, or, in our terminology, between theory and practice. Theory would thus include Taylor's ideas of articulation and self-interpretation, and practice would include Taylor's ideas of engaged, embodied and situated agency. The model assumes a view of discourse that distinguishes between reflection and action.

In linguistics research, social practice can be seen as a unit of analysis which is larger than the single discourse or text. A social practice such as the card game of bridge is associated with several types of text. For instance, there are books containing the rules of bridge, and daily newspapers often have a bridge column which describes actual games of bridge. These are different kinds of reflective discourse. When people play the game of bridge they use action discourse. A discourse study of a social practice may use a number of different types of text as data.

There are two discourse contrasts in our model. Reflection versus Action contrasts what is talked about ("the topic") with speech action ("speech act") (See Halliday and Matthiessen, 1999, p. 321). Generic Reflection versus Specific Reflection contrasts what is generic or general (e.g., a rule) vs. what is specific or particular (e.g., advice about a specific case) (See Hasan 1999, Cloran, 2000). Theory includes tacit knowledge as well as reflection discourse. Practice includes nonverbal action as well as action discourse. The relation between theory and practice is dynamic, with theory reshaping practice and practice reshaping theory.

The model is a basic starting point for relating social practice, interpretive research and discourse. It is also a point of departure for more elaborate analyses drawing on a systemic functional view of language. For example, Hasan (1999) and Cloran (2000) incorporate the distinction between action and reflection in a much more elaborate set of distinctions that concern event orientation and central entity in rhetorical units. Leung

& Mohan (2004) discuss the analysis of decision-making in action discourse. Mohan & Slater (in press) discuss the role of knowledge structures in reflection discourse. In our discussion of the narrative of an informal learning project we have briefly referred to the use of appraisal analysis (Martin & Rose 2003) to analyse values and the notion of good in a social practice. We also made brief mention of the grammatical analysis of agency. Human agency in texts like the narrative can be analyzed more finely using transitivity analysis (Halliday, 1994, p. 106ff.). Its best known example is Halliday's (1971) study of William Golding's *The Inheritors* which shows how the Neanderthals' weak agency and control of their world is conveyed through transitivity processes due to an external cause, an agency other than the person involved. In Williams (1998) primary school children, native speakers of English with little prior explicit knowledge of grammar, were able to use transitivity analysis to show different degrees of agency in characters in *Piggybook* (Brown, 1986). The mother in the story does all of the work around the house (e.g., she "made all the beds") while her husband and sons do none.

The model draws on a systemic functional linguistics (SFL) view of language (see Derewianka, 2001) which is based on the functions that language serves within our lives. SFL sees language as a resource for making meaning and sees discourse in relation to its context of situation and culture. The model sees a social practice as a semantic unit of culture. SFL takes a language socialization view of learning, seeing the learner as learning language, learning through language and learning about language. It can thus analyse language as a medium of learning as well as language as a focus of learning. That is, it can address the learning of content (i.e., meanings) as well as the learning of language and it offers a theoretical and analytical frame to analyse content-based language learning.

APPLYING THE MODEL

Following her reflections on playing the card game and analysing its discourse, Grace's diary continues:

> All of this led me to reflect upon my own teaching in Taiwan. My lectures were always quite popular with the students because I carried the class in a cheerful and lively atmosphere. However, after I learned the framework [i.e., the model in Figure 16.1], I thought I needed to revolutionize my lesson plan. In terms of engaging the students to learn through the language and use the language to accomplish tasks, my strategy was not functioning at all.

In writing this, Grace has gone some way to answering her questions about the relevance of social practice. She sees how this view of discourse presents a picture of how students can learn a social practice through language and can use language to accomplish the practice. Looking critically at the teaching situation she is most familiar with, she sees a need to develop language as a medium of learning and of action in it. But how can this be done? How can she develop the potential of what is normally done within these classrooms? She struggled with this problem for some time and finally chose it as the topic of her term paper for the course.

As it happened, Grace was enrolled in a program for training International Teaching Assistants. Each of the students in the program was asked to microteach a brief lesson for discussion by the group. Grace decided to teach pronunciation, a standard part of her normal teaching in Taiwan. She decided to tape record her teaching and analyse her discourse for her term paper. She realized that she had an opportunity to review her familiar teaching situation and revise her normal teaching strategies and to aim for the development of language as a medium of learning and action. When she considered how to do this, she used her experiences in the card game as an example. Her term paper critiqued her familiar teaching situation for its over-emphasis on memorizing the formal system of English and its neglect of its relation to discourse and meaning.

> Our students come from a mono-language environment, where Mandarin is the predominant language at home and in the community. They start to learn English formally in Junior High school where grammar rules and vocabulary memorization are over-emphasized. In almost every classroom activity, the content of the texts is taught in a superficial level. Most teachers simply read them through and give nothing more than Chinese translation because they want to spare more time for sentence pattern practice and quizzes.

Her lesson covered the pronunciation of the sounds [i:] and [i]. As her essay pointed out, teaching pronunciation in schools can be seen as teaching a social practice, where the action was actually pronouncing the sounds and the knowledge included knowledge about the articulation and spelling of the sounds.

Her plan for her lesson was in two parts. In the first part she would teach the social practice in her usual, teacher –centered way: "This was what I always did in Taiwan when I was teaching pronunciation." This way, she felt, ignored the potential for students to use English as a medium of learning. Therefore, in the second part, she would change to a more learner-centered approach at the beginning. Then, she started with theory and moved to pronunciation practice. She illustrated in her discourse analysis how she, as the teacher, produced general reflection, as in:

> T: It is a long tensed sound which is usually represented by letters ee as in "cheese" or ea as in "teacher."

Then she showed how she, as the teacher, produced specific reflection and the students did the action:

> T: Open your mouth a little bit and move your tongue higher and say, [i:]
> (The students pronounce the vowel i.e., do the action)
> T: Yes, very good.

In other words, she showed how in this approach the teacher did all of the reflection and directed all of the actions of the students.

In the second half of the ITA presentation, she says: "I purposely reduced my talking in order to make the lesson more *learner-centered.* I attempted to elicit information from the students and avoid direct teaching." An example of this occurred when she asked a student to comment on a mispronunciation who then offered the diagnosis that there was a smile on her face when she pronounced "sheet," but there was no smile when she pronounced "neat." In her discourse analysis she showed how she guided them to work in pairs, "start from Action along with Specific Reflection relating to their task" and to build towards general principles. To aid this process, "I started to pay more attention to the decisions students made when they were doing a task." She involved students in commentary on tasks "so that they can decide jointly between alternatives." "This appears so significant to me because many of the students in Taiwan, in doing tasks such as true or false questions or multiple choices, seldom think about the reasons that lead them to their decision—most of the time they just guess." By "learner-centered," Grace does not simply mean that the students talked more. Instead, she encouraged the students to engage in focussed discussion that articulated what they were doing and why, so that they could make informed decisions. In addition, she herself had developed the discourse analysis competence to identify the language needed for this discussion and to track and guide these decision-making processes in the classroom.

Summarising the flow of her work across the graduate course, we can see how Grace moved from a learning project to a teaching project. Moving through a broad cycle of reflection and action applied to her self and her situation, she reflected on her informal learning project and acted by developing her teaching project, a project to critically review and rework her own teaching. She made a connection between her experience with her own informal adult learning projects and her experience of teaching in Taiwan. She demonstrated how she could modify her teaching so that it incorporated some of the features of her learning projects; she thought about learner agency and inquiry and opened up spaces where her students could be more active and reflective. Of course, there are many connections that could have been made. This one made sense in her personal and practical world. To make this connection, Grace used the model of social practice and discourse. She began by applying this model to her adult learning project, developed her understanding of it by working with the card game exercises, and then applied it to her pattern of teaching in Taiwan. By viewing these activities as social practices, she was able to compare them in a fruitful way and develop an understanding of their discourse. Across the flow of her work she moved repeatedly between the roles of learner, researcher, and teacher.

CONCLUSION

The connection between a teacher's experiences of learning and teaching is vitally important. If teachers do not make this connection for themselves, it is difficult to see how they can understand the nature and potential of project learning and begin to foster it in their classrooms. Taylor's view of the knower as an engaged and embodied agent throws light on the fundamental value of understanding one's own informal learning and on why making this connection might be difficult to achieve. The graduate course we described aimed to support four processes for teachers: (1) narrating informal learning projects; (2) analyzing these from the perspective of social practice, action research, and interpretive research; (3) analyzing the discourse of social practices from a functional linguistic perspective; and (4) critiquing familiar learning practices in formal education and working for greater learner agency and learner inquiry. These processes are also important for learners, though they would have to be suitably modified.

More generally, the graduate course processes were based on a model of social practice and discourse. This model links action and reflection, and at a more abstract level, links interpretive research and functional discourse analysis. It thus links central themes of PBL research that underlie many of the chapters of this book. It is hard to overstate the significance of linking interpretive research and functional discourse analysis. This allows us to connect educational goals with *appropriate* language analysis, and explore how reflective learners use reflective discourse, for example, or trace the discourse processes of learner decision-making in the social practice.

Project learning is not a teaching method but a natural way of engaging with our world. It is a major presence in our lives, as the evidence of adult informal learning projects shows. We are involved in it as engaged agents in the fundamental form of knowing that Taylor has identified. If we are to counteract some of the commodified pathologies of knowing and learning that educational institutions can give rise to, we need to understand this fundamental form of knowing more adequately by inquiring and researching into our own learning and our own teaching. Interpretive research and functional linguistics provide appropriate research approaches to do so. These approaches can mutually reinforce each other through the concepts of social practice, reflection, and action.

REFERENCES

Abbey, R. (2000). *Charles Taylor*. Princeton, NJ: Princeton University Press.

Altrichter, H., Posch, P., & Somekh, B. (1993). *Teachers investigate their work*. London: Routledge.

Beckett, G. H., & Slater, T. (2005). The Project Framework: A tool for language and content integration. *The English Language Teaching Journal, 59*, 108–116.

Benner, P. (1994). The role of articulation in understanding practice and experience as sources of knowledge in clinical nursing. In J. Tully (Ed.). *Philosophy in an age of pluralism: The philosophy of Charles Taylor in question* (pp. 136–155). Cambridge, UK: Cambridge University Press.

Browne, A. (1986). *Piggybook*. London: Julia McRae.

Cloran, C. (2000). Socio-semantic variation: Different wordings, different meanings. In L. Unsworth (Ed.). *Researching language in schools and communities: Functional linguistic perspectives* (pp. 152–183). London: Cassell.

Crotty, M. (1998). *The foundations of social research*. London: Sage.

Derewianka, B. (2001). Pedagogical grammars: Their role in English language teaching. In A. Burns & C. Coffin (Eds.). *Analysing English in a global context: A reader* (pp. 240–269). London: Routledge.

Dewey, J. (1916). *Democracy and education*. New York: Macmillan

Flick, U. (1998). *An introduction to qualitative research*. London: Sage.

Halliday, M. A. K. (1971) Linguistic function and literary style: An inquiry into the language of William Golding's *The Inheritors*. In S. Chatman (Ed.). *Literary style: A symposium* (pp. 330–368). Oxford: Oxford University Press.

Halliday, M. A. K. (1994). *An introduction to functional grammar* (2nd ed.). London: Edward Arnold.

Halliday, M., & Matthiessen, C. (1999). *Construing experience through meaning*. London: Cassell.

Hasan, R. (1999). Speaking with reference to context. In M. Ghadessy (Ed.). *Text and context in functional linguistics* (pp. 219–328). Amsterdam: Benjamins.

Leung, C., & Mohan, B. (2004). Teacher formative assessment and talk in classroom contexts: Assessment *as* discourse and assessment *of* discourse. *Language Testing, 20*(3), 335–359.

Livingstone, D. (2001). Adults' informal learning: Definitions, findings, gaps and future research. NALL Working Paper #21. Retrieved November 30, 2005, from http://www.nall.ca/res/21adultsifnormallearning.htm

Martin, J. R., & Rose, D. (2003). *Working with discourse*. London: Continuum.

Mohan, B., & Slater, T. (In press). A functional perspective on the critical theory/practice relation in teaching language and science. *Linguistics and Education*.

Taylor, C. (1989). *Sources of the self: The making of the modern identity.* Cambridge, MA: Harvard University Press.

Taylor, C. (1991). *The malaise of modernity.* Concord, Ontario: Anansi Press.

Tiles J. E., (1988) *Dewey.* London: Routledge

Tough, A. (1971). *The adult's learning projects: A fresh approach to theory and practice in adult learning.* Toronto: OISE.

Tough, A. (1978). Major learning efforts: Recent research and future directions. *Adult Education Quarterly, 28*(4), 250–263.

Williams, G. (1998). Children entering literate worlds. In F. Christie & R. Misson (Eds.). *Literacy in schooling* (pp. 18–46). London: Routledge.

ABOUT THE EDITORS

Gulbahar H. Beckett is Assistant Professor of Sociolinguistics and Applied Linguistics in the TESL/Literacy Graduate Program at the University of Cincinnati. She holds a Ph.D. in TESL from the Department of Language and Literacy Education at the University of British Columbia. Her doctoral and postdoctoral research was on project-based instruction in English as a second language education. Her book (co-edited with Guofang Li), *"Strangers" of the Academy: Asian Women Scholars in Higher Education*, was recently published by Stylus Publishing. Gulbahar has published in such journals as *TESOL Quarterly, Modern Language Journal, The Canadian Modern Language Review, TESL Canada Journal, English Language Teaching Journal, The Journal of Asian Pacific Communication, Journal of Research on Computing in Education, Canadian Higher Education Profile,* NABE *Journal of Research and Practice, Journal of School Leadership,* and *Applied Measurement in Education.* She also has published several book chapters and has other works in press. Her research interests include project-based and conent-based second/foreign language education, second/foreign language acquisition and socialization, and second/foreign language policy.

Paul Chamness Miller is Assistant Professor of Foreign Language Education in the Division of Teacher Education at the University of Cincinnati. He received his Ph.D. in Foreign Language Education at Purdue University in 2003. Prior to pursuing his doctorate, he taught French in the K–12 setting in both rural and urban schools. He has taught French at the college level, as well as foreign language and TESOL methods courses at the undergraduate and graduate levels. He has also taught courses in teacher education on exploring teaching as a career and educational technology, in addition to supervising field experiences and student teaching. His scholarly work appears in *Phi Delta Kappan, Multicultural Perspectives, Multicultural Education,* and the *Electronic Magazine of Multicultural Education.* His

Project-Based Second and Foreign Language Education, pages 281–282
Copyright © 2006 by Information Age Publishing

first edited volume, *Narratives from the Classroom: An Introduction to Teaching,* was published by Sage in 2004. His research interests include multicultural education issues with immigrant children and second language instruction and acquisition.

ABOUT THE CONTRIBUTORS

Carolyn Aufderhaar is an Adjunct in Teacher Education at the University of Cincinnati. She has taught children, university students, and adult community members in Korea, Ukraine, and the United States. She earned a Master of Arts from Bowling Green State University and a Doctorate of Education from the University of Cincinnati. She also teaches English language learners in the K–12 system, and is a private piano instructor. Her research interests include English phonology and online learning.

Becky Brown is Associate Professor of Linguistics at Purdue University. Her research centers on varieties of French and language contact and appears in *Language in Society, Journal of Sociolinguistics, Francophonies d'Amérique, Plurilinguismes,* and *Radical Philosophy Review.* She is a two-time recipient of her department's Outstanding Teaching Award and has recently been awarded her school's Educational Excellence Award. She has received six grants relating to her French gastronomy course, which has garnered national and international recognition.

Mary Brydon-Miller is Associate Professor in Educational Foundations and Urban Educational Leadership in the Division of Educational Studies at the University of Cincinnati. She has a Ph.D. in Environmental Psychology and Statistics from the University of Massachusetts, Amherst. Brydon-Miller is editor of two volumes on participatory action research and has worked in a variety of community settings. Her most recent research focuses on work in refugee resettlement.

Rod Case is Assistant Professor at the University of Nevada, Reno. He earned his Ph.D. in Literacy Education with a focus on TESOL from Washington State University in 1998, and his research focuses on the connections between language and identity. He teaches courses in second

Project-Based Second and Foreign Language Education, pages 283–286
Copyright © 2006 by Information Age Publishing

language acquisition, curriculum development, ESL methods, and language assessment.

Kip A. Cates is Professor in the Faculty of Regional Studies at Tottori University. He has a B.A. in Modern Languages (University of British Columbia) and an M.A. in Applied Linguistics (Reading University, England). He teaches graduate courses on global education for the MA-in-TESOL program of Teachers College Columbia University (Tokyo). He coordinates the "Global Issues" SIG of the Japan Association for Language Teaching (JALT) and publishes the *Global Issues in Language Education Newsletter.*

Doreen Doherty is an ESL Instructor in the School of Continuing Education for the North Orange County Community College District and for Santiago Canyon College. She develops curricula for adult ESL literacy and writing in addition to teaching English language skills, grammar, and composition. Her continuing interest is in the application of newly developed pedagogical theories and language acquisition methodologies in the adult ESL classroom in order to facilitate students with diverse learning styles.

Beatrice Dupuy is Associate Professor of French/Foreign Language Education and a faculty member in the interdisciplinary Ph.D. program in Second Language Acquisition and Teaching at the University of Arizona, Tucson. She holds a Ph.D. in Education (Language, Literacy, and Learning) from the University of Southern California. Her research interests include incidental vocabulary acquisition and reading, experiential learning, and understanding language/culture development. She has published in *Foreign Language Annals, System,* and *The Canadian Modern Language Review.*

Janet Eyring is Department Chair of the Department of Modern Languages and Professor in the M.S. TESOL Program at California State University, Fullerton. She has taught most of the courses in the TESOL master's program, from methodology to program design to assessment. Her main professional interests are in the areas of pedagogical grammar and the teaching of literacy and writing. Her recent publication activities include applications of service learning to the second language classroom.

Yan Guo is Assistant Professor in the TESL program of the Faculty of Education at the University of Calgary. She teaches courses in second language learning, ESL special topics, and L2 reading and writing. Her research interests include intercultural inquiry with pre-service teachers, ESL parent involvement, L2 writing and identity, and the settlement of immigrants.

Masaki Kobayashi is Lecturer in the Language Center at Rikkyo University. He holds a Ph.D. in TESL from the Department of Language and Literacy Education at the University of British Columbia. His current research interests include L2 academic discourse socialization, task-based and project-based L2 teaching and learning, sociocultural theories of learning, the functional analysis of classroom discourse, and the development of language and learning awareness.

George Jacobs is a board member and the newsletter editor of the International Association for the Study of Cooperation in Education, a networking organization for cooperative learning, and consults with schools in Singapore on cooperative learning implementation. On global education and language instruction, George's main efforts concern promoting compassion for our fellow animals and environmental protection via leadership positions in the Vegetarian Society (Singapore), and the Centre for Language and Ecology.

Valerie Jakar is a lecturer at David Yellin College in Israel where she teaches in the areas of EFL pedagogic studies, multicultural education, applied linguistics, and English for academic purposes. She holds a Ph.D. in Language Education from the University of Pennsylvania. She has also served as coordinator of English Studies for Israel's Ministry of Education.

Grace I-chia Lee graduated from the English Department at National Taiwan Normal University, and taught high school English in Taiwan for 8 years. She is presently completing a Master's degree in TESL at the Language and Literacy Education Department, University of British Columbia.

Bernard A. Mohan is Emeritus Professor in the Department of Language and Literacy Education at the University of British Columbia. His areas of research interest include educational linguistics, language socialization, language learning and the computer, and functional linguistics. He holds a doctorate in linguistics from the University of London and has published widely on linguistic aspects of learning, including the seminal book *Language and Content* (1986).

Tammy Slater is affiliated with the Department of Language and Literacy Education at the University of British Columbia, where she completed her Ph.D. and is currently teaching in the TESL program. Her research examines discourse interactions in the classroom and adopts a systemic functional linguistic approach to understanding, assessing, and promoting academic language development.

Fredricka L. Stoller is Professor of English at Northern Arizona University where she teaches in the M.A. in Teaching English as a Second Language and Ph.D. in Applied Linguistics programs. Her scholarly interests include content-based instruction, project work, reading instruction, and disciplinary writing. She has published on project work in the *English Teaching Forum*, is co-author of *Teaching and Researching Reading* (Longman), and co-editor of *A Handbook for Language Program Administrators* (Alta Book Center).

Leo van Lier is Professor in the Graduate School of Language and Educational Linguistics at the Monterey Institute of International Studies. His expertise is in educational linguistics, second language acquisition, contrastive studies, computer-assisted instruction, discourse analysis, and bilingual education. He has a Ph.D. in Linguistics from the University of Lancaster, England. He is the author of *The Classroom and the Language Learner, Introducing Language Awareness,* and *Interaction in the Language Curriculum,* and has articles in numerous national and international journals. His most recent book is entitled, *The Ecology and Semiotics of Language Learning: A Sociocultural Perspective* (Kluwer Academic, 2004). His current interests include ecological linguistics, semiotics, project-based language learning, and equitable uses of technology in education.

Gail Weinstein is Professor in the English Department at San Francisco State University. She has a Ph.D. in Educational Linguistics from the University of Pennsylvania. She teaches courses on English for nonacademic purposes, "Language, Literacy and Citizenship," sociolinguistics, and the teaching of listening/speaking and reading/writing skills. Her research has focused on a range of issues in the ethnography of language and literacy, adult and family literacy in multilingual communities, and learner-centered education for community building.

Printed in the United States
91873LV00028B/7/A